36.95

D1601669

Intergovernmental
Relations
and Public Policy

Recent Titles in
Contributions in Political Science
Series Editor: Bernard K. Johnpoll

Intergovernmental Relations and Public Policy

Edited by

J. Edwin Benton
and David R. Morgan

*Prepared under the auspices
of the Policy Studies Organization*

JK
325
.I575
1986
West

Contributions in Political Science, Number 156

GREENWOOD PRESS
New York • Westport, Connecticut • London

Library of Congress Cataloging-in-Publication Data

Intergovernmental relations and public policy.

(Contributions in political science, ISSN 0147–1066 ;
no. 156)
 Bibliography: p.
 Includes index.
 1. Federal government—United States.
2. Federal-city relations—United States.   3. State-
local relations—United States.   I. Benton, J. Edwin,
1950–   .   II. Morgan, David R.   III. Policy
Studies Organization.   IV. Series.
JK325.I575   1986   353.9′29   86-3155
ISBN 0-313-25443-5 (lib. bdg. : alk. paper)

Copyright © 1986 by the Policy Studies Organization

All rights reserved. No portion of this book may be
reproduced, by any process or technique, without the
express written consent of the publisher.

Library of Congress Catalog Card Number: 86-3155
ISBN: 0-313-25443-5
ISSN: 0147-1066

First published in 1986

Greenwood Press, Inc.
88 Post Road West, Westport, Connecticut 06881

Printed in the United States of America

The paper used in this book complies with the
Permanent Paper Standard issued by the National
Information Standards Organization (Z39.48-1984).

10 9 8 7 6 5 4 3 2 1

Acknowledgment

Figure 1.1 originally appeared in *Understanding Intergovernmental Relations,* 2nd Ed. by D. S.
Wright. Copyright © 1982, 1978 by Wadsworth, Inc. Reprinted by permission of Brooks/Cole
Publishing Company, Monterey, Ca.

Contents

Tables and Figures

TABLES

FIGURES

Intergovernmental
Relations
and Public Policy

Part 1
The Intergovernmental Setting of Public Policy

1

The Intergovernmental Dimension of Public Policy

J. Edwin Benton and David R. Morgan

What an exciting time to study intergovernmental relations (IGR). According to one specialist, the system of relations among units of government in this country has become so complex and involved as to constitute a whole "new system of domestic government" (Walker, 1981:xiii). Practitioners agree. For example, former Utah Governor Scott Matheson, writing recently in *Intergovernmental Perspective,* describes the past eight years as a period of "dramatic turnaround" in American federalism. He mentions changes in peoples' attitudes, where less confidence is expressed in federal solutions to domestic ills. He also notes major shifts in intergovernmental financial arrangements and the increased capacity of states to deal with new and difficult challenges.

These enormous changes of the past two decades are so far-reaching as to constitute a "definite break with the past," according to the Advisory Commission on Intergovernmental Relations' David Walker (1981:xiii-xiv). As might be expected, this enormous ferment and flux has also brought a re-evaluation and reassessment of the study of IGR. In the past, political scientists tended to view national, state, and local politics as virtually distinct fields of inquiry. The result of such an approach, according to Hanson (1983:27) was that scholars carried out specialized research into national, *or* state, *or* local politics, and they taught courses and wrote textbooks that reflected these concerns. The study of IGR suffered as a result of the way in which the term was conceptualized. For many years, IGR was considered as being synonymous with federalism. Now, however, federalism is viewed as a more limited term, concerned mainly with national/state relations and occasionally with interstate relations. IGR is a much broader concept, and according to Anderson (1960:4), it refers to the "activities or interactions occurring between governmental units of all types and levels within the federal system." In short, IGR includes not only national/state and interstate relations, but also national/local, state/local, national/ state/local, and interlocal relations.

To understand the full dynamics of IGR requires more than identifying the various combinations of relations among units of government in our system; it necessitates a focus on *persons,* the major governmental officials who control the course of IGR actions. Anderson (1960:4) notes that "it is human beings clothed with office who are the real determiners of what the relations between units of government will be." As a result, Anderson (1960:4) concludes that "the concept of intergovernmental relations necessarily has to be formulated largely in terms of human relations and human behavior." Wright (1982:11) reiterates these views when he says: "Strictly speaking, then, there are no relationships among *governments;* there are only relations among officials who govern different units." Elsewhere, Wright (1974:2) depicts IGR as "continuous, day-to-day patterns of contact, knowledge, and evaluation of the officials who govern." Implicit in the observations of Anderson and Wright is that IGR involves both formal and informal interactions and public officials' attitudes. Moreover, IGR encompasses political, economic, and administrative interactions as well as legal ones, in addition to including all elected public officials as well as administrators. In sum, elected public officials' and administrators' attitudes and actions are at the heart of IGR, and according to Glendening and Reeves (1984:13) "they must be seen in the light of the environment in which public officials operate, including all the constraints and stimuli within that environment as well as those imposed from the outside."

Aside from its focus on persons, IGR is also characterized by a policy component. Dye (1976:1) has defined policy as "whatever governments choose to do or not to do." In the context of IGR, policy is the result of interaction among intergovernmental actors. Traditionally, intergovernmental policy has been the product of interaction among elected public officials. However, Wright (1982:19) asserts that this has changed in the last few decades because "economic and political complexity have combined with rapid rates of social and technological change to reduce the capacity of courts and legislatures to deal with continuous pressures for policy change." These changes have resulted in more pressure being put on and more latitude being given to administrators in both the formulation and implementation of IGR policy. Therefore, any analysis of IGR policy should contain a description and explanation of the causes and consequences of interaction among all IGR actors.

COMBINING THE STUDY OF PUBLIC POLICY AND IGR

With the recent emergence of public policy as a principal area of study in political science, a wedding of IGR and public policy was inevitable. Invariably, as we now direct more attention to such concerns as what governments do, why they do it, and what difference it makes (Dye, 1976:20–21), we are immediately struck by the intergovernmental context within which the making, implementation, and impact of public policy is set. For example, various analyses of the Elementary and Secondary Education Act of 1965—ESEA (Comfort, 1982; Munger and Fenno, 1962; Eidenberg and Morey, 1969; Mercanto, 1967; Price, 1962; Bendiner, 1965) indicate that, aside from the many private interests, a multitude of intergovernmental actors (e.g., the president; governors; state legislators; congressmen; school superintendents; teachers; principals; state and local school board members; members of congressional committees and subcommittees; administrators in federal, state, and local departments of education; and even federal and state judges), government departments and agencies (e.g., federal, state, and local departments of education; United States Department of Justice; Bureau of the Budget; Bureau of the Census), and all levels of governments (federal, state, local, and even foreign governments) had an input in formulating this policy as well as hammering out a definition of the problem that was to be addressed by this act.

Although initial directives and ultimate oversight for the implementation of the ESEA came from and rested with the United States Office of Education, much of the nitty-gritty, day-to-day implementation of the law was carried out by state and local departments of education, commissions and boards, school districts, school superintendents, principals, and teachers (see Comfort, 1982; Bailey and Mosher, 1968; Berke and Kirst, 1972; Mazmanian and Sabatier, 1983). Moreover, the impact of the ESEA had a very strong intergovernmental flavor about it, as the rippling effect of this policy had a bearing on the actions and behaviors of numerous government agencies and countless elected officials and administrators at all levels of government. Such matters as the nature, scope, and delivery of school curricula, course content, method of instruction, values and beliefs imparted to students—affairs normally within the discretion of both elected and appointed state and local school officials and administrators—as well as the attitudes of these individuals on a variety of education-related topics were influenced by the new federal role in education. Numerous other illustrations, of course, could be given, but the point meriting emphasis is that intergovernmental relations permeate—in fact, some would say are at the very center of—public policies.

In sum, the quest to develop sound and accurate theories about public policy (i.e., our ability to understand, explain, and predict its making, implementation, and impact) has been enhanced in large measure by viewing the policy process from an intergovernmental perspective. But, what has contributed to making IGR a relevant concern for the study of public policy? Specifically, what has changed about the nature of the making, implementation, and impact of policy decisions that has made the employment of an intergovernmental perspective a *necessity* rather than a mere *convenience?*

FACTORS CONTRIBUTING TO INCREASED RELEVANCE OF IGR

A simple, straightforward answer to the questions posed above would be to assert that the very increase in the incidence of IGR and its subsequent bearing on policy has brought about the need to study the public policy process from an IGR perspective. Yet, for all of its simplistic niceties, this answer leaves something to be desired. Perhaps, a more adequate answer could be found by examining those conditions that initially gave rise to IGR and, more importantly, those factors that eventually led to its increased incidence. At any rate, a fuller explanation is warranted, which should assist in demonstrating the relevance, indeed the necessity, of studying policy from an IGR perspective.

Initially, we can look to constitutions as the source of IGR. After all, constitutions lay down the fundamental rules by which the game of IGR is played. As Hanson (1983:28) notes, constitutions "determine who the players will be, what the permissible moves are, and what stakes are involved." Therefore, it is important that we understand the nature of constitutions.

Under the terms of many constitutions, certain governmental functions must be performed jointly by two or more levels of government, thus ensuring some IGR. Constitutions do vary in both the number and importance of programs that are to be jointly administered. For example, the United States Constitution requires federal-state cooperation in only a few areas (e.g., elections, militia, judiciary), while state constitutions in this country often mandate considerably more interaction (either of a state-local or interlocal nature). A point of greater significance to IGR, however, is that constitutions in many federated republics require *powers and responsibilities in general be shared among specific governments.* In many instances, the sharing of responsibility is neither equal nor unchangeable. As a consequence, a rather loose structure of authority in IGR results, and it enhances the likelihood of clashes between governments over the prerogative to make certain kinds of decisions. Conflict is always looming on the horizon as these governments from time to time seek to define or redefine the boundaries of their authority and their relationships with one another. In short, such constitutional arrangements create the potential for expansions of IGR.

Unlike other nations with a federal form of government, the United States experienced very few episodes of IGR during its formative years and throughout most of the nineteenth century. This epoch, usually referred to as a period of "dual federalism," was also characterized by the notions of divided government and two separate spheres of governmental authority and autonomous activity (Walker, 1981:46–65). However, all of this changed in the Unites States and elsewhere (it actually occurred earlier in more socialistic countries) as governments in general experienced an avalanche of service demands from their citizens in the wake of the Industrial Revolution, social and political reform movements (e.g., Progressive movement in the United States), collapse of the economic system (e.g., the Great Depression), rejection of such doctrines and philosophies as laissez-faire and "survival of the fittest," and the increase in urbanization and the problems associated with that phenomenon. In only a few short years, governments were transformed from entities that best fit the exhortation of Jefferson (i.e., government which governs best, governs least) to what many have variously called the positive or welfare state. (For an excellent discussion on why governments grow, see Savas, 1982:11–26.)

Though one can detect a modest rise in the number and array of government services in the United States by as early as the late nineteenth century, Roosevelt's New Deal was a turning point in both the growth of government and IGR. In fact, Howitt (1984:5) concludes that "the New Deal represented a major reorientation of political attitudes by American citizens and public policy makers alike, [whereby] there was an increasing philosophical acceptance of government activism, in general, and federal activism, in particular." Faced with the most profound and widesweeping national economic crisis in history, the federal government vastly expanded the scope of its activity. For example, it either initiated or expanded its activity in the areas of agriculture, conservation, social security, public works, urban renewal, public assistance, unemployment compensation, child welfare, public housing, highways, vocational education, and rehabilitation. At the same time state and local governments—either upon urging from the federal government or from citizen demands—also increased their involvement in existing programs or ventured into wholly new service areas.

As the size and service component of all governments have increased dramatically since the New Deal, so has the interaction among a wide variety of intergovernmental actors. This largely owes to two side-products of the increase in government activism—intergovernmental aid and statutory mandates. Federal grants-in-aid in the United States have encouraged (some would say "bribed") state and local governments to jointly participate in the administration of literally thousands of programs that address pressing needs and problems identified by the national government. Eventually, state and local officials and administrators contribute to the making of congressional federal aid policies (e.g., seeking more money, demanding less federal "red tape" and fewer restrictions). Similarly, expansions in state-local and interlocal relations result from state aid programs. Historically, many of the authorizing statutes of programs receiving federal aid (and to a lesser degree those receiving state aid) have tended to mandate planning activities and impose other administrative requirements on recipient governments. Moreover, many states (without offering financial assistance or other incentives) require that local governments perform certain functions (e.g., prisoner housing, budgetary audits, property reassessments) or participate with one another or with the state government in a number of programs (e.g., retirement systems; solid waste disposal; police, and fire personnel training). In short, intergovernmental aid and statutory mandates (whether in the United States or elsewhere) served to promote the expansion of IGR.

In the end, federal and state aid and mandates, though designed to assist state and local governments to meet rapid increases in citizen demands and needs, also served to centralize power in Washington and state capitals. By the late 1960s, as tensions mounted in the intergovernmental system in response to the centralization of authority, attempts were made to expand the involvement of state and local governments in both the making and implementation of policy. For all of these good intentions, these efforts at decentralization brought on what Reeves (1981) has called "galloping intergovernmentalization" as well as renewed concerns for manageability, accountability, program efficiency, and effectiveness in the intergovernmental system (see ACIR, 1981; Walker, 1981; Benton, 1985). More recently, under the leadership of the Reagan administration, a major re-evaluation of the intergovernmental system has taken place, and both practitioners and scholars alike have sought to deal with some of these problems brought on by a rapid escalation in intergovernmentalization.

As a testimony to the recognition that joint action on the part of federal, state, and local governments in formulating and implementing public policy was becoming more and more common (or perhaps as an attempt to understand, cope with, or somehow be able to control or manage the intergovernmental quagmire), most state, city, and county governments by 1970 had created agencies for the intended purpose of overseeing relations with other levels of government (Wright, 1982). Yet, until recently, it was customary for political scientists to consider national, state, and local politics as more or less distinct fields of study, and thus they promoted the assumption that "politics at one level could be safely studied in virtual isolation from the politics of other levels of American governments" (Hanson, 1983:27). Unfortunately, this practice coincided with a period in which all levels of government were becoming increasingly interdependent. But, according to Hanson (1983:27), as

the inadequacy of old ways of thinking about American politics became apparent [with] increased interdependence among American governments, scholars began to emphasize the study of *intergovernmental relations,* in which the actions of a particular government or government agency were placed in a more general context of interaction between governments in order to capture the complexities of such a highly interdependent system of governments as that in the United States.

As a means to further clarify our understanding of the full dynamics, operation, and relevancy of IGR for analyzing public policy as well as to assist in putting the remaining chapters into perspective, we need to introduce a model of IGR.

A MODEL OF IGR

Lave and March (1975:3) have defined a model as "a simplified picture of a part of the real world . . . [which contains] some of the characteristics of the real world but not all of them." Being fully cognizant that a model, like a picture, is simpler than the phenomenon it is supposed to represent or explain, we will utilize a model that best captures the intergovernmental relationships and interactions described in the following chapters. Such a model will assist in the following endeavors: simplifying and clarifying our thinking about government and politics; identifying important forces in the policy process; communicating relevant knowledge about the policy process; directing inquiry into policy matters; and suggesting explanations for policies and their outcomes. In short, our IGR model should enhance our ability to think about, understand, explain, and predict the formulation, implementation, and impact of public policy.

The model that we will employ (see Figure 1.1) has been called the overlapping-authority model by Wright (1982:38–40). (This model, though depicting authority relationships existent in the United States, can be easily adapted to identify relationships in other nations, if one replaces the word "state" with other analogous levels of government, e.g., province, district, canton, republic.) As Wright (1982:38) notes, the overlays among the circles connote three characteristic features of the model:

1. Substantial areas of governmental operations involve national, state, and local units (or officials) simultaneously.
2. The areas of autonomy or single-jurisdiction independence and full discretion are comparatively small.
3. The power and influence available to any one jurisdiction (or official) is substantially limited. The limits produce an authority pattern best described as bargaining.

In this context bargaining is defined as "negotiating the terms of a sale, exchange, or agreement." From an IGR perspective, exchange and agreement are the most pertinent terms because numerous areas of IGR entail either one or both of these actions. For example, state and local governments may take advantage of a multitude of assistance programs made available by the federal government, provided they agree to implement a program, carry out a project, or follow any one of a large variety of activities. In addition, as part of the bargain, recipient governments must normally consent to conditions such as providing matching funds and satisfactorily meeting accounting, reporting, auditing, and performance requirements.

Analyzing the policy process from the perspective of the overlapping-authority model (as do the authors of the following chapters) reveals several additional features of the model that merit mention. First, it is possible to change authority relationships among intergovernmental officials whenever exchanges transfer resources and influence from one

Figure 1.1   Overlapping-Authority Model of IGR

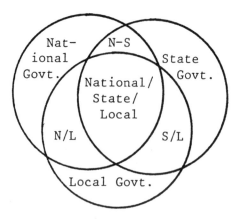

SOURCE: Deil S. Wright, Understanding Intergovernmental Relations, 2d ed. (Monterey, CA: Brooks/Cole, 1982), p. 29.

level of government to another. Second, power in the overlapping model is usually broadly spread and nearly uniformly divided. Third, this model does not assume in advance that relationships among participants are characterized as being either cooperative or competitive. Finally, as the model indicates, areas of autonomous action (the nonoverlapping areas of the circles) are small for each respective jurisdiction, while national/state/local relations appear to dominate. This distribution signifies the interdependence that tends to penetrate IGR, for as Lovell (1979:14) notes: "Policy is no longer made mostly in a single governmental unit but is hammered out through a negotiating, bargaining relationship among multiple governmental units."

In a nutshell, the major characteristics of the overlapping-authority model are as follows: (1) widely distributed power and authority; (2) large degree of interdependence; (3) few areas of autonomy; (4) ever-present bargaining-exchange relationships; and (5) possibility of either or both cooperation and competition.

CONCLUSION

Theories and models are accepted only after rigorous and repeated testing and as a result of their consistent ability to clearly and accurately describe and predict political behavior. Given the nature of the public policy process, it is imperative that both the theorizing we do and the models we develop should be tempered by an understanding and appreciation of the role played by IGR. While reporting on a wide variety of recent developments in IGR policy, the ensuing chapters in this book (which are grouped under four basic headings—federal-state-local relations, federal-state relations, federal-local relations, and state-local relations) conform to this exhortation as the authors seek to accent intergovernmental officials interactions in their quest to explain and predict the formulation, implementation, and impact of public policies.

REFERENCES

Advisory Commission on Intergovernmental Relations. 1981. *The Federal Role in the Federal System: The Dynamics of Growth, an Agenda for American Federalism: Restoring Confidence and Competence* (Washington, D.C.: Government Printing Office).

Anderson, William. 1960. *Intergovernmental Relations in Review* (Minneapolis: University of Minnesota Press).

Bailey, Stephen K., and Edith K. Mosher. 1968. *ESEA: The Office of Education Administers a Law* (Syracuse, N.Y.: Syracuse University Press).

Bendiner, Robert. 1965. *Obstacle Course on Capitol Hill* (New York: McGraw-Hill).

Benton, J. Edwin. 1985. "American Federalism's First Principles and Reagan's New Federalism Policies," *Policy Studies Journal* 13: 568–75.

Berke, Joel S., and Michael W. Kirst. 1972. *Federal Aid to Education: Who Benefits? Who Governs?* (Lexington, Mass.: D. C. Heath).

Comfort, Louise K. 1982. *Education Policy and Evaluation: A Context for Change* (New York: Pergamon Press).

Dye, Thomas R. 1976. *Policy Analysis: What Governments Do, Why They Do It, and What Difference It Makes* (University, Ala.: University of Alabama Press).

Eidenberg, Eugene, and Robert D. Morey. 1969. *An Act of Congress* (New York: W. W. Norton).

Glendening, Parris N., and Mavis Mann Reeves. 1984. *Pragmatic Federalism: An Intergovernmental View of American Government*, 2d ed.(Pacific Palisades, Calif.: Palisades Publishers).

Hanson, Russell L. 1983. "The Intergovernmental Setting of State Politics," in Virginia Gray et al. (eds.), *Politics in the American States: A Comparative Analysis*, 4th ed. (Boston: Little, Brown): 27–56.

Howitt, Arnold M. 1984. *Managing Federalism: Studies in Intergovernmental Relations* (Washington, D.C.: Congressional Quarterly, Inc.).

Lave, Charles A., and James G. March. 1975. *An Introduction to Models in the Social Sciences* (New York: Harper and Row).

Lowell, Catherine. 1979. "Where We Are in Intergovernmental Relations and Some of the Implications," *Southern Review of Public Administration* 3: 6–20.

Matheson, Scott. 1984. "View From the Commission," *Intergovernmental Perspective* 10: 2.

Mazmanian, Daniel A., and Paul A. Sabatier. 1983. *Implementation and Public Policy* (Glenview, Ill.: Scott, Foresman).

Mercanto, Philip. 1967. *The Politics of Federal Aid to Education in 1965: A Study in Policy Innovation* (Syracuse, N.Y.: Syracuse University Press).

Munger, Frank J., and Richard F. Fenno, Jr. 1962. *National Politics and Federal Aid to Education* (Syracuse, N.Y.: Syracuse University Press).

Price, Hugh D. 1962. "Race, Religion, and the Rules Committee: The Kennedy Aid-to-Education Bills," in Alan F. Westin (ed.), *The Uses of Power* (New York: Harcourt, Brace, and World): 1–71.

Reeves, Mavis Mann. 1981. "Galloping Intergovernmentalism as a Factor in State Management," *State Government* 54: 102–8.

Savas, E. S. 1982. *Privatizing the Public Sector: How to Shrink Government* (Chatham, N.J.: Chatham House Publishers).

Walker, David B. 1981. *Toward a Functioning Federalism* (Cambridge, Mass.: Winthrop).

Wright, Deil S. 1974. "Intergovernmental Relations: An Analytical Overview," *The Annals* 416: 1–16.

———. 1982. *Understanding Intergovernmental Relations*, 2d ed. (Monterey, Calif.: Brooks/Cole Publishing).

Part 2
Federal (Central)-State (Regional)-Local Relations

2
Federal Aid Cutbacks and State and Local Government Spending Policies

J. Edwin Benton

Much comment about and discussion of the Reagan New Federalism has occurred during the first five years of this decade.[1] A sizable portion of the scholarly literature on this subject (Benton, 1986, 1985; Conlan and Walker, 1983; Fairchild and Hutcheson, 1983; Williamson, 1983, 1981; Davis and Howard, 1982) has sought to explain Reagan New Federalism initiatives in terms of his asserted goal to restore the balance of power between the national government and the states in the American federal system—that is, a reinstitution of federalism's "first principles." One recent article (Benton, 1985), which examined the Reagan administration's "Big Swap" proposals, block grants, and attempts at deregulation and federal aid cutbacks, concluded that these efforts were consonant with Reagan's interpretation of the founding fathers' intent for American federalism. Now that some of these initiatives have resulted in policies and have been implemented for a few years, it is time that we begin an examination of their impact.

Following the lead of several researchers who have already begun to study the effects of some of the Reagan New Federalism policies (Beam, 1985; Lovell, 1985; Agranoff and Pattakos, 1984; Liebschutz, 1983; Rothenberg and Gordon, 1983), this chapter proposes to make a preliminary assessment of the effects produced by one of the administration's policies—federal grant-in-aid cutbacks. Specifically, we will examine the short-term impact that federal aid reductions have had on direct total state-local spending as well as direct state-local expenditures in the areas of education and public welfare. Before we turn to this task a review of the pertinent literature is presented.

PREVIOUS LITERATURE

Although there are some (Fisher, 1964; Pogue and Sgontz, 1968; Oates, 1968) who question the use of federal aid as a determinant of state and local spending, those who do employ this variable are not in agreement as to how it should be conceptualized. A number of scholars (Benton, 1978; Dye, 1976, 1974; Sachs and Harris, 1964; Osman, 1968; Bahl and Saunders, 1965) have argued that federal grants should be viewed as outside money, which tends to free states from some of the constraints of their own limited economic resources, thus allowing them to spend more money on public services. Hence, they consider federal aid to be an economic variable. Others (Strouse and Jones, 1964) have contended that it is a political variable. However, all of these scholars agree that federal aid is a major determinant of state-local spending policies.

Economists were the first to note the important effect that federal aid had on state-local expenditure policies. In their study of state and local government spending for 1960, Sachs and Harris (1964) found that economic resources were losing some of their explanatory power, namely in the areas of public welfare and health. In particular, they noticed that such variables as income, population density, and urbanization were losing their explanatory power vis-à-vis total state and local spending (i.e., explained variance dropped from 72 percent in 1942 to 53 percent by 1960). Of particular note was the decline in explained variance attributed to these three variables in welfare (from 45 percent in 1942 to 11 percent in 1960) and health (from 72 percent in 1942 to 44 percent in 1960). They contended that the reduction in explanatory power of economic resources could be explained by the intervening effect of federal grants-in-aid, particularly in the welfare and health fields. In sum, Sachs and Harris suggested that federal grants, which should be viewed as "outside money" and free the states from the limits of their own economic resources, allow state and local officials to fund programs at levels beyond their own economic resources.

In a replication of the Sachs and Harris study for 1970, Dye (1978:270) confirmed their findings. By including federal grants-in-aid as independent variables along with environmental variables (income, education, and urbanization), the proportion of explained variance in the policy areas of health and welfare increased appreciably. For instance, the amount of explained variance increased from 17 to 48 percent as a result of including federal aid in the regression equation. In interpreting this finding, Dye concludes that "economic resources had relatively little to do with its *welfare* spending; federal policy is the primary determinant of state and local spending in this field."

The findings of a large body of research, which has focused exclusively on the impact of federal grants-in-aid on local government spending, indicate that federal aid has an important stimulative effect. For example, Henderson (1968) reports this to be the case for all levels of local government. More importantly, most research on the effect that federal grants have on city spending policies (Stein, 1982, 1981a, 1981b; Weicher, 1972; Smith, 1968; Wilde, 1968; Osman, 1966) reveals that increases in federal aid tend to lead to increases in local expenditures for both aided and nonaided functions. Finally, a recent study (Benton and Rigos, 1985) shows that increases in federal aid produce increases in central county spending and hence enhance these governments' roles as major service providers in Standard Metropolitan Statistical Areas (SMSAs) with populations over 200,000.

Although there is a wealth of research which demonstrates that a considerable proportion of the variance in state-local and/or local spending policies can be explained by the level of federal aid, only a few studies (Hansen and Cooper, 1980; Bahl and Saunders, 1965) have focused on the relationship between *changes* in the level of federal aid and *changes* in state and local government expenditures. One early study (Bahl and Saunders, 1965) reported that changes in federal aid to state and local governments have the greatest effect on both level of and changes in these governments' expenditures. A more recent study (Hansen and Cooper, 1980) found that changes in federal grants proved to be the major variable that accounted for increases in state spending between 1960 and 1976. Moreover, in his review of the literature in this area, Gramlich (1977:219–240) concludes that a significant portion of the growth in state and local spending—between 25 and 50 percent—can be attributed to the stimulation of federal grants of various types. In short, changes in federal policy, which result in different patterns of federal grant-in-aid revenues, have the most direct and immediate effect on changes in state and local government spending policies.

However, all of these studies were conducted during a period when federal aid was still increasing. For the most part, these studies report that a large proportion of the variance in increases in state-local spending could be explained by increases in federal aid. What happens to direct state-local expenditures when either the rate of growth or overall level of federal aid decreases? State and local governments have been forced to deal with an unprecedented reduction in federal aid during the early 1980s. What, if any, changes in state-local expenditure policy have resulted?

MEASURES OF STATE-LOCAL SPENDING

When seeking to assess the influence that a whole host of independent variables (including federal aid) have on changes in state-local expenditure policy, careful attention must be given to the selection of the measure(s) of this dependent variable. Warning of this fact, Benton (1983) and

Jacob (1976) have noted that the measures we use will inevitably have a significant bearing on the conclusions of our research. Much of the research on changes in state and local spending has employed changes in per capita expenditures as the dependent variable. On the other hand, the literature on the much broader topic of public spending (Jennings, 1979; Dawson and Gray, 1971; Fry and Winters, 1970; Cnudde and McCrone, 1969; Dye, 1969, 1966, 1965; Sharkansky and Hofferbert, 1969; Hofferbert, 1966; Jacob, 1964; Dawson and Robinson, 1963) features a wide variety of empirical measures of state-local expenditure policy. However, according to Benton (1983:242) the utilization of a number of various measures of public spending "appears to have been done without either the consideration or realization that each represents a different dimension of public spending." In sum, previous research to a large extent failed to view the multifaceted nature of public spending and therefore conceptualized state and local government spending activity as a simple rather than multidimensional phenomenon and process.

Given that the present study seeks to examine the impact of federal grants-in-aid cutbacks on state and local direct total, education, and public welfare spending from as many perspectives as possible, we will employ (where applicable) the four dimensions of public spending identified by Benton (1983, 1978) and seek to determine if these measures of spending activity declined during 1982 (a year in which federal aid dropped) and 1983 (a year in which federal aid increased only slightly— .3 percent) as compared to 1981 (a year of continued growth for federal grants). These dimensions—levels, burdens, priorities, and benefits— will be broken down as follows:

Dimension	All Functions	Education	Public Welfare
Levels	Per capita total expenditures	Per capita education expenditures	Per capita public welfare expenditures
Burdens	Total expenditures per $1,000 of personal income	Education expenditures per $1,000 of personal income	Public welfare expenditures per $1,000 of personal income
Priorities		Education expenditure as a percentage of total expenditures	Public welfare expenditures as a percentage of total expenditures
Benefits		Education expenditures per pupil in average daily attendance (ADA)	Average monthly payment per family, aid to families with dependent children (AFDC)

Each of these dimensions presents us with a different profile of government spending or different way of comparing expenditure activity across governments. For instance, whereas the dimension "levels" provides us with a common measure of state-local expenditure activity in relation to the general population, the "burdens" dimension enables us to compare the relative sacrifice or hardship incurred as a result of state-local spending. Additionally, while "priorities" allows us to compare relative emphasis assigned to or effort made by state and local governments in regard to various functional areas, the dimension "benefits" helps to identify for comparative purposes the dollar level of benefits provided to specific clientele or recipients of sundry state and local targeted programs. In short, each of the four dimensions tells us something different about state-local spending as well as provides us with different information about how and why these governments spend money (Benton, 1983:243).

A macroanalysis (i.e., the U.S. state-local average) and a microanalysis (i.e., the fifty states individually) of the impact that changes in federal aid had on the various dimensions of state-local total, education, and public welfare spending during 1981, 1982, and 1983 will be presented in the next section.

IMPACTS OF FEDERAL AID CUTBACKS

One can gain initial insight into the impact that federal aid reductions have had on various state-local spending policies by comparing changes in per capita federal aid to changes in the various dimensions of state-local spending for the period 1979–83. These data, which are displayed in table 2.1, present evidence of an association between reductions in federal aid and several measures of state-local total, education, and public welfare spending.

Upon viewing the relationship between changes in federal aid and total state-local spending, one sees that per capita federal aid increases from 7.3 to 8.7 percent for the 1979–80 to 1980–81 time period, while state-local spending levels also increased over the same time frame from 9.5 to 10.4 percent; burdens continued a decline that had begun two years previously. By the 1981–82 time period, the level of federal aid showed a 3.8 percent overall decline. Correspondingly, the growth rate in state-local spending levels dropped to 6.9 percent, and the rate of overall decline of burdens accelerated from −1.1 to −4.3 percent. In 1982–83, the level of federal aid increased by a mere .3 percent. On the other hand, the growth rate in spending levels continued to decline from 6.9 to 3.8 percent, whereas a slight increase (.6 percent) in spending burdens occurred.

With reference to state-local education spending, one sees a similar

Table 2.1   Percent Change in Per Capita Federal Aid and Dimensions of State-Local Spending

	Federal Aid (Percent Change)	Total State-Local Spending (Percent Change)	
		Levels	Burdens
1979–80	7.3	9.5	−.5
1980–81	8.7	10.4	−1.1
1981–82	−3.8	6.9	−4.3
1982–83	.3	3.8	.6

	Federal Aid (Percent Change)	State-Local Education Spending (Percent Change)			
		Levels	Priorities	Burdens	Benefits
1979–80	14.3	8.3	0.0	−1.4	12.6
1980–81	9.3	9.5	.5	−2.9	9.3
1981–82	−8.6	5.9	.1	−4.5	9.6
1982–83	−3.1	2.6	−.4	0.0	8.1

	Federal Aid (Percent Change)	State-Local Public Welfare Spending (Percent Change)			
		Levels	Priorities	Burdens	Benefits
1979–80	7.8	8.2	−.4	0.0	6.5
1980–81	17.3	14.9	−.3	0.0	.7
1981–82	8.5	7.4	−.4	−4.2	7.4
1982–83	1.4	1.2	−.4	0.0	N.A.*

SOURCE: Computations based on data from the U.S. Department of Commerce, Bureau of the Census, Governmental Finances, 1978–79: 90–91, 94; 1979–80: 90–91, 94; 1980–81: 90–91, 95; 1981–82: 91–92; 95; 1982–83: 77–78, 81; U.S. Department of Commerce, Bureau of the Census, Statistical Abstract of the United States, 1980: 356; 1984: 395; 1985: 381; U.S. Department of Education, Office of Educational Research and Improvement, Digest of Education Statistics 1981: 81; 1982: 81; and unpublished data.

*Not available.

pattern. By as early as 1980–81 the growth rate in per capita federal aid was declining (i.e., from 14.3 to 9.3 percent). During this time frame, the growth rate in state-local spending benefits decreased somewhat, while burdens continued an overall decline that began in the previous period; the growth in the levels and priorities dimensions continued to increase. But, by the 1981–82 period, when the overall level of per capita federal aid for education dropped sharply (i.e., by 8.6 percent), the benefits dimension was the only one not to record either a decrease in the growth rate or an overall decline. With per capita federal aid to education continuing to drop in the 1982–83 period, two measures of spending (levels and benefits) showed declines in their growth rates, one measure (priorities) had an overall decline, and burdens experienced no change. In sum, all of the dimensions of state-local education spending responded—at one time or another—to changes in per capita federal aid but particularly to decreases in the growth rate or overall declines.

Finally, looking at state-local public welfare spending, one also detects that changes in the various dimensions of spending in this functional area tend to coincide with changes in per capita federal grants for welfare. From the 1979-80 to the 1980-81 period, the growth rate in per capita federal aid to welfare increased by almost 10 percent. Over the same period levels of spending also increased, while spending burdens showed no change. On the other hand, the growth rate in benefits decreased and priorities continued an overall decline. By the 1981–82 period there was a drop in the growth rate of per capita federal aid. During this same time frame, one sees that all of the dimensions of state-local welfare spending except benefits experienced either a decrease in the growth rate or an overall decline. Finally, the table indicates that further reductions in state-local spending in the 1982–83 period accompanied a continued decrease in per capita federal aid.

Although these cumulative figures are helpful in our quest to probe the relationship between changes in federal aid and changes in state-local expenditure policy, a more important concern for both students of intergovernmental relations fiscal policy and government officials may be the effect that either decreases in the growth rate or overall reductions in federal aid since 1981 have had on state-local spending policies when the states are viewed on an individual basis. To guide our approach it will be useful to hypothesize about possible federal aid impacts. Reference to the relevant literature, which was summarized above, would lead us to offer the following hypotheses:

Hypothesis 1: In 1982 (the year of the first overall decline in federal aid), a larger number of states were more likely to show either a decrease in the growth rate (DGR) or an overall decline (OD) in spending policies as compared to 1981.

Hypothesis 2: In 1983 (a year in which federal aid rebounded modestly), a larger number of states were more likely to show either a decline in the growth rate (DGR) or an overall decline (OD) in spending policies as compared to 1981 but fewer than was the case for 1982.

Hypothesis 3: States which experienced a decrease in the growth rate (DGR) or an overall decline (OD) in federal aid (as opposed to those that experienced an increase in the growth rate) are more likely to experience either a decrease in the growth rate (DGR) or an overall decline (OD) in state-local spending.

Hypothesis 4: A larger number of states that experience either a decrease in the growth rate (DGR) or an overall decline (OD) in spending will also be those states that have experienced a decrease in the growth rate (DGR) or an overall decline (OD) in federal aid (as opposed to those experiencing an increase in the growth rate).

At this juncture, we now proceed to a testing of these hypotheses with the pertinent data for total spending levels and burdens as well as education and public welfare levels, priorities, burdens, and benefits.

Total Spending

We begin by testing these hypotheses vis à vis total state-local spending levels and burdens. Table 2.2 reveals strong support for Hypotheses 1 (for both spending levels and burdens) and 2 (for spending levels only). Somewhat less conclusive support is found for Hypothesis 2 when using spending burdens. More states in both 1982 (37) and 1983 (33) showed either a DGR or an OD with regard to spending levels as

Table 2.2 Relationship between Changes in Federal Aid and Changes in State-Local Total Spending

Changes in State-Local Spending	Decrease in Growth Rate or Overall Decline in Federal Aid (DGR or OD)			Changes in Federal Aid	Decrease in Growth Rate or Overall Decline in State-Local Spending (DGR or OD)		
Levels	1981	1982	1983	Levels	1981	1982	1983
Increase in Growth Rate (IGR)	11[a] (44.0)[b]	13 (29.5)	5 (29.4)	Increase in Growth Rate (IGR)	8 (36.4)	6 (16.2)	15 (44.5)
Decrease in Growth Rate or Overall Decline (DGR or OD)	14 (56.0)	31 (70.5)	18 (78.3)	Decrease in Growth Rate or Overall Decline (DGR or OD)	14 (63.6)	31 (83.8)	18 (54.5)
Total	25[c]	44	23	Total	22	37	33
Burdens				Burdens			
Increase in Growth Rate (IGR)	4 (16.0)	4 (9.1)	9 (39.1)	Increase in Growth Rate (IGR)	20 (48.8)	5 (11.1)	10 (41.7)
Decrease in Growth Rate or Overall Decline (DGR or OD)	21 (84.0)	40 (90.9)	14 (60.9)	Decrease in Growth Rate or Overall Decline (DGR or OD)	21 (51.2)	40 (88.9)	14 (58.3)
Total	25	44	23	Total	41	45	24

SOURCE: Computations based on data from the U.S. Department of Commerce, Bureau of the Census, Governmental Finances, 1978-79: 18-26, 90, 94; 1979-80: 18-26, 90, 94-95; 1980-81: 18-26, 90, 95; 1981-82: 20-28, 91, 95; 1982-83: 6-14, 77, 81.

[a]These figures represent the number of states.

[b]These figures are percentages.

[c]Total figures do not equal 50, since state experiencing an increase in federal aid have been excluded from analysis.

opposed to 1981 (22). Moreover, as predicted, fewer states fell into this category for 1983 than for 1982 but more than was the case for 1981. With respect to spending burdens, the data do confirm support for Hypothesis 1, as more states in 1982 (45) displayed either a DGR or an OD. This happened in only 41 states in 1981. On the other hand, one sees but partial support for Hypothesis 2. Whereas it was predicted that fewer states in 1983 as compared to 1982 would have either a DGR or an OD, this was the case when comparisons are made to *both* 1982 and 1981. It is evident that some intervening factor(s) caused an unusually large number of states in 1981 to have either a DGR or an OD in total spending burdens because they were declining a year before the massive cuts in federal aid occurred. Quite likely, the DGR or OD in burdens for many of the 41 states in 1981 can be attributed to a cutback in state-local spending as a result of the states anticipating revenue shortfalls brought on by the recession of 1980–82 (Benton, 1986).

The data necessary for testing Hypothesis 3 are displayed in the left side of table 2.2. From the table one sees strong support for the prediction that federal aid reductions are associated with changes in state-local spending. Initially, one notes, that of the total number of states in 1981, 1982, and 1983 that experienced either a DGR or an OD in federal aid, a large percentage of them reported either a DGR or an OD in state-local spending. Additionally, one discovers that, in the case of both levels and burdens, this percentage is higher in 1982—the year of the first overall cut in federal aid—than for 1981. Therefore, it is apparent that the message coming from Washington—a change in federal aid policy was in the making—had a strong effect on state-local spending policies in 1982 and spending levels in 1983.

Turning once again to the right hand side of table 2.2, one finds data that lends considerable support to Hypothesis 4. Specifically, one sees that those states in 1981, 1982, and 1983 which reported either a DGR or an OD in state-local spending were more likely to have experienced either a DGR or an OD in federal aid. Also, one will detect that 1982 marked the time when federal aid reductions had their greatest impact on spending levels and burdens. In 1982, 83.8 percent of the states that saw either a DGR or an OD in federal aid ended up with either a DGR or an OD in spending levels as compared to 1981 (63.6 percent) or 1983 (54.5 percent). The differences are more pronounced for spending burdens, as 88.9 percent of the states recorded either a DGR or an OD in 1982 as opposed to 51.2 percent in 1981 and 58.3 percent in 1983.

Overall it appears that cutbacks in federal grants-in-aid had a noticeable impact on the amount of money state and local governments spent on a per capita (i.e., levels) basis as well as the relative sacrifice states made (i.e., burdens). But, how did the DGR or OD in federal dollars affect state-local spending policies in the areas of education and welfare?

Education

Since state and local governments consistently spend more money on education than any other functional category, let us see what impact federal grant-in-aid cutbacks have had on state-local expenditures in this area. Data for this purpose are presented in table 2.3.

Looking at the "Total" figures on the right-hand side of the table, one sees that, while no support is found for Hypothesis 1 among priorities and benefits of education spending, support is detected for both the levels and burdens dimensions. As the table indicates, more states in 1982 (33) had either a DGR or an OD in spending levels as compared to 1981 (22). The same pattern is seen for spending burdens—though the contrast was not quite as impressive—as 41 states showed either a DGR or an OD in 1982, while this was the case for only 38 states in 1981.

Hypothesis 2—a logical follow-up to Hypothesis 1—predicted that more states in 1983 as opposed to 1981 (but less than for 1982) would report either a DGR or an OD. Complete confirmation of this hypothesis is found for none of the dimensions, though the data provide limited support for burdens and levels. First, contrary to our prediction, one notices that a large number of states recorded either a DGR or an OD in 1983 (35) as compared to both 1981 (22) and 1982 (33). Perhaps the larger figure for 1983 represents the lingering effect of the federal aid cuts experienced the previous year. Secondly, one sees partial support for this hypothesis among burdens. As hypothesized, the number of states for 1983 (35) is smaller than for 1982 (41); however, contrary to the hypothesis, fewer states in 1983 (35) had either a DGR or an OD, when a comparison is made to 1981 (38). Here, again this contradictory finding—particularly the much larger than expected numbers for 1981—may be the result of state-local spending cutbacks induced by fiscal problems during the recession of 1980–82.

A tentative conclusion one may draw from the lack of support among priorities and benefits of spending for Hypothesis 2 is that the major federal aid cutbacks of 1982 had no appreciable effect on spending reductions for these two dimensions. However, the number of states with either a DGR or an OD increased from 1982 to 1983 (i.e., from 32 to 41 for priorities and from 21 to 29 for benefits). In fact, the number for 1983 priorities is larger than for even 1981. This pattern, as Tucker (1982:182–88) suggests, may be the result of a lagged effect that changes in federal aid had on these dimensions of spending.

The data relevant to Hypothesis 3 are found on the left-hand side of table 2.3. Here one finds strong support for the prediction that reductions in federal aid are related to changes in state-local spending. In all cases (except for benefits of spending in 1982), the figures are in the hypothesized direction. Furthermore, one notices that the percentage is

Table 2.3 Relationship between Changes in Federal Aid and Changes in State-Local Education Spending

Changes in State-Local Spending	Decrease in Growth Rate or Overall Decline in Federal Aid (DGR or OD)			Changes in Federal Aid	Decrease in Growth Rate or Overall Decline in State-Local Spending (DGR or OD)		
Levels	1981	1982	1983	Levels	1981	1982	1983
Increase in Growth Rate (IGR)	17[a] (48.6)[b]	14 (31.8)	13 (38.2)	Increase in Growth Rate (IGR)	4 (18.2)	3 (9.1)	14 (40.0)
Decrease in Growth Rate or Overall Decline (DGR or OD)	18 (51.4)	30 (68.2)	21 (61.8)	Decrease in Growth Rate or Overall Decline (DGR or OD)	18 (81.8)	30 (90.9)	21 (60.0)
Total	35[c]	44	34	Total	22	33	35
Burdens				Burdens			
Increase in Growth Rate (IGR)	8 (22.9)	7 (15.9)	12 (35.3)	Increase in Growth Rate (IGR)	11 (28.9)	4 (9.8)	13 (37.1)
Decrease in Growth Rate or Overall Decline (DGR or OD)	27 (77.1)	37 (84.1)	22 (64.7)	Decrease in Growth Rate or Overall Decline (DGR or OD)	27 (71.1)	37 (90.2)	22 (62.9)
Total	35	44	34	Total	38	41	35
Priorities				Priorities			
Increase in Growth Rate (IGR)	12 (34.3)	16 (36.4)	7 (20.6)	Increase in Growth Rate (IGR)	10 (30.3)	4 (12.5)	14 (34.1)
Decrease in Growth Rate or Overall Decline (DGR) or OD)	23 (65.7)	28 (63.6)	27 (79.4)	Decrease in Growth Rate or Overall Decline (DGR or OD)	23 (69.7)	28 (87.5)	27 (65.9)
Total	35	44	34	Total	33	32	41
Benefits				Benefits			
Increase in Growth Rate (IGR)	10 (28.6)	26 (59.1)	12 (35.3)	Increase in Growth Rate (IGR)	11 (30.6)	3 (14.3)	7 (24.1)
Decrease in Growth Rate or Overall Decline (DGR or OD)	25 (71.4)	18 (40.9)	22 (64.7)	Decrease in Growth Rate or Overall Decline (DGR or OD)	25 (69.4)	18 (85.7)	22 (75.9)
Total	35	44	34	Total	36	21	29

SOURCE: Computations based on data from the U.S. Department of Commerce, Bureau of the Census, Governmental Finances, 1978-79: 18-26, 90-91, 94; 1979-80: 18-26, 90-91, 94-95; 1980-81: 18-26, 90-91, 95; 1981-82: 20-28, 91-92, 95; 1982-83: 6-14, 77-78, 81; U.S. Department of Education, Office of Educational Research and Improvement, Digest of Education Statistics 1980-81; 1982: 81; and unpublished data.

[a] These figures represent the number of states.

[b] These figures are percentages.

[c] Total figures do not equal 50, since states experiencing an increase in federal aid have been excluded from analysis.

highest for both levels and burdens in 1982. As was noted with total state-local spending, it would appear that the signal from Washington, indicating that a major change in federal aid policy was in the offing, had a strong impact on spending levels and burdens in 1982 and on spending levels, priorities, and benefits in 1983. (The impact for priorities and benefits for 1983 was a lagged one.)

Returning to the right-hand side of table 2.3, one finds the data that allows us to test Hypothesis 4. Here we see conclusive evidence that those states which reduced state-local spending (for all four dimensions) were more likely to have experienced either a DGR or an OD in federal aid. Another viewing of these data will also reveal that reductions in federal aid seemed to have their strongest effects on all dimensions in 1982, thus coinciding with the first time that the states had experienced overall cuts in federal grant-in-aid monies.

Public Welfare

Let us now look at the effect that federal aid cutbacks had on a state-local function that traditionally has been more dependent on federal support—welfare. The appropriate data for testing our four hypothesis are found in table 2.4.

From the "Total" statistics on the right-hand side of this table, one notices support for Hypotheses 1 and 2 among levels, burdens, and priorities of welfare spending. (The unavailability of data for 1983 prevents us from fully testing these hypotheses for benefits; however, from what we are able to see, no support appears for Hypothesis 1.) In all instances (except for benefits of spending), more states report either a DGR or an OD in 1982 as compared to 1981, thus confirming the expectation that the 1982 cutbacks in federal aid would lead to a reduction in spending for a large portion of the states. Moreover, the data for levels, burdens, and priorities confirm the prediction in Hypothesis 2, as more states ended 1983 with either a DGR or an OD when compared to 1981; however, consonant with our hypothesis, these figures for 1983 were smaller than was the case for 1982.

Careful examination of the left-hand side of table 2.4 reveals support for Hypothesis 3 in all but three instances (levels and burdens for 1981 and benefits for 1982). Furthermore, federal aid reductions appear to have had their greatest impact on changes in state-local spending levels, burdens, and priorities in 1982. This underscores the importance that state and local officials placed on what they interpreted as a major shift in federal aid policy. Finally, one should recognize the lingering effect that the federal aid reductions in 1982 had on the three dimensions during 1983, for more states as compared to 1981 reported either a DGR

Table 2.4 Relationship between Changes in Federal Aid and Changes in State-Local Public Welfare Spending

Changes in State-Local Spending	Decrease in Growth Rate or Overall Decline in Federal Aid (DGR or OD)			Changes in Federal Aid	Decrease in Growth Rate or Overall Decline in State-Local Spending (DGR or OD)		
Levels	1981	1982	1983	Levels	1981	1982	1983
Increase in Growth Rate (IGR)	12[a] (57.1)	4 (9.8)	4 (14.8)	Increase in Growth Rate (IGR)	8 (47.1)	4 (9.8)	5 (17.9)
Decrease in Growth Rate or Overall Decline (DGE or OD)	9 (42.9)	37 (90.2)	23 (85.2)	Decrease in Growth Rate or Overall Decline (DGR or OD)	9 (52.9)	37 (90.2)	23 (82.1)
Total	21[c]	41	27	Total	17	41	28
Burdens				Burdens			
Increase in Growth Rate (IGR)	11 (52.4)	9 (22.0)	2 (7.4)	Increase in Growth Rate (IGR)	15 (51.7)	7 (15.9)	14 (36.8)
Decrease in Growth Rate or Overall Decline (DGR or OD)	10 (47.6)	32 (78.0)	25 (92.6)	Decrease in Growth Rate or Overall Decline (DGR or OD)	14 (48.3)	37 (84.1)	24 (63.2)
Total	21	41	27	Total	29	44	38
Priorities				Priorities			
Increase in Growth Rate (IGR)	7 (33.3)	4 (9.8)	3 (11.1)	Increase in Growth Rate (IGR)	12 (54.5)	4 (11.1)	7 (21.9)
Decrease in Growth Rate or Overall Decline (DGR or OD)	14 (66.7)	37 (90.2)	24 (88.9)	Decrease in Growth Rate or Overall Decline (DGR or OD)	10 (45.5)	32 (88.9)	25 (78.1)
Total	21	41	27	Total	22	36	32
Benefits				Benefits			
Increase in Growth Rate (IGR)	6 (28.6)	3 (80.5)	N.A.*	Increase in Growth Rate (IGR)	25 (62.5)	2 (20.0)	N.A.*
Decrease in Growth Rate or Overall Decline (DGR or OD)	15 (71.4)	8 (19.5)	N.A.*	Decrease in Growth Rate or Overall Decline (DGR or OD)	15 (37.5)	8 (80.0)	N.A.*
Total	21	41	N.A.*	Total	40	10	N.A.*

SOURCE: Computations based on data from the U.S. Department of Commerce, Bureau of the Census, Governmental Finances, 1978-79: 18-26, 90-91, 94; 1979-80: 18-26; 90-91, 94-95; 1980-81: 18-26, 90-91, 95; 1981-82: 20-28, 91-92, 95; 1982-83: 6-14, 77-78, 81; U.S. Department of Commerce, Bureau of the Census, Statistical Abstract of the United States 1980: 356; 1984: 395; 1985: 381.

*Not available.

[a]These figures represent the number of states.

[b]These figures are percentages.

[c]Total figures do not equal 50, since states experiencing an increase in federal aid have been excluded from analysis.

or an OD in spending. (In fact, more states were in this category in 1983 than 1982 for spending burdens.)

Shifting attention once again to the right hand side of table 2.4, one sees support for Hypothesis 4 in all cases except for burdens, priorities, and benefits for 1981. (Perhaps this is a sign that after 1981 state and local governments were more cognizant of federal aid cuts and were hence more deliberate in their efforts to tie state-local spending to shifts—particularly downward—in federal aid.) In the instances where support is found for Hypothesis 4, one finds that most of those states that recorded either a DGR or an OD in spending also experienced a shrinkage of federal aid. Further scrutiny of the table reveals that this association is most pronounced in 1982. Finally, the figures for 1983 demonstrate the strong effect that federal aid reductions in 1982 continued to have on state-local spending policies.

Degree of Impact

In the previous sections we saw that both decreases in the growth rate and overall declines for many of the dimensions of total, education, and welfare spending in 1982 and 1983—and to a certain extent 1981—are associated with similar changes in per capita federal aid. Moreover, it is apparent that reductions in federal aid in 1982 may have had a lagged effect. That is, in some instances, changes in 1983 state-local spending seem to be linked to 1982 reductions in federal aid. However, as a last step in our analysis, we need to examine the strength of the association between changes in the level of federal aid and changes in the various dimensions of state-local spending.

The data for this purpose are found in table 2.5. Several striking features are found among the contingency coefficients in the table.[2] First, in most cases, the strength of the relationship increases markedly for 1982 and 1983 as compared to 1981. This indicates that changes in the level of federal aid had their most pronounced impacts on state-local spending patterns during 1982 and 1983. In short, it appears that fiscal decisions of state and local governments are more closely linked to reductions (as opposed to increases) in federal aid.

A second pattern among the data in this table is that the strength of the association is greatest for measures of spending during 1983, a year in which federal aid increased slightly and fewer states (as compared to 1982) experienced either a DGR or an OD in federal aid. This may portend that the federal aid cuts of 1982 may continue to have a major impact on state-local spending in the immediate future, as these governments play a game of "wait and see" with regard to federal aid policy. In essence, state and local governments are probably going to exercise

Table 2.5 Contingency Coefficients for the Association between Changes in Federal Aid and State-Local Spending

	State-Local Total Spending	
	Levels	Burdens
1981	.025	.052
1982	.214	.082
1933	.232	.231

	State-Local Education Spending			
	Levels	Burdens	Priorities	Benefits
1981	.223	.041	.009	.019
1982	.124	.146	.021	.060
1983	.253	.166	.098	.194

	State-Local Public Welfare Spending			
	Levels	Burdens	Priorities	Benefits
1981	.157	.148	.148	.179
1982	.416	.146	.276	.026
1983	.537	.311	.546	N.A.*

SOURCE: Computations based on data from the U.S. Department of Commerce, Bureau of the Census, Governmental Finances, 1978-79: 18-26, 90-91, 94; 1979-80: 18-26, 90-91, 94-95; 1980-81: 18-26, 90-91, 95; 1981-82: 20-28, 91-92, 95; 1982-83: 6-14, 77-78, 81; U.S. Department of Commerce, Bureau of the Census, Statistical Abstract of the United States 1980: 356; 1984: 395; 1985: 381; U.S. Department of Education, Office of Educational Research and Improvement, Digest of Education Statistics 1981: 81, 1982: 81; and unpublished data.

*Not available.

extreme caution in their spending for those programs receiving federal funds.

A final observation meriting our attention is that changes in federal aid have their strongest association with levels, priorities, and burdens of welfare spending, particularly the first two of these measures. This is not too surprising, since federal aid consistently constitutes over 50 percent of state-local expenditures in this area. Hence, one would logically expect any state-local program that is so heavily dependent on federal funding to readily respond to changes in the level of federal aid. On the other hand, education, which receives much less federal support (typically federal aid makes up around 10 percent of such expenditures), would be expected to be much less responsive to fluctuations in federal funding.

SUMMARY AND CONCLUSIONS

Based upon a reading of the relevant literature, this study began from the premise that changes in state-local spending were attributable in large measure to changes in levels of federal aid. Unlike other work in this area, our research sought to gauge the specific impact of *reductions* in federal assistance. Therefore, given the uniqueness of our approach, a number of our major findings bear repeating. First, our data indicate that a larger number of states in 1982 (the year of the first overall decline in federal aid) as opposed to 1981 reported either a DGR or OD in state spending. This major change in state-local spending behavior coincided with the sharp drop in federal aid that occurred in 1982. Second, the number of states experiencing either a DGR or OD in expenditures was greater for 1983 (a year in which federal aid rebounded slightly) than for 1981, as the after-shock of federal aid cutbacks continued to have a pronounced effect on state-local spending. Third, states whose federal aid was reduced (either a DGR or an OD) were more likely to make an overall cut in spending or decrease the growth rate in such spending. Fourth, these states that decreased their spending from 1981–83 were to a large degree the same states experiencing a reduction in federal aid. Fifth, federal aid cutbacks had their greatest effect on state-local welfare spending. In sum, our findings clearly demonstrate that state-local spending activity responds not only to increases, but also to *decreases* in federal aid.

As profound as these findings are, one must remember that this research represents only an initial effort to analyze the impact of changes in federal aid on changes in state-local spending. Confidence in these findings will be determined by future research that examines the relationship between reductions in federal aid and state and local expenditure patterns over the long run. Of course, this will necessitate analyzing both aggregate and cross-sectional data in a longitudinal fashion. In short, the employment of an interrupted time-series design with a number of control variables (e.g., changes in state income, revenue elasticity, and population growth, measures of a state's economic health) will be required. Moreover, in such an endeavor researchers would be wise to use a variety of indicators of expenditure policy because, as was seen in the present research, changes in federal aid do not always effect different measures of state-local spending activity in the same manner.

Although it is not possible to predict with any certainty the effect that federal aid cutbacks will have on state-local spending behavior over the long run, we can speculate about several possible scenarios. One possibility would entail the federal government reversing its cutback posture and embarking on a course that would restore federal aid to pre--

1982 levels. This action in turn would spur state and local governments to resume a pattern of increased spending from their own revenue sources for those programs that are the recipients of increased levels of federal assistance. In other words, state and local governments would be encouraged to increase direct state-local spending as a result of perceiving a renewed commitment to a variety of programs. However, given the jolting effect that federal cutbacks have had on state and local budgets, these governments would probably proceed with a modicum of caution and increase spending at a modest pace over a period of time rather than immediately restoring the rate of spending to pre-1982 levels.

Another scenario would involve a continuation of federal aid cutbacks, and state and local governments, sensing a moral obligation or political pressure, deciding to continue program services at pre-1982 levels by picking up the fiscal slack left by the exit of the federal government. Under this scenario the states and their communities would become the senior (if not exclusive) fiscal partners in a number of programs. The chances of this happening for all or most programs sustaining federal cuts is quite remote, since there appears to be tremendous constituency pressure on state and local governments to cut taxes and hold the line on spending. Moreover, one recent study (Benton, 1986) reports that many state and local governments probably do not possess the capacity to assume the federal government's earlier monetary share of aided programs.

A third scenario, at the opposite end of the spectrum, would have state and local governments curtailing benefit levels and even totally eliminating programs as federal aid continues to decline. Simply put, states and their localities would be unwilling to maintain service levels in the wake of federal aid cutbacks. As attractive as this option would be to those concerned with holding down increased state-local outlays, the prospects of this scenario being realized (like the second scenario) is remote because in most cases the clientele of programs experiencing cuts in federal funding would have enough political clout to stave off such a drastic state and local response.

The most plausible scenario relates to the present and projected state of flux and uncertainty that surrounds the question of the appropriateness, feasibility, and desirability of federal aid to state and local governments. This situation evolves out of a whole host of issues, such as competing philosophical views as to governments' role in society and the economy; documented failure, waste, and inefficiency in federally supported programs; practical need to cut government spending; preservation of federalism's "first principles." Since a consensus vis-à-vis the role (if any) for federal grants-in-aid in the system of intergovernmental relations does not appear to be readily obtainable, the federal government, quite conceivably, will keep the grant-in-aid system in limbo. Given this state of affairs, state and local governments will react in a variety of ways. First, they will likely fill the fiscal void in those programs that traditionally have received only minimal federal funding. Second, they probably will cut back services or eliminate entire programs in response to reduced federal funding for those programs which have been heavily dependent on aid from Washington. Third, there is sure to be some swap of functions with the federal government or between the states and their local governments. Finally, state and local governments will certainly engage in a continual process of re-evaluation of their role as service providers and will be cautious in their financial commitments to programs that have been largely financed through federal assistance.

NOTES

1. This research was supported in part by a grant from the University of South Florida Research and Creative Scholarship Program.

2. Like Cramer's V, the *contingency coefficient* C is a measure of association between nominal-level variables. For a 2×2 table, it has a minimum value of zero and a maximum value of .707 (See Nie et al., 1975:225). No chi square tests of significance are provided for the coefficients, since we are dealing with the universe of states rather than a sample of them.

REFERENCES

Agranoff, Robert, and Alex N. Pattakos. 1983. "Intergovernmental Management: Federal Changes, State Responses, and New State Initiatives," *Publius: The Journal of Federalism* 14: 49–84.

Bahl, Roy W., and Robert J. Saunders. 1965. "Determinants of Change in State and Local Government Expenditures," *National Tax Journal* 18: 50–57.

Beam, David R. 1985. "After New Federalism, What?" *Policy Studies Journal* 13: 584–90.

Benton, J. Edwin. 1978. "Concepts of Spending in the American States," Ph.D. diss. Florida State University, Tallahassee.

———. 1983. "Dimensions of Public Spending," *Policy Studies Journal* 12: 233–46.

———. 1985. "American Federalism's First Principles and Reagan's New Federalism Policies," *Policy Studies Journal* 13: 568–75.

———. 1986. "Economic Considerations and the Reagan New Federalism Swap Proposals," *Publius: The Journal of Federalism* 16: (forthcoming).

Benton, J. Edwin, and Platon N. Rigos. 1985. "Patterns of Metropolitan Service Dominance: Central City and Central County Service Roles Compared," *Urban Affairs Quarterly* 20: 285–302.

Cnudde, Charles F., and Donald J. McCrone. 1969. "Party Competition and Welfare Politics in the American States," *American Political Science Review* 63: 858–66.

Conlan, Timothy J., and David B. Walker. 1983. "Reagan's New Federalism: Design, Debate and Discord," *Intergovernmental Perspective* 8:6–22.

Davis, Albert., and S. Kenneth Howard. 1982. "Perspectives on a 'New Day' for Federalism," *Intergovernmental Perspective* 9: 9–21.

Dawson, Richard E., and Virginia Gray. 1971. "State Welfare Politics," in Herbert Jacob and Kenneth Vines (eds.), *Politics in the American States*, 2nd ed. (Boston: Little, Brown).

Dawson, Richard E., and James A. Robinson. 1963. "Interparty Competition. Economic Variables, and Welfare Policies in the American States," *Journal of Politics* 25: 265–89.

Dye, Thomas R. 1965. "Malapportionment and Public Policy in the States," *Journal of Politics* 27:586–601.

_____. 1966. *Politics, Economics, and the Public* (Chicago: Rand McNally).

_____. 1969. "Executive Power and Public Policy in the States," *Western Political Quarterly* 22:926–39.

_____. 1974. *Understanding Public Policy*, 3d ed. (Englewood Cliffs, N.J.: Prentice-Hall).

_____. 1976. *Policy Analysis: What Governments Do, Why They Do It, and What Differences It Makes* (University, Ala.: University of Alabama Press).

Fairchild, Donald L., and John D. Hutcheson, Jr. 1983. "Another New Federalism? Madison, Block Grants and Urban Policy," *Policy Studies Review* 3:57–61.

Fisher, Glenn W. 1964. "Interstate Variation in State and Local Government Expenditures," *National Tax Journal* 17:71–73.

Fry, Brian R., and Richard R. Winters. 1970. "The Politics of Redistribution," *American Political Science Review* 64: 508–22.

Gramlich, Edward M. 1977. "Intergovernmental Grants: A Review of the Empirical Literature," in Wallace Oates (ed.), *The Political Economy of Fiscal Federalism* (Lexington, Mass.: D. C. Heath).

Hansen, Susan B., and Patrick Cooper. 1980. "State Expenditure Growth and Revenue Elasticity," *Policy Studies Journal* 9: 26–33.

Henderson, James M. 1968. "Local Government Expenditures: A Social Welfare Analysis, *The Review of Economics and Statistics* 50: 156–63.

Hofferbert, Richard I. 1966. "The Relationship between Public Policy and Some Structural Environmental Variables in the American States," *American Political Science Review* 60: 73–82.

Jacob, Herbert. 1964. "The Consequences of Malapportionment: A Note of Caution," *Social Forces* 43: 256–61.

_____. 1976. "Public Policy in the American States," in Herbert Jacob and Kenneth N. Vines (eds.), *Politics in the American States*, 3d ed. (Boston: Little, Brown).

Jennings, Edward T. 1979. "Competition, Constituencies, and Welfare Policies in American States," *American Political Science Review* 73: 414–29.

Liebschutz, Sarah F. 1983. "New Federalism Modified: Jobs and Highways in New York," *Publius: The Journal of Federalism* 14: 85–98.

Lovell, Catherine H. 1985. "Deregulation of State and Local Government," *Policy Studies Journal* 13: 607–15.

Nie, Norman, et al. 1975. *Statistical Package for the Social Sciences*, 2d ed. (New York: McGraw-Hill).

Oates, Wallace E. 1968. "The Dual Impact of Federal Aid on State and Local Government Expenditures: A Comment," *National Tax Journal* 21: 220–23.

Osman, Jack W. 1966. "The Dual Impact of Federal Aid on State and Local Government Expenditures," *National Tax Journal* 19: 362–72.

————. 1968. "On the Use of Intergovernmental Aid as an Expenditure Determinant," *National Tax Journal* 21: 437–47.

Pogue, Thomas R., and L. G. Sgontz. 1968. "The Effects of Grants-in-Aid on State-Local Spending," *National Tax Journal* 21: 190–99.

Rothenberg, Irene Fraser, and George J. Gordon. 1983. "The New Federalism, Intergovernmental Coordination, and Executive Order 12372," *Publius: The Journal of Federalism* 14: 31–48.

Sachs, Seymour, and Robert Harris. 1964. "The Determinants of State and Local Government Expenditures and Intergovernmental Flow of Funds," *National Tax Journal* 17: 75–85.

Sharkansky, Ira, and Richard I. Hofferbert, 1969. "Dimensions of State Politics, Economics and Public Policy," *American Political Science Review* 63: 867–79.

Smith, David L. 1968. "The Response of State and Local Governments to Federal Grants," *National Tax Journal* 22: 349–57.

Stein, Robert M. 1981a. The Allocation of Federal Aid Monies: The Synthesis of Demand-Side and Supply-Side Explanations," *American Political Science Review* 75: 334–43.

————. 1981b. "The Impact of Federal Grant Programs on Municipal Functions: An Empirical Analysis," in Advisory Commission on Intergovernmental Relations, *The Federal Influence on State and Local Roles in the Federal System* (Washington: U.S. Government Printing Office).

————. 1982. "The Political Economy of Municipal Functional Responsibility," *Social Science Quarterly* 63: 530–48.

Strouse, James C., and Philippe Jones. 1974. "Federal Aid: The Forgotten Variable in State Policy Research," *Journal of Politics* 36: 200–207.

Tucker, Harvey J. 1982. "It's About Time: The Use of Time in Cross-Sectional State Policy Research," *American Journal of Political Science* 26: 176–96.

Weicker, John C. 1972. "Aid, Expenditures, and Local Government Structure," *National Tax Journal* 25: 573–84.

Wilde, James A. 1968. "The Expenditure Effects of Grant-in-Aid Programs," *National Tax Journal* 21: 340–48.

Williamson, Richard S. 1981. "1980: The Reagan Campaign—Harbinger of a Revitalized Federalism," *Publius: The Journal of Federalism* 11: 147–51.

————. 1983. "The 1982 New Federalism Negotiations," *Publius: The Journal of Federalism* 13: 11–32.

3

The Burger Court's View of Intergovernmental Relations

Louise Byer Miller

This chapter examines two aspects of the Burger Court's view of intergovernmental relations. First, it will consider the Burger Court's view of the constitutional relationship between the states and the national government. In certain key decisions the Burger Court has protected and enhanced state authority vis-à-vis national authority. The issue is whether this Court, as compared to previous Supreme Courts, is theoretically motivated in its decision making. Corwin's (1950) axioms of "dual federalism" provide the methodology for determining whether the Court has a theoretical perspective on federalism or if the Court's jurisprudence is characterized by ad hoc decision making. Another issue considered in this section is whether the Court has been consistent in upholding states' rights.

Second, it investigates the Burger Court's decisions concerning the relationship between the states and their municipalities. A preliminary examination of Burger Court jurisprudence in this area indicates that the Court has a distinct conception of that relationship. By focusing on the judicial parameters of municipal antitrust immunity, this section intends to examine whether the Burger Court is theoretically motivated in its decision making. In short, is the Court engaged in a theoretical affirmation of Dillon's Rule through its jurisprudence, or is the Court merely engaged in ad hoc decision making?

STATE POWER VERSUS NATIONAL POWER

This section examines key decisions of the Burger Court in which state power in the federal system was protected and increased. The aim is to determine whether or not this Court is presenting a new vision of federalism. More specifically, has the Burger Court, as compared to the post-1937 Courts, developed a new theoretical construct of the constitutional position of the states in relation to the national government?

Edward S. Corwin's (1950) four axioms of "dual federalism" are used as a methodological framework for organizing relevant material. The axioms provide a way of comparing the constitutional dimensions of an era in history (characterized by the "dual federalism" label), with the decisions of the post-1937 Courts, and subsequently with the decisions of the Burger Court in order to contrast these differing judicial views concerning state power in the federal system.

Corwin's axioms also are one means of determining whether a substantive judicial theory on federalism exists. This can be achieved by analyzing the extent to which the Burger Court decisions do or do not reflect those axioms and also the extent to which the Burger Court decisions contrast with the post-1937 Courts' decisions in the axiom areas to present a new vision of federalism.

Corwin, in his classic article "The Passing of Dual Federalism," wrote of an era in constitutional history when the Supreme Court of the United States enhanced state authority in the federal system. He labeled this hundred year period the era of "dual federalism." The substance of the Court's actions during this period was summarized by Corwin through four axioms. To Corwin those axioms, or constitutional aspects of Court decisions, appeared in Supreme Court opinions from the period of the Taney Court through 1937. Surveying the overall trend of the era, Corwin maintained that the states were accorded a certain deference by the Court, and that the state interest in the federal system was upheld. Corwin observed that the Court did not merely augment state authority during this period; it adhered to a philosophical view concerning state power in relation to national power.

Thus in Axiom I (the national government is one of only enumerated powers and the states are governments of residual powers), Corwin maintained that in the era of "dual federalism" the Supreme Court's interpretation of the enumerated powers concept, combined with its broad reading of the Tenth Amendment, functioned as a limitation on national power. This can be seen when examining the history of the enumerated Commerce Clause power. The Commerce Clause, with its accompanying effects on state power, has been used both to expand and to contract national power. During the era of "dual federalism" Congress's enumerated Commerce Clause power was viewed narrowly by the Court (e.g., see *Adair v. U.S.*, 1908, and *Carter v. Carter Coal Company*, 1936), and activities involving production such as mining, manufacturing, agriculture, and labor relations were seen as intrastate matters without a direct bearing on interstate commerce; these were reserved to the states under the Tenth Amendment.

A change in the Court's posture was signaled in *N.L.R.B. v. Jones and Laughlin Steel Corporation* (1937), as the Court began to interpret the commerce power expansively. The post-1937 Courts saw the clause as a grant of power and not a limitation on Congress's ability to implement its policy objectives with a regard to economic enterprise. In *U.S. v. Darby* (1941) the Tenth Amendment was relegated to just a truism—a mere guide to interpretation. The post-1937 Courts saw no state sphere of operations untouchable by Congress's lawful exercise of its commerce power, and there was no judicial consideration of the states' reserved powers under the Tenth Amendment (e.g., see *Maryland v. Wirtz*, 1968).

The 1970s ushered in another judicial approach concerning the parameters of national authority vis-à-vis state authority in the exercise of congressional power over interstate commerce. The Burger Court for the first time in 40 years not only curtailed Congress's Commerce Clause power, but also focused on the states' role within a federal framework. But the Court developed a distinct construct of the integrity of the states in the federal system without reliance on the enumerated powers doctrine and the reserved powers of the state.

National League of Cities v. Usery (1976) centered on the constitutionality of the 1974 Fair Labor Standards Act amendments, which extended the minimum wage and maximum hour requirements to almost all public employees of the states and their various political subdivisions. The Court asserted that in enacting these amendments, Congress had exceeded its Commerce Clause power. The Court based its limitation of national powers on a "state sovereignty" doctrine inferred from the structure of the federal system and the relationship emanating from that structure. The structure and relation implicit in the principles of federalism necessarily limit even Congress's plenary power over commerce when states act in their capacities as sovereign governments and perform governmental functions essential to their separate and independent existence. Examples of such functions are the right of elected leaders to make policy choices concerning the hours, wages, and overtime requirements for state workers engaged in traditional governmental functions. The ability to set hours, wages, and overtime requirements are aspects of state sovereignty. Displacing these choices interferes with the functions these governments were created to provide and impairs their ability to function effectively in the federal system.

This position at first might seem to indicate that the Court has a substantive judicial view of why the protection of state power is critical to federalism. Arguably, this is not so. The Court never developed its thesis in terms of structure and relationship in constitutional law.[1] It also is unclear as to the source of state sovereignty. The Court is incorrect in its assumption that state sovereignty emanates from the Tenth Amendment. The wording of the Tenth Amendment says nothing at all about state sovereignty. Historically, the Court has long rejected the notion that the Tenth Amendment imposes limitations on Congress's plenary power based on state sovereignty.[2] Nor do the precedents cited in this case lend support to the Court's assumption. For example, one of the cases cited to substantiate the Court's position (*Coyle v. Smith*, 1911) dealt with a constitutional provision of admitting states under Article 4, section 3, and did not specifically deal with the question of the scope of federal power to regulate state governmental activities under Article 1, section 8.[3]

Nor does the reader know from *National League of Cities v. Usery* why policy preferences concerning wages, hours, and overtime requirements are so essential to state sovereignty. The deficiency in the Court's reasoning is especially apparent because the federal government calls the tune in so many other areas that seem just as integral to state sovereignty. The Court's logic in this case does not indicate what other governmental services will fit under the Court's category of "traditional" and therefore constitute other attributes of state sovereignty.

More importantly, the decision loses credibility because of its inflexibility. The Court's categorical approach (identifying wages, hours, and overtime requirements as aspects of state sovereignty) leaves little room for consideration of the federal objective when dealing with serious problems that are national in nature and which may be the product of state activity. Considerations of federalism mandate judicial recognition of this factor. In sum, *National League of Cities v. Usery* leaves us with a murky view of the Court's position on federalism. Moreover, the Burger Court changed its view on the necessity of applying the Fair Labor Standards Act to state and local governments in the 1985 case, *Garcia v. San Antonio Metropolitan Transit Authority*.

Corwin's second axiom of dual federalism is that the purposes which the national government may constitutionally promote are few. In essence, Corwin asserts that the national government was strictly limited to direct grants of power found in the Constitution. The power to impose and collect taxes was the example Corwin used to illustrate how the Court limited congressional objectives. When ruling on tax issues in *Bailey v. Drexel Furniture Company* (1922), the Court kept Congress within the confines of power as explicitly delegated in Article 1, section 8. But in *Steward Machine Company v. Davis* (1937), the Court reversed its position, ruling that Congress no longer was to be constrained by the specific grant of power in achieving its policy goals.

In delineating his second axiom, Corwin did not exhaust the issues that can be examined in order to discern whether the Court still is determined to limit national goals. Congressional powers other than the enumerated powers can provide relevant examples, such as the congressional power stemming from Article 3. That article allows Congress to define the jurisdiction of the federal courts. Pursuant to this power,

Congress has specifically asserted a national dimension. It has enacted legislation reflecting its policy determination that federal courts having habeas jurisdiction should protect federal constitutional rights.

In the pre-1937 era, the Court limited the scope of federal habeas review available to state prisoners in the cases of *Ex parte Siebold* (1879) and *Ex parte Royall* (1886). In contrast, in the post-1937 era the Warren Court, through *Townsend v. Sain* (1963) and *Fay v. Noia* (1963), effectively broadened the federally mandated protection. It denied finality to any state criminal conviction so long as the prisoner made a constitutional claim that a federal judge agreed might not have been adjudicated fairly at the state level.

The Burger Court, in *Stone v. Powell* (1976), *Francis v. Henderson* (1976), and *Wainwright v. Sykes* (1977), has limited the remedies available to individuals who have recourse to state courts to raise constitutional claims in federal courts. All three cases indicate a determination by the Burger Court to limit the broad scope of federal habeas corpus relief and to open up a wider area where states can exercise final authority with respect to the constitutional rights of individuals. But again, after analyzing the decisions, it seems evident that the Burger Court never promulgated a substantive judicial theory concerning the nature of the national-state relationship. The Court never addressed the question of whether the federal government is limited in the objectives it may pursue. It said nothing about state sovereignty and did not frame its arguments in terms of affirmative limits that must be placed on national authority to protect the states. For example, in the *Stone* case the Court asserted the need to maintain state judicial integrity, but not directly in the name of state power or state sovereignty. The Court merely ruled that there is no reason not to trust the states to fairly adjudicate constitutional rights.

The only rationale that does emerge from these decisions is a pragmatic one. Resort to federal habeas corpus has the potential of wasting judicial resources by having federal courts retry matters already decided upon in the state courts. Also, resort to habeas relief may prove too costly to society. It could downgrade the state trial procedure and encourage evasive legal tactics. The Court concluded that in the past broad use of federal habeas procedures had freed some individuals who undoubtedly were guilty. The latter point in particular seems to be the crux of these decisions.

In Axiom III Corwin related that the Supreme Court, in the era of "dual federalism," frequently ruled that the national and state governments were sovereign and hence equal within their respective spheres. Relying on the Tenth Amendment, powers reserved to the states were considered by the Court to be sovereign powers: complete, unqualified, and exclusive. Through them the states could realize their objectives without the interference of national authority. Certain subject matter under the concept of "police power," for example, could not be reached by the federal government. By 1937, however, state equality was no longer a substantive issue; Congress was free to pursue its objectives in certain fields without regard to the reserved powers of the states.

Even if the Court no longer uses the Tenth Amendment to enhance state authority in the federal system, the Eleventh Amendment can protect the states. That amendment embodies a formal declaration of federalism because it places specific textual restraints on federal power. The amendment can be used by the Court to place limits on congressional authority by protecting nonconsenting states from private suits in federal courts.

The Eleventh Amendment can enhance state authority in another way. Although a literal interpretation suggests that the Eleventh Amendment should be understood as a jurisdictional question, the doctrine of sovereign immunity is interlined in the wording of the amendment or has been interpreted to be in most Eleventh Amendment jurisprudence (Tribe, 1976). Sovereign immunity is a doctrine under which the Court can express its views about the nature of the national-state relationship. The Court's willingness to view this Amendment as an aspect of state sovereignty is one way in which the Court can enhance state power in the federal system. The question remains, however, of whether the Burger Court actually envisions the states as being sovereign entities on a par with federal authority.

The pre-1937 Court in both *Monaco v. Mississippi* (1934) and *Hans v. Louisiana* (1890) interpreted the Eleventh Amendment to allow the states a fair amount of freedom from lawsuits.[4] The Supreme Court protected the states in that it required very specific proof of state consent to suit before it would permit the action in federal courts. In the post-1937 era, the Warren Court interpreted the Eleventh Amendment differently. When Congress acted within its lawful commerce authority, state immunity was automatically and absolutely waived in cases arising under statutes passed pursuant to the Commerce Clause. In *Parden v. Terminal Railroad* (1964) the Court ruled that Congress was not compelled to specifically delineate in such enactments an intent to subject a state to suit, nor was specific consent to suit by the state required. In sum, the Warren Court saw no special position for the states in the federal system. As far as this Court was concerned, the states surrendered a portion of their sovereignty when their citizens ratified the Constitution and granted Congress enumerated powers.

The Burger Court's view of state power vis-à-vis national power with regard to the Eleventh Amendment is different from that of the Warren Court. In *Edelman v. Jordan* (1974) the Court protected, via the Eleventh Amendment, state treasuries from retroactively having to give up funds to rectify intentional or unintentional noncompliance with federal regulations. The Court intimated that Congress must clearly indicate its intention to make a state amenable to private suit in federal courts and the state itself must consent to such suit by explicit language or by overwhelming implications from the text of the state law so that no other interpretation could be possible. The Court claimed that a state's immunity was a "constitutional right" that cannot be brushed lightly aside or automatically waived. However, this statement was just rhetoric. There was no well developed position as to why the states in the name of federalism should be immune to federal suit or equal to national power in this regard.

The Burger Court also protected state immunity in *Pennhurst State School and Hospital v. Halderman* (1984). In that case the Court ruled that the Eleventh Amendment prohibited a federal court from ordering state officials to conform their conduct to state law. The Court asserted that the importance of the doctrine of sovereign immunity to federalism governed not only whether a state may be sued, but also where a state may be sued. However, the Court never addressed the issue of comity nor gave any indication of why the doctrine of sovereign immunity prohibits the federal government from enforcing state policy.

Corwin's fourth axiom stated that under "dual federalism" tension rather than collaboration characterized relations between the two centers of power. Federal preemption is an area that exemplifies the fourth axiom, where the Court can add to a milieu of tension or of cooperation in the federal system. Federal preemption can add to tension if the Court's approach continually mandates national dominance over state activities. Court determinations along those lines will enhance the frustration the states experience when their enactments, designed to remedy a specific problem, are struck down. On the other hand, when the Court does not rigidly construe its scope, the Court's preemption doctrine can add to an atmosphere of cooperation. Cooperation in the federal system will increase as, in the absence of overriding federal concerns, the Court adopts a more flexible approach to problem-solving (and continually reevaluates which level of government can cope best with a particular problem area). State objectives designed to facilitate problem-solving then can be given more credence by the Court.

In ruling on the Copyright Clause of the Constitution, the Burger Court has added to cooperation in the federal system by upholding state determinations. In two decisions—*Goldstein v. California* (1973) and *Kewanee Oil v. Bicron* (1974)—the Burger Court departed from the Warren Court standard, which stated that an item not protected by a federal copyright or patent cannot be protected by state law. These two cases mark the emergence of a state-oriented preemption doctrine, as the Court insisted on a showing of necessary conflict with federal law and subject matter necessarily national in character before it would strike down a state law. The Court implied in its rationale that federalism must involve respect for some state determinations, but it did not speak directly about federalism or frame its decision in terms of cooperative efforts needed to solve pressing problems in the federal system. Thus, the Court did not squarely address the importance of state sovereignty or state power in the federal system to bolster its position, nor did the Court define the proper balance in authority between the competing centers of government.

In sum, as the above cases indicate, the Burger Court has enhanced state authority. For the first time in 40 years it has placed limits on Congress's power over commerce. The Court has limited access to broad federal habeas relief and in effect has granted to states final authority in some areas with respect to the protection of constitutional rights of individuals. It has protected, via the Eleventh Amendment, state treasuries and has placed limits on where a state may be sued. In the copyright field, the Court has allowed states more leeway in pursuing their objectives.

Although the policy direction in these cases is clear, the federalism-based justifications for the conclusions are vague. The Burger Court has not formulated its position in terms of Corwin's axioms. It has not based its rationale on the enumerated-reserved powers, nor on the concepts of a limited national government or equality of governing units. Although the Court has increased the cooperative milieu in the federal system through two decisions in the copyright area, its rhetoric is not actively directed toward a climate of collaboration. Moreover, the Burger Court appears to have no conception of why the protection of state power is critical to the federal system. The Court says little about state entities, their importance, or the need to protect and preserve them as independent governing units. The decisions do not provide any coherent rationale as to what the concept of state sovereignty encompasses or how, when, or why state sovereignty limits congressional power. The only decision that substantively addresses this issue is *National League of Cities v. Usery*, but that decision is inadequately reasoned and unsupported by the precedents cited.

It seems that the Court has been inconsistent in protecting state power vis-à-vis national power for several reasons. For example, depending on the nature of the constitutional question, a consensus may exist among Court members not to uphold the state's interest. In *United Transportation Union v. Long Island Railroad Co.* (1982), a unanimous Court ruled that the Tenth Amendment did not prohibit federal regulation of a state-owned railroad engaged in intrastate commerce. In *Hodel v. Virginia Surface Mining and Reclamation Association* (1981), the Court (without dissent) rejected the argument that the Surface Mining Control and Reclamation Act of 1977 violated the Tenth Amendment by displacing the traditional state function of land use planning.

The Court may not afford the states protection because there is lack of a cohesive states' rights coalition on the Court. In the cases examined in this chapter Justices Burger, Rehnquist, Powell, and Stewart signed the majority opinion upholding the states' interest (with the exception of *Pennhurst,* where Justice O'Connor substituted for Justice Stewart). The Burger-Rehnquist-Powell-Stewart (O'Connor) alliance is a shaky one. In *Massachusetts v. United States* (1978), both Justices Stewart and Powell's positions indicated that they will not automatically support the states' interest and will weigh the federal objective carefully before making a determination.

The Court may not rule in favor of the states because the "state-oriented" members of the Court may not be able to gather enough support to formulate the majority opinion. In *EEOC v. Wyoming* (1983), the Court ruled that the federal Age Discrimination in Employment Act extension to state and local governments was a valid exercise of Congressional powers under the Commerce Clause. In that case, Justices Brennan, White, Marshall, Blackmun, and Stevens formed the five-member majority. In *Federal Energy Regulatory Commission v. Mississippi* (1982), the majority (Justices Brennan, White, Marshall, Blackmun, and Stevens) upheld the constitutionality of the Public Utility Regulatory Policies Act of 1978. The majority ruled that requiring states to enforce the regulations of the Federal Energy Regulatory Commission did not violate the Commerce Clause or the Tenth Amendment.

The most recent example of this phenomenon is *Garcia v. San Antonio Metropolitan Transit Authority* (1985), which overruled *National League of Cities v. Usery.* In *Garcia,* Justice Blackmun, (who provided the fifth vote in *NLC*) sided with the *NLC* minority (Brennan, White, Marshall, and Stevens), thus upholding the application of the Fair Labor Standards Act to the employees of San Antonio's mass transit system. *Garcia* completely rejected the "traditional governmental functions" analysis of *NLC* and asserted protection for the states lies in the structure of the federal government itself and in the political process.

STATES AND THEIR MUNICIPALITIES

The Burger Court's view of this relationship necessarily involves an explication of Dillon's rule. Although the United States Constitution divides governance between the states and the national government, it does not acknowledge the constitutional existence of local governments that have always been considered "creatures of the state." States may choose to delegate some of their power to localities, take powers away, or entirely abolish units of local government. The legal relationship between the states and their municipalities was defined further by Judge John F. Dillon in 1872. Under Dillon's rule, local governments may exercise only those specific powers delegated to them and are prohibited from exercising powers not delegated. Specifically, Dillon (1911:448) stated that "any fair, reasonable, substantial doubt concerning the exercise of power is resolved by the courts against a corporation, and the power is denied."

States have found it necessary to delegate to local governments substantial authority to govern. Through either constitutional provisions or legislation most of the states have enacted home rule charters. Under home rule, power is vested in a locality, usually a city, to draft or change its own charter and to manage its own affairs. It weakens Dillon's rule in that under home rule the city has control over local matters. Yet, in general ordinances passed under home rule, authority cannot be in conflict with state law.

Although states legally possess the power to endow local governments with the ability to act for states in strictly local matters, it is often unclear as to what constitutes a local matter and whether in some circumstances the municipality derives from the state the same legal status as the state possesses in the federal system. A relevant question pertaining to the derivative status of municipalities is the parameters of municipal antitrust immunity. The Burger Court, in recent cases concerning cities' antitrust immunity, has refused to grant municipalities the "state action" exemption allowed states under the Sherman Act. The issue is whether the jurisprudence has theoretical underpinnings, given the fact that states have taken affirmative steps to dilute the force of Dillon's rule by allowing municipalities the exercise of a broad range of powers.

The "state action" exemption allowed states under the Sherman Act stems from the Supreme Court's decision in *Parker v. Brown* (1943). In that case the Court held that a state law restricting competition in the marketing of agricultural commodities was immune from the Sherman Act. That Court recognized a "dual system of government," in which the states possess a degree of sovereignty, by interpreting congressional intent under the Sherman Act as only applying to the anticompetitive actions of the private sector.

In 1978 for the first time the Supreme Court considered the application of *Parker v. Brown* to municipalities. The issue in *City of Lafayette v. Louisiana Power and Light Company* (1978) was the extent to which the Sherman Act prohibits a state's cities from imposing anticompetitive restraints. The Court ruled that a city operating its electric utility was not automatically exempt from federal antitrust laws simply because of its status as a political subdivision of the state and could be held liable for anticompetitive activities that cause injury to a privately owned electric company. The plurality decision stated that *Parker* exempts only anticompetitive conduct engaged in as an act of government by the state as sovereign, or by its political subdivision pursuant to a state policy to displace competition with regulation or the monopolizing of public services. If the state's authorization of anticompetitive conduct is absent, the municipality is subject to antitrust laws.

In *Lafayette,* the Court reaffirmed the *Parker* decision as it declared the states "as sovereign" and, in imposing certain anticompetitive restraints, immune from federal penalty. But the Court viewed cities differently. They are not sovereign entities; they are created by the state and not entitled to the same deference the states receive from the national government. The Court noted that historically it has never viewed the states' subdivisions as the equivalent of the states themselves. Cities are delegated certain power from the state and legitimately may exercise that power.

In *Community Communications v. City of Boulder* (1982), the Court rejected the notion that an ordinance enacted by a home rule municipality constituted state action eligible for exemption from federal antitrust laws. Boulder is a "home rule" municipality. The Constitution of the state of Colorado granted Boulder extensive powers of self-government in local and municipal matters. In these matters the city's charter and ordinances enacted pursuant to that charter supersede the laws of the state. In this case the Court held that the city's action can be immune from antitrust scrutiny only if it constitutes the action of the state of Colorado itself or if it constitutes municipal action in furtherance or implementation of clearly articulated or affirmatively expressed state policy.

The Court reasoned that when a home rule city acts on local matters, that is, the regulation of a cable television within its boundaries, its action does not make it the equivalent of state action eligible for exemption under the *Parker* doctrine. *Parker* reflects Congress's intention to embody in the Sherman Act the federalism prescription that states are sovereign, but the prescription makes no allowance for sovereign cities. The Court asserted that our nation is not one of city-states but one of states. In short, municipalities are not sovereign entities.

Given the Court's reasoning in the above cases, it is apparent that the unitary nature of the relationship between the states and their municipalities has been reinforced. Although the states have delegated broad governing authority to their municipalities, the Court adheres to a strict construction of the parameters of municipal power. In both cases the Court has reinforced (without directly addressing) Dillon's rule by declaring that cities, as creatures of their states, are entitled to only the specific powers the states have intended them to possess. If there is any doubt concerning the existence of the power—in this instance the power of immunity from federal antitrust legislation—the power is denied.

In an age of complexity, states have found it increasingly necessary to delegate to their municipalities comprehensive responsibility for governance. In fact, Elazar (1984:203) notes that "over 80 percent of the states reject Dillon's rule or have modified it to constitutionally recognize the residual powers of local governments." Therefore, it seems logical to assume that states can endow municipalities with broad power without detailing every specific aspect of that power.

In contrast to *Lafayette* and *Boulder,* Court action supporting broad delegation of power would seem consistent with recent trends in Burger Court jurisprudence as documented in this study. The Burger Court has been concerned with the erosion of state autonomy reflected in the jurisprudence of the post-1937 Court and has taken affirmative steps to remedy its federalism concerns. In *National League of Cities v. Usery,* the Court's concern was national interference with the ability of state governments to conduct integral operations in areas of traditional governmental functions. It is no less integral to the effective functioning of the states in the federal system to allow states the freedom to broadly grant their municipalities power to govern within their proper sphere of authority.

But even though municipalities are governmental entities and can derive broad authority from their respective states, it does not logically follow that they also automatically derive attributes of sovereignty from those states. In the two cases delineated above, it is the lack of municipal sovereignty that causes Court intrusion on state prerogatives to broadly delegate authority.

CONCLUSIONS

The Constitution contains few provisions concerning the states and does not directly address state sovereignty, but it is clear that states are an integral part of the federal system and are afforded protection from federal intrusion. The Tenth Amendment grants states residual power; the Eleventh Amendment in some instances has protected the states from suit; and Court interpretations have upheld state sovereignty, although the degree of judicial protection has varied in constitutional history.

In contrast, municipalities are constitutionally and legally not sovereign entities, only creatures of their states. They can exercise power within their sphere of authority, but the extent of that power is determined by the state and ultimately by the courts. Theoretically, home rule maximizes the reach of municipal power, but it is not an absolute determinant of municipal authority.

In the field of antitrust immunity, *Parker v. Brown* established that states possess sovereignty and that the congressional intent was not to subject states to federal antitrust legislation. The states' immunity is not automatically passed to their political subdivisions unless states very specifically indicate their intention to do so. Moreover, the Court in *Goldfarb v. Virginia State Bar* (1975) has ruled that not every act of a state agency is that of the state as sovereign.

In a sense the Burger Court has reduced municipal power and set back the home rule movement. From the Court's jurisprudence in the above decisions, it seems that in issues of municipal concern the Court may rely on Dillon's rule and will leave municipalities unprotected. In contrast to its jurisprudence of the national-state relationship, the Court is consistent in its reasoning and in its vision of the relationship between the states and their municipalities. But it is likely that the impact of *Boulder* and *Lafayette* will be limited to questions of municipal immunity from federal antitrust suits. In fact, recent cases (e.g., see *Newport v. Fact Concerts*, 1981; and *City of Los Angeles v. Lyons*, 1983) indicate that the Court will not ignore municipal interests. Similar to the Burger Court's jurisprudence of the national-state relationship, future decisions may turn on the issues or coalitions of Court members rather than any dogmatic judicial affirmation of Dillon's rule or any other construct. Based upon the evidence presented, there is no indication that the Burger Court intends to eviscerate municipal power any more than the Court intends to uphold state authority on a consistent basis.

The Burger Court has not clarified its stance on the relationship between intergovernmental entities. The Court's view of the national-state and state-municipal relationship lacks an overall theoretical framework. The Court has asserted in several decisions that the states are "sovereign," but that concept is vaguely defined. Thus, the Burger Court's conception of how state power places limits on national authority is unclear. In contrast, in the area of municipal antitrust immunity, the jurisprudence in two significant cases indicates that the Court has a distinct conception of the relationship between the states and their municipalities. It is a unitary relationship. States can endow municipalities with substantial power, such as the power to be immune from federal antitrust laws, but their intention to do so must be clearly indicated. However, there is no evidence that Dillon's rule or any other construct is a conscious element in the Court's reasoning. In sum, it is questionable whether any theory will emerge from Burger Court jurisprudence or if future decisions will show the judicial clarity that will give lower courts guidance in ruling on issues of intergovernmental relations.

NOTES

1. This would involve an argument centering on implicit assumptions in the Constitution itself. See Miller (1982:50–55) for a more cogent reargument in terms of a structure and relationship mode of analysis.

2. See Justice Brennan's dissent in *National League of Cities v. Usery* (1976).

3. See Miller (1982:42–46) for other examples of the misuse of precedents.

4. However, see *Ex parte Young* (1908) as an example of an instance when a state can be sued.

REFERENCES

Corwin, Edward S. 1950. "The Passing of Dual Federalism," *Virginia Law Review* 36: 1–23.

Dillon, John F. 1911. *Commentaries on the Laws of Municipal Corporations*, 5th ed. (Boston: Little, Brown and Co.)

Elazar, Daniel J. 1982. *American Federalism: A View From the States*, 3d ed. (New York: Harper and Row)

Miller, Louise Byer. 1982. "The Burger Court's Vision of the Constitutional Position of the States in Relation to the National Government," Ph.D. diss., State University of New York, Albany.

Tribe, Laurence H. 1976. "Intergovernmental Immunity in Litigation, Taxation and Regulation," *Harvard Law Review* 89: 682–713.

_____. 1978. *American Constitutional Law* (Mineola, N.Y.: The Foundation Press).

4

Environmental Policy and Aspects of Intergovernmental Relations

Sheldon Kamieniecki, Robert O'Brien, and Michael Clarke

Previous research on environmental policy has uncovered considerable tension and conflict in intergovernmental relations. Rosener (1980), for example, has shown how the "pull of local control" can lead to conflict between administrators in coastal zone management programs. She explains that, "While intergovernmental tension can be productive by forcing public debate and generating responsive regulation, successful coastal management will require intergovernmental cooperation and a minimum of state/local conflict" (1980:95–96).

Other research indicates that a significant amount of intergovernmental friction is present in radioactive waste policymaking. Kearney and Garey's (1982:15) study of radioactive waste management suggests that this policy issue "has perhaps bred more federal-state conflict than any other since the battle over desegregation in the South." They believe this tension is created by the complexity of the issues involved, the indecisiveness of federal responses, and perceptions of inequity among state officials on matters relating to the disposal of radioactive wastes. They conclude that "the conventional operating model of cooperative federal-state relations is being supplanted by the rise of contentious federalism" (1982:21).

Worthley and Torkelson (1981, 1983) report similar findings in their investigations of intergovernmental relations concerning hazardous waste site management in New York State. They focused their attention primarily on Love Canal and the Old Bethpage landfill in Oyster Bay. Based on their analysis, tension has grown between state officials and the Environmental Protection Agency (EPA) over the cleanup of these two sites due to the slow transfer of authorized "Superfund" money and the qualifying procedures employed by the EPA (1983:104). Consequently, government action has been largely ineffective. From Worthley and Torkelson's vantage point: "The great need is . . . to discover and develop processes and mechanisms that enable, facilitate, and hasten the collaboration and cooperation that seems to be the only feasible strategy. It is in this area that policy and management researchers and analysts can make major contributions to the solution of our hazardous waste problem" (1983:110).

In addition, Bowman (1984) has examined how tension in intergovernmental relations affected the implementation of "Superfund" at four toxic waste sites in South Carolina. She found numerous instances of conflict between participants, which served to delay the cleanup of these sites.

This chapter develops and tests six hypotheses concerning the conditions that stimulate or inhibit intergovernmental cooperation in toxic waste policymaking. The conditions addressed in this study include: (1) the perception on the part of public officials of the urgency of the problem and the need to act immediately, (2) the costs and potential financial and legal liabilities involved in the abatement and cleanup procedures, (3) the extent to which government agencies must rely on other government agencies at different levels for expertise and financial assistance, (4) the public and political pressures to act, (5) the degree of openness of communication between government agencies, and (6) the degree to which a specific governmental unit or groups of units has or have jurisdiction or responsibility for involvement in the area. The results of six case studies of toxic waste sites are used to test the hypotheses.

HYPOTHESES

This study identifies six conditions that may promote or hinder intergovernmental cooperation in the management of toxic waste sites. The conditions examined in this study are not mutually exclusive, and they are not the only factors affecting the association between governments. They are, however, *major* factors, which we theorize color the nature of intergovernmental relations in toxic waste policymaking.[1]

One of the most important conditions influencing intergovernmental contacts is the *perceived urgency of the problem*. Early research on intergovernmental collaborations during the Great Depression and World War II seems to bear this out. Vieg (1941), for example, revealed how agricultural researchers, extension agents, and soil conservationists cooperated closely across governmental boundaries in agricultural-related activities of promotion, inspection, and regulation during the severe "dust bowl" crisis of the 1930s. Bane (1942) and Bromage (1943) also noted a blending of national, state, and local activities (e.g., civil defense and rationing) during the wartime emergency. More recent studies on public housing programs (Reeves, 1974) and the regulation of hazardous wastes (Tyson, 1980; Lester et al., 1983) report similar findings. Apparently, the perception of crisis usually forces public officials at various levels of government to set aside their differences, band together, and cooperate. Thus:

> *Hypotheses 1:* When the level of danger at a toxic waste site is perceived to be increasing, there is a greater probability that different levels of government will cooperate with one another.

The *estimated costs and potential financial and legal liabilities* of toxic waste site abatement is a second condition that can affect intergovernmental relations. Wright (1978) and Hanson (1983) cite the importance to the states of assessing costs and liabilities in their interactions with national and local government in general. More specifically, Kearney and Garey (1982) cite the example of a privately owned radioactive waste facility at West Valley, New York, that had to be shut down in 1971 because of financial difficulties, thus forcing the state to take over control of the site. Friction between the state of New York and the federal government has developed over who will pay the estimated costs and accept the liability for relocating the abandoned radioactive waste. Williams (1983), Getz and Walter (1982), and Walter and Getz (1986) argue that the major problem concerning the EPA's implementation of the 1976 Resource Conservation and Recovery Act involves the calculation and distribution of charges to both state governments and private interests. Disagreements in this area have resulted in clashes between federal and state policymakers over how best to manage the transportation and disposal of hazardous wastes in this country.

Love Canal further highlights the potential impact of expected costs and potential liabilities on intergovernmental relations (Worthley and Torkelson, 1981). For a long time officials in Washington, D.C., and Albany, New York, argued over who should assume primary responsibility for cleaning up the site and compensating homeowners in the area. Both the federal and state governments, as well as the Hooker Chemical Company, tried to avoid this expensive commitment, especially because of the precedent-setting nature of the situation. The Carter administration eventually agreed to pick up the tab.

Although "Superfund" is supposed to provide funds for the cleanup of abandoned toxic waste sites like Love Canal, its ineffective application during the Reagan administration and its relatively small budget have caused serious conflicts between all levels of government. Future deliberations over the extension of "Superfund" and similar programs at the state level will have to address the question of liability for the cleanup of abandoned sites (Worthley and Torkelson, 1983). The huge expense required to abate the nation's two-thousand-plus toxic waste dumps no longer in use and the intense conflicts between all concerned parties has led Cohen (1984) to recommend the formation of a set of private or quasi-public corporations to handle hazardous waste. Until such measures are adopted:

> *Hypothesis 2:* As the estimated costs and potential financial and legal liabilities for the abatement of a toxic waste site increase, there is a greater likelihood that intergovernmental conflict will occur.

The *need for technical expertise and financial assistance* on the part of state and local governments represents a third condition that affects the tone of intergovernmental relations. Cohen and Grodzins (1963) and Glendening and Reeves (1977) have noted the importance of this variable in federal and state associations. Reeves (1974) has pointed to the need for and availability of federal grants-in-aid in public housing as a primary trigger for intergovernmental interactions. After reviewing the extent of intergovernmental cooperation in several federal programs, Glimer, Guest, and Kirchner (1975:78) conclude that, "Programs in which states are assigned a technical assistance role further improve state/local relations when adequate funding is provided to enable the state to do more than a token job."

The need for technical and economic assistance by state and particularly local governments is perhaps most evident in toxic waste management (Lieber 1983; Williams, 1983; Lester et al., 1983). The abatement of toxic waste disposal sites is extremely complex and requires scientific, engineering, and planning input. Naturally, federal, state, and local agencies are likely to differ significantly in their technical expertise and laboratory facilities. More often than not, state and local governments lack the money, specialized personnel, and facilities necessary to test and monitor waste sites on a continuous basis or to develop cleanup procedures. In most cases, state and local officials are forced to approach the EPA or other federal agencies to obtain such help. When this type of assistance is perceived to be available but is withheld, tension between levels of government is likely to result. But when federal agencies are able to provide technical and economic assistance and state and local officials require such help, intergovernmental relations are likely to be stimulated. In those rare situations where a governmental unit at a lower level can adequately oversee the cleanup of a site by itself, there is likely to be little or no intergovernmental contact. In most circumstances, however:

Hypothesis 3: When state and local officials need technical expertise and financial assistance and federal agencies are able to offer such assistance, intergovernmental relations are likely to be stimulated.

The presence of *public and political pressure* also has been shown to influence intergovernmental relations on various issues (Glendening and Reeves, 1977). While public and political pressure can sometimes lead to "buck passing," this factor has promoted cooperation between different levels of government in public housing programs in Maryland (Reeves, 1974). Moreover, Tyson (1980) has demonstrated how political pressure by the Love Canal Homeowners Association, led by Lois Gibbs, eventually forced government agencies at separate levels to cooperate and take action. Due to the efforts of this organization, those living near the site were finally evacuated and compensated for the loss of their homes. Mobilization at the grassroots level at other sites has resulted in meaningful exchanges between agencies as well (Worthley and Torkelson, 1983). Following the fiasco at Love Canal, elected leaders have become increasingly sensitive to claims by organized citizens groups that a toxic waste site is threatening the natural environment and especially the public health. As a result:

Hypothesis 4: Public and political pressure will tend to promote intergovernmental cooperation in hazardous waste management.

In addition, *the openness of communication* between decision makers can act as a catalyst in intergovernmental relations. Gilmer, Guest, and Kirchner (1975), Glendening and Reeves (1977), and Wright (1978) have discussed the importance of frequent and open exchanges between levels of government in policy development and implementation. Prior contact builds trust and respect, which, in turn, leads to greater cooperation, particularly when a serious problem arises. Reeves (1974) showed this to be true in the formulation of public housing programs. The absence of prior communication between agencies, in contrast, inhibited intergovernmental relations at Love Canal at the beginning (Worthley and Torkelson, 1981), and a lack of contact between federal and state officials currently hampers efforts to dispose of radioactive wastes (Kearney and Garey, 1982). Based on the findings of previous research:

Hypothesis 5: Frequent and open communication between policymakers will tend to improve intergovernmental relations in the cleanup of toxic waste sites.

A final condition that is likely to promote or hinder intergovernmental relations is whether an agency or level of government has *clear jurisdic-*

tion or responsibility for managing a specific toxic waste site. Scholars have recognized the importance of this factor as a determinant of the tone of intergovernmental relations (e.g., Gilmer, Guest, and Kirchner, 1975; Glendening and Reeves, 1977; Buntz and Radin, 1983). When legal requirements exist and are well defined, there tends to be more collaboration than when mandates are ambiguous or nonexistent. Reeves (1974) has found this to be the case in her analysis of intergovernmental contacts in public housing programs. According to Gilmer, Guest, and Kirchner (1975), legislation creating federal grant-in-aid programs, such as the Safe Streets Act, provided clear-cut roles for states and cities, thereby facilitating intergovernmental relations. In contrast, Wright (1967) has argued that a lack of clear legal jurisdiction or responsibility in early attempts to maintain or improve environmental quality in the United States resulted in little or no intergovernmental cooperation and ineffective policies. Indeed, the absence of clear jurisdiction and responsibility interfered with attempts to establish a joint governmental effort to handle the Love Canal problem at the outset (Worthley and Torkelson, 1981, 1983). Accordingly:

> *Hypothesis 6:* The presence of a governmental unit that has clear jurisdiction or responsibility for the abatement of a given toxic waste site is likely to facilitate intergovernmental relations in the management of that site.

Appropriate indicators will be used to test the six hypotheses. While some are obvious others are not. When the perception of crisis is considered, for instance, the study will address the number of leaders and citizens who perceive a problem exists as well as the extent to which they believe a problem is serious. Also, the number of contacts and the nature of the contacts will help determine the degree of openness of communication between government agencies. Actual intergovernmental cooperation and not the appearance of cooperation is the dependent variable.

THE HAZARDOUS WASTE SITES

We analyzed six case studies of toxic waste sites to determine the extent to which our six hypotheses shape intergovernmental relations in toxic waste management.[2] The sites are Woburn, Massachusetts; Jackson Township, New Jersey; "Valley of the Drums" near Louisville, Kentucky; the Denver radium sites in Colorado; Stringfellow in Southern California; and Alkali Lake in South Central Oregon. In addition to being widely dispersed geographically, the sites exhibit rather different case histories. The case histories of the sites are discussed in Clarke,

Kamieniecki, and O'Brien (1984) and in O'Brien, Clarke, and Kamieniecki (1984).

THE ANALYSIS

The perception of urgency or crisis tended to affect intergovernmental relations at all six sites. When decision makers felt an emergency existed, they usually forgot their differences and cooperated with one another. Probably the best example of this is the Denver radium sites. After the first site was discovered, there was an immediate mobilization of the Interagency Regulatory Liaison Group (IRLG), a federal agency coordination unit. Surveys of Denver were made using a specially equipped Department of Energy helicopter and a sophisticated EPA scanning van. The Colorado State Department of Health became the center for coordinating intergovernmental efforts, and those involved (from journalists to rival public officials) praised the high degree of collaboration. The fact that the perceived crisis was sudden and posed an unknown danger to public health led to a rapid mobilization of agencies at different levels cooperating with one another.

Similar emergencies occurred at the Valley of the Drums and Stringfellow sites. Severe flooding at the Valley of the Drums disposal area prompted the EPA's Region IV office and the Kentucky Department of Natural Resources and Environmental Protection (KDNREP) to join together and develop a plan of action. Officials from these agencies decided to assess the extent of the environmental damage at the site and to explore possible remedies. The EPA, Kentucky Water Supply, and Jefferson County Health Department made a joint reconnaissance of groundwater users within a one-mile radius of the site. This case is especially telling because intergovernmental cooperation decreased noticeably once the perception of the seriousness of the crisis had declined (in part due to a partial cleanup at the site). Analogous events took place at the Stringfellow site in California. The greatest degree of intergovernmental cooperation at this site occurred when heavy rains fell in March of 1980. The EPA, United States Coast Guard, and Regional Water Quality Control Board (RWQCB) were immediately brought to the site to correct flooding, overflow, and leachate conditions. An intensive 12-day operation was financed with 311 K emergency funds (through the Clean Water Act of 1977). In comparison to the Valley of the Drums, however, the overall level of cooperation at Stringfellow has been fairly high since the perceived seriousness of the problem was reduced. Less intergovernmental collaboration took place at the other three sites, to a large extent because the perceived urgency to abate these sites was never very great. The evidence, therefore, appears to support Hypothesis 1.

While the perception of crisis has promoted intergovernmental cooperation and action, the estimated costs and potential liabilities involved in the abatement of the sites have had a mixed effect on intergovernmental cooperation and have prevented action. At the Denver radium sites, for example, the solution to the problem is relatively clear both technically and politically. The buried uranium tailings must be removed to an unpopulated area. The cost of complete removal, however, is estimated to be between $2.6 and $25 million, and state and local officials maintain that they cannot afford to pay this amount. As a result, the federal government has agreed to participate in developing a solution to the problem, and it will appropriate "Superfund" money to remove the contents of the sites.

The fear of becoming involved in a costly cleanup program often results in "buck passing." At the Stringfellow site in California, the Riverside County Board of Supervisors, which had been involved in overseeing the operation of the dump, relinquished all responsibility after 1974 on the advice of its own legal counsel. There was deep concern on the part of the county's attorney that continued maintenance of the site could eventually hold the county liable for damages to the environment or public health at a later point in time. The state of California took sole control over the site and, through the State Water Resources Control Board, has appropriated $4 million of the estimated $14 million required to abate the site. Intense lobbying by the state and the removal of Ann (Gorsuch) Burford and Rita Lavelle from the EPA resulted in the release of "Superfund" money to clean up the waste.

The high cost of cleanup (several million dollars) has led to buck passing at the Jackson Township site in New Jersey as well. The state and the township each believe the other must pay for cleanup of the site, and the state is suing the township over this issue. In contrast to the position of the state, local officials have argued that the township's landfill is not the source of groundwater contamination and that illegal dumping on an adjoining property is responsible. Since Jackson Township established the landfill and has always overseen its operation, local officials fear that action by them to abate the site might be construed by the courts as an admission of liability. Private residents, whose drinking wells have been contaminated and who may have experienced health problems as a result, would then have greater success in bringing suit against the township. In general, the projected high cost of abatement and the potential liabilities have impeded intergovernmental relations and have led to conflict at the remaining sites. With the possible exception of the Denver radium sites, where other factors seem to be more important, the findings tend to support Hypothesis 2.

The need for technical expertise and financial assistance has also helped to shape intergovernmental relations at all six sites. In the six cases examined, not one local government possessed the scientific and economic resources necessary to clean up its toxic waste dump. Excluding Oregon (for reasons we will discuss shortly), each state has asked the EPA and, on occasion, other federal agencies for technical and financial support and has received some form of assistance. Therefore, as noted in Hypothesis 3, when state and local officials need this type of aid and federal agencies are able to provide such aid, intergovernmental relations are likely to be stimulated.[3]

A fourth condition that was expected to further intergovernmental cooperation was public and political pressure. At four of the six sites studied, citizen groups have organized and have actively argued for abatement of the sites. Only at Alkali Lake, which is 60 miles from the nearest town, and the Denver radium sites, where swift action was taken, have such indigenous groups failed to form. The isolation of Alkali Lake and the corresponding lack of organized public pressure addressing the abatement issue help explain why there has been little intergovernmental activity involving the site.

Lobbying by citizens at Woburn and Stringfellow has tended to have a positive impact on intergovernmental exchanges. However, pressure by citizens can sometimes pit different governmental units against one another. Jackson Township residents, for example, felt the township (which has owned and operated the landfill) was unresponsive to their demands. As a result, they have brought a $51.5 million suit against the local government.[4] This, in turn, prompted the state to bring suit against the township to have the site permanently capped. Local officials, however, argue that the state was acting only to give the appearance of being responsive to the public.

In the Valley of the Drums dispute, a petition drive and appearances in court by citizens played a major role in preventing the rezoning of the land around the site to allow for the installation of an incinerator. Public pressure on county officials persuaded them to oppose the plan, and a county court ruled against the proposal in the end. In this instance public pressure actually prevented the implementation of an abatement solution by placing local officials in direct opposition to state and EPA administrators who supported the proposal. Thus, the results of the study offer only partial confirmation of Hypothesis 4.

The degree of openness of communication between various levels of government has molded intergovernmental relations as well. On the positive side, communication at the Denver radium sites was excellent. The Colorado State Department of Health served as a center for information about the sites for both the public and other governmental agencies. The Department of Health kept records of confirmed sites and, along with the IRLG, helped coordinate the survey of Denver for radium sites. Clearly, the frequency of contacts between agencies facilitated intergovernmental cooperation in this case.

Exchanges between federal, state, and local officials involving the Woburn site in Massachusetts have also been open and fruitful. The EPA appointed a full-time coordinator for the site who channeled citizen concerns to the correct governmental branch and coordinated intergovernmental interactions. Fear and distrust between concerned parties were minimized, thus promoting intergovernmental cooperation.

Unfortunately, the same observations cannot be made about the remaining sites. At the Valley of the Drums, for example, information disseminated by the EPA and state officials has been primarily channeled through the media. For the most part, local elected leaders have not been kept informed about the planning process. For instance, when the EPA and KDNREP failed to consult the county about the state's plan to install an incinerator at the site, tension increased between federal, state, and local officials. This lack of communication made local officials suspicious about the intentions of the EPA and KDNREP, causing them to reject the proposal. Intergovernmental relations were therefore hindered.

In general, the results of the six case studies lend support for Hypothesis 5. When contacts were frequent, such as at the Denver radium and Woburn sites, constructive intergovernmental collaboration took place. A lack of communication at the other four sites, however, appeared to obstruct intergovernmental cooperation.

The last condition that can influence the nature of intergovernmental relations in toxic waste policymaking is whether a particular governmental agency or set of agencies has clear jurisdiction or responsibility for managing a site. The IRLG in the Denver case had clear jurisdiction to act in this emergency situation. The behavior of this organization induced a high degree of cooperation between federal, state, and local governmental units by fulfilling certain coordinating functions. Similarly, the RWQCB took lead responsibility at Stringfellow because flooding of the site was threatening an underground aquifer and nearby surface water. Through the efforts of the agency, intergovernmental cooperation has been high and abatement of the site has progressed in an orderly manner.

In contrast, however, it is less clear which agency has legal jurisdiction over the Jackson Township site. Although the township had opened and operated the landfill, it claims the contamination is originating from another source. The state, of course, disagrees. At the same time, the EPA refuses to intervene because the contaminated wells are privately rather than publicly owned. Hence, all those involved in the dispute are polarized, and almost no intergovernmental interaction has taken place. The absence of a coordinating body at the other sites has limited intergovernmental cooperation at those sites as well. Taken together, the findings of this investigation underscore the value of an overseeing agency and appear to confirm Hypothesis 6.

CONCLUSION

We recognize that six case studies of toxic waste sites do not provide sufficient background upon which to construct an elaborate theory of intergovernmental relations. However, these studies do, in general, support our hypotheses that intergovernmental relations are significantly influenced at the policy level by the perception of the urgency of the situation, the costs and potential financial and legal liabilities of abatement, the necessity for technical and financial assistance at the state and local level, the existence of public and political pressure, the nature of communication between governmental units, and whether an agency has clear jurisdiction or responsibility for the cleanup of a site.

While the current study concerned itself with toxic waste problems, the typology of contingencies could be extended to other policy areas, both inside and outside of the environmental policy domain, affected by the structure of intergovernmental relations. Of course, the interaction between the variables examined in this study is quite complex and deserves further investigation. The importance of these variables in the decision-making process is obviously, as Reeves (1974) argues in her micro-level study of public housing, influenced by the attitudes and values of the actors in the process. This fact makes it difficult to formulate accurate predictions. Finally, more emphasis needs to be placed on this form of micro analysis in order to understand adequately the dynamics of intergovernmental relations as they affect major policy decisions that refuse to conform to existing policymaking structures.

NOTES

1. This investigation focuses on a particular period (the early 1980s) and, as Reeves (1974) reminds us, conditions that affect intergovernmental relations tend to take on different complexions with the passage of time.

2. These studies were financed by the EPA and three of the six investigations were conducted by the authors of this chapter. The EPA sponsored these studies so that it could better design a realistic program of participation for citizens, interest groups, and local government in toxic waste projects. The case studies consisted primarily of personal interviews with relevant local, state, and federal officials, citizens' and environmental group leaders, industry and business leaders, and members of the media. In addition, media reports, various government documents, and other technical material were analyzed. The six case studies were comprehensive and focused on nearly every aspect of toxic waste manage-

ment, thus allowing EPA officials to gain a full understanding of the decision-making process within the toxic waste policy area.

3. Additional information about the technological complexity of abating the six sites can be found in Clarke, Kamieniecki, and O'Brien (1984) and O'Brien, Clarke, and Kamieniecki (1984).

4. The residents of Jackson Township won this suit in court following the completion of this investigation.

REFERENCES

Bane, Frank. 1942. "Cooperative Government in Wartime," *Public Administration Review* 2: 95–103.

Bowman, Ann O'M. 1984. "Intergovernmental and Intersectoral Tensions in Environmental Policy Implementation: The Case of Hazardous Waste," *Policy Studies Review* 4: 230–44.

Bromage, Arthur W. 1943. "Federal-State-Local Relations," *American Political Science Review* 37: 35–48.

Buntz, C. Gregory, and Beryl A. Radin. 1983. "Managing Intergovernmental Conflict: The Case of Human Services," *Public Administration Review* 43: 403–10.

Clarke, Michael, Sheldon Kamieniecki, and Robert O'Brien. 1984. "Decision Making in a Complex Sociotechnical Environment: The Case of Toxic Waste Management" in Lloyd G. Nigro (ed.), *Decision Making in the Public Sector* (New York: Marcel Dekker): 187–207.

Cohen, Jacob, and Morton Grodzins. 1963. "How Much Economic Sharing in American Federalism?" *American Political Science Review* 57: 5–23.

Cohen, Steven. 1984. "Defusing the Toxic Time Bomb: Federal Hazardous Waste Programs" in Norman J. Vig and Michael E. Kraft (eds.), *Environmental Policy in the 1980s: Reagan's New Agenda* (Washington, D.C.: Congressional Quarterly Press): 273–91.

Getz, Malcolm, and Benjamin Walter. 1982. "Perilous Waste" in Dean E. Mann (ed.), *Environmental Policy Implementation: Planning and Management Options and Their Consequences* (Lexington, Mass.: D. C. Heath): 51–64.

Gilmer, Jay, James W. Guest, and Charles Kirchner. 1975. "The Impact of Federal Programs and Policies on State-Local Relations," *Public Administration Review* 35: 774–79.

Glendening, Parris N., and Mavis Mann Reeves. 1977. *Pragmatic Federalism: An Intergovernmental View of American Government* (Pacific Palisades, Calif.: Palisades Publishers).

Hanson, Russel L. 1983. "The Intergovernmental Setting of State Politics" in Virginia Gray, Herbert Jacob, and Kenneth N. Vines (eds.), *Politics in the American States: A Comparative Analysis* (Boston: Little, Brown): 27–56.

Kearney, Richard C., and Robert B. Garey. 1982. "American Federalism and the Management of Radioactive Wastes," *Public Administration Review* 42: 14–24.

Lester, James P., James L. Franke, Ann O'M. Bowman, and Kenneth W.

Kramer. 1983. "Hazardous Wastes, Politics, and Public Policy: A Comparative State Analysis," *Western Political Quarterly* 36: 257–85.

Lieber, Harvey. 1983. "Federalism and Hazardous Waste Policy" in James P. Lester and Ann O'M. Bowman (eds.), *The Politics of Hazardous Waste Management* (Durham: Duke University Press): 60–72.

O'Brien, Robert, Michael Clarke, and Sheldon Kamieniecki. 1984. "Open and Closed Systems of Decision Making: The Case of Toxic Waste Management," *Public Administration Review* 44: 334–40.

Reeves, Mavis Mann. 1974. "Change and Fluidity: Intergovernmental Relations in Housing in Montgomery County, Maryland," *Publius* 4: 5–44.

Rosener, Judy B. 1980. "Intergovernmental Tension in Coastal Zone Management: Some Observations," *Coastal Zone Management Journal* 7: 95–109.

Tyson, Rae. 1980. "The Intergovernmental Cleanup at Love Canal: A First Crack at 'The Sleeping Giant of the Decade'," *Publius* 10: 101–109.

Vieg, John Albert. 1941. "Working Relationships in Governmental Agricultural Programs," *Public Administration Review* 1: 141–48.

Walter, Benjamin, and Malcolm Getz. 1986. "Social and Economic Effects of Toxic Waste Disposal" in Sheldon Kamieniecki, Robert O'Brien, and Michael Clarke (eds.), *Controversies in Environmental Policy* (Albany: State University of New York Press).

Williams, Bruce A. 1983. "Bounding Behavior: Economic Regulation in the American States" in Virginia Gray, Herbert Jacob, and Kenneth N. Vines (eds.), *Politics in the American States: A Comparative Analysis* (Boston: Little, Brown): 329–372.

Worthley, John A., and Richard Torkelson. 1981. "Managing the Toxic Waste Problem: Lessons from the Love Canal," *Administration and Society* 13: 145–60.

_____. 1983. "Intergovernmental and Public-Private Sector Relations in Hazardous Waste Management: The New York Example" in James P. Lester and Ann O'M. Bowman (eds.), *The Politics of Hazardous Waste Management* (Durham: Duke University Press): 102–11.

Wright, Deil S. 1967. "Intergovernmental Action on Environmental Policy: The Role of the States," Papers on the Politics and Public Administration of Man-Environment Relationships, Institute of Public Administration, Indiana University 2: 1–69.

_____. 1978. *Understanding Intergovernmental Relations: Public Policy and Participants' Perspectives in Local, State, and National Governments* (North Scituate, Mass.: Duxbury Press).

5

The Rise and Emerging Fall of Metropolitan Area Regional Associations

Charles P. Shannon

Certain recent activities and programs undertaken by metropolitan area regional associations, commonly known as regional planning commissions or councils of governments, indicate a change in substate relations with implications for policy formulation and implementation. Regional associations (henceforth referred to as COGs), which historically have been heavily dependent on federal funding for their viability, have been forced to reexamine their purpose and relations with local (i.e., member) governments in the midst of major federal program cutbacks since at least 1977. Recent Reagan administration cutbacks in domestic programs have further accentuated the need for reexamination.

At a time when many COGs are being reduced to paper organizations or disincorporating, an intense effort is being made to redefine their relations with local governments and hence find new and different purposes for operation. To better understand why these different relations are developing, it is important to look at the type and mix of services currently offered to local governments by COGs. These services are classified under the following general types:

1. planning (e.g., housing, land use, economic development, and environmental quality);
2. nonplanning
   - issue and crisis management (i.e., multijurisdictional problems requiring immediate resolution);
   - direct service delivery (e.g., building inspection, engineering services, and circuit rider management); and

- management support services (e.g., joint purchasing, centralized recruitment, computer services and training).

Traditional local government-COG relations built around planning services are proving to be insufficient to preserve historic working relationships. Increased emphasis is being given to development of new relations associated with issue and crisis management, the direct delivery of services, and provision of management support services. These new areas of service emphasis notwithstanding, COGs face a major challenge to remain viable. The first part of this chapter explores the implications of new substate relations between local governments and COGs in the context of a declining partnership (i.e., funding) between the federal government and COGs.

The Advisory Commission on Intergovernmental Relations (ACIR, 1976) reports that substate regionalism represents one of the greatest contemporary challenges to the American federal system. ACIR has a long-standing interest in regionalism that goes back to the 1950s and 1960s when metropolitan consolidation was somewhat seriously discussed throughout the country but, with few exceptions, rejected. In the wake of that rejection, ACIR began a search for new models of metropolitan governance, and in large part due to its advocacy, COGs emerged proliferously. The cynical view at that time held that COGs were created primarily to avoid suburban consolidation with inner cities, not to address meaningful metropolitan problems. Today, in light of the new service arrangements offered by COGs, it is important to examine the historical performance and capacity of these associations to solve metropolitan public policy issues. The second focus of this chapter, therefore, is on the contribution, or absence thereof, that COGs have made to metropolitan area problem solving.

COGs have not been the focus of widespread scholarly study, but among those who have studied them, opinion varies considerably. They have been referred to as "modern-day nether regions, existing in the limelight of American governance" (Atkins, 1983). Proponents of COGs claim that they are an answer to efforts to reorganize fragmented local governments into a more coordinated and unified system (Hartman, 1983) and that "they have carved out a place for themselves because they have been useful without being painful to member governments" (Hawley and Zimmer, 1970:115). One student of COGs argues that they have demonstrated cooperation and represent an "incremental" reform for metropolitan government (Wikstrom, 1977:130). By contrast, in a sarcastic tone, it has been argued that the illusion of the COG as a government is a necessary "psychological" response to the problems of our metropolitan areas because there is an "assumed capability" to do something (Mogulof, 1971:3). The hardline criticism claims that "when change cannot be prevented, one defensive stratagem is to foster harmless change, and that COGs are, in part, such a stratagem allowing the appearance of dealing with metropolitan problems" (Hanson, 1974:33). ACIR (1966) supports this view by claiming that COGs are frequently formed for defensive purposes to prevent any more powerful or drastic regional governmental reorganization. These views tend to cover the range of opinion on COGs and therefore set the stage for our examination.

GROWTH AND DECLINE OF COUNCILS OF GOVERNMENTS

In the mid-1950s, several metropolitan areas experienced the creation of COGs. Approximately 60 such organizations were formed in the 1960s, and the number mushroomed to approximately 650 by the end of the 1970s. During the 1950s and 1960s, the most common federal programs that COGs participated in included the Housing Acts of 1954 and 1959 that provided urban planning assistance, the Highway Act of 1962, the Public Works and Economic Development Act of 1965, the Demonstration Cities and Metropolitan Development Act of 1966, and the Intergovernmental Cooperation Act of 1968.

The federal-COG partnership peaked in 1977, when up to 40 programs were operating. Eight key federal programs included housing planning assistance, highway and mass transit planning and programming, areawide planning for services to the aging, economic development planning, air and water pollution control planning, manpower development planning, criminal justice planning, and A-95 program review and comment coordination. That same year, federal funding assistance to COGs was approximately $800 million, which represented 75 percent of the nation's total COG funding. By contrast, in the 1980s only two (i.e., aging and transportation) of the key programs continued without dramatic cuts in budget or operation; and federal support to COGs declined to $350 million by 1984, a 56 percent drop since 1977, which represents only 40 percent of total funding of COGs (Hartman, 1983). The number of such organizations has also declined in the 1980s to approximately 450 from a high of 650. Defining a role and relationship to local governments within the context of a particular federal program was relatively easy, but doing so in the absence of such programs is proving very challenging.

DECLINING IMPORTANCE OF TRADITIONAL PLANNING

The Metropolitan Council of the Minneapolis-St. Paul area probably comes closest to a metropolitan planning model envisioned by ACIR and others a few decades ago, but it cannot be considered a true COG. It has several coordinating powers, budgetary and policy control over single-purpose special districts, comprehensive planning powers relating to a number of developmental functions, authority to set standards for environmental quality, and a role in fiscal equalization among the region's local governments through a tax-sharing plan. It also serves as a regional housing authority. The Metropolitan Council, however, is an exceptional case. Few other metropolitan areas even approach this model. By contrast, the COG model is characteristically a voluntary organization with no taxation power or ordinance authority, requires no political reorganization or voter referendum, and has limited ability and authority to link planning with implementation. As such, ACIR (1977a:35) states, "they have become classic examples of organizations with responsibilities which far surpass their authority to carry them out."

COGs are both the cause and victim of reduced federal planning assistance programs. There is a veritable smorgasbord of factors to explain this phenomenon. The first factor has to do with the expectation of regional planning. Coordinated metropolitan area planning started too late and without adequate tools. Zoning and general land use planning were not readily available as effective tools for inner cities and some suburban communities. When these planning tools became popular, they were generally limited to the most infant suburban communities. Formal metropolitan planning efforts were then often dominated, if not rendered insignificant, by market forces and decisions of private land developers.

Additionally, in an effort to address the intergovernmental impact of an individual jurisdiction's action on another jurisdiction or other jurisdictions, the federal government implemented a "review and comment" process established by the Office of Management and Budget (OMB), known as Circular A-95, to look at the implications of federal grants to local projects. COGs were often designated as metropolitan clearinghouses by federal agencies for the purpose of soliciting local comments on development projects and in order that the agencies themselves might comment on local project consistency with regional or metropolitan plans when appropriate. The process, although desirable in concept, has never lived up to expectations. Local governments participated inconsistently, COGs bureaucratized the process, and federal agencies often disregarded formal comments associated with grant award decisions. The A-95 process was recently rescinded by the federal government, and states have been given the opportunity to develop their own regional review structure apparatus.

A preference by COGs for, in relative terms, noncontroversial planning problems is a second factor contributing to deflated expectations of metropolitan planning cooperation. Low- and moderate-income housing planning is a classic example of a policy issue that, in general, COGs would rather avoid. This policy issue illustrates traditional inner city and suburban differences that make it a controversial policy area. Although partisan political differences are rarely exhibited among such bodies, policy areas with stark differences between inner cities and suburbs tend to be avoided. By contrast, genuine metropolitan issues, such as air quality and transportation, generally involve noncontroversial policy areas for planning. That is not to say that the planning is necessarily well done, but rather it is not avoided because of inherent metropolitan area conflicts. Common public interests (e.g., improved air quality and transportation systems) as opposed to selected public interests (e.g., more low- and moderate-income housing) usually dictate the status and importance of a planning effort.

Clearly, COGs owe much of their existence to federal programs. But those very programs represent a third cause or problem associated with metropolitan area planning. At the same time that federal planning programs were making funds available to COGs, they were, de facto, establishing local agendas. These agendas, however, were often artificial in the sense that they were not necessarily genuine or priority local issues (e.g., aging services planning and manpower development planning). In recognition of this relationship, COGs often developed a strategy of playing local interests against federal interests and vice versa (i.e., federal agencies needed COGs to relate to local governments and, conversely, local governments needed COGs to relate to federal agencies). By the mid-1970s, ACIR estimated that over 600 COGs were created indirectly through federal contributions. During that same time, however, federal agencies were also responsible for creating over 1,800 single-purpose regional planning organizations, thus contributing to further fragmentation in metropolitan area planning (ACIR, 1977b). So, although COGs have been highly dependent on federal agencies, those same agencies ultimately have helped prevent the logical and sustained growth of such organizations. Consequently, as federal programs have declined, so have the number of COGs.

A fourth but related factor affecting the planning function is the source of authority acquired by COGs. Federal agencies have been the usual but limited source of authority often in defiance of locally perceived legitimacy. That dichotomy between federally derived authority and locally sought legitimacy has been an ongoing dilemma for COGs. The problem has been accentuated through gradual efforts at defederalizing domestic programs, often resulting in an increase in categorical grant programs administered by states and a concomitant decline in block grants administered by COGs. In response, COGs have experienced a declining role as sites of regional and local expertise for federal agencies.

The decision by most states not to provide sufficient funding to COGs is a fifth factor contributing to the inability of most of them to emerge as comprehensive planning agencies. ACIR expected these organizations to acquire strength and purpose from new state legislation and funding. By and large, that has not happened. In fact, approximately one-third of the states provide no state funding to COGs for general planning activity. State governments have failed, in general, however, to provide guidelines for sensible planning at the metropolitan, local, and neighborhood levels. Criteria associated with economies-of-scale, efficiency, fiscal equity, political accountability, and administrative effectiveness would contribute to a better understanding of and role for COGs.

The role of representatives to COGs is a sixth factor influencing their performance. They are rarely directly elected (i.e., usually appointed by member governments), often have limited interest in their representative role, or worse, are interested in only a single issue. Turnover is high among COG representatives, and they often participate with a "protectionist" mentality for their own local government. This general characterization contributes little to the commitment or continuity necessary for comprehensive, coordinated metropolitan planning.

Finally, despite the fact that COGs have created some sense of a regional or metropolitan community, the term "region" is a weak concept and even more difficult to operationalize as a product of planning. It has very little political or administrative identification value. The unofficial partnership between federal agencies and COGs evolved faster than public perception or expectation of the value of metropolitan planning. Increased awareness of metropolitan area problems has not coincided with a comparable interest in metropolitanwide planning institutions. Additionally, the outcome of regional planning is most difficult to document in concrete terms and, therefore, such planning is of minimal interest to those public policy officials who require visible evidence and/or dollar savings as a test of utility. These and other factors have led to a search for new identity among COGs.

EFFORTS TO DEVELOP NEW SERVICE RELATIONSHIPS

The motivation of COGs in response to seven or more years of defederalization is clearly one of survival. That COGs are in peril if viewed as "unnecessary federal appendages" but enhanced if viewed as "allies in dealing with local problems" (Bender, 1982:92) is a message that sets the stage for their future. As they seek new service relationships with member governments, which have been referred to as crises or issue management, direct service delivery, and management support services, they confirm the view of ACIR (1977a) that the characteristics of substate regionalism continue to change rapidly. More importantly, COGs are aware that they are badly in need of creating a more substantial record of actual accomplishments. Improved effectiveness and efficiency of services within their regions must be shown to have resulted from regional council activity (ACIR, 1977a). One of the most meaningful claims made for COGs is that they are, at least institutionally, a legitimate forum for addressing regional issues. Member governments generally have a sense of ownership in the processes of COGs, and they tend to have a commendable history of nonpartisan decision making. As such, they are appropriate institutional settings to address crisis management issues. A recent example associated with the Denver Regional Council of Governments (DRCOG) illustrates the role of a COG in crisis management.

For many years the Denver Public Library (DPL) received funding from the Colorado Legislature to support services for non-Denver residents using the Colorado Resource Center, a special collection of reference material housed at the DPL. When the legislature refused in 1982 to provide Denver with its full request of financial support for non-Denver users, DPL decided to exclude non-Denver residents unless they paid a substantial daily or annual admittance fee. This was contrary to tradition and the services expected of a publicly supported library. DRCOG was then asked to form a task force to develop a plan that would restore access to DPL for non-Denver residents and identify an equitable funding arrangement. In brief, the plan specified a short-term (i.e., two years) funding arrangement and a long-term (i.e., permanent) funding arrangement, both of which guaranteed nonfee access to all users. Funding for the first year came from the Colorado Legislature and a combination of suburban counties. Second year funding came from increased support from five of seven counties, and the policy of nonfee access to those respective non-Denver residents was continued. Fee access, however, was reinstated for residents of the other two counties. A permanent funding and nonfee access arrangement may be provided under the auspices of a metropolitan library district currently being explored. However, the legislature has resumed funding for support of non-Denver users of DPL during FY '85-'86.

The role of DRCOG was that of a facilitator for Denver and other members. It facilitated dialogue and encouraged the development and examination of alternative solutions and did so in immediate response to the crisis. The ability of DRCOG to serve as a successful facilitator was due, in part, to the fact that it was not a true decision-making entity with the authority to implement its plans. Such a status would have dissuaded many member governments from agreeing to use DRCOG in a crisis management role. This example represents a new and different type of role for COGs.

Direct service delivery and the provision of management support services are increasingly popular and competitive roles for COGs. The types of direct delivery and support services being provided are varied and extensive, from services to individuals such as rideshare match and low- and moderate-income housing locator services to cooperative multijurisdictional services and contract services to individual jurisdictions. An argument advanced in the mid-1970s stated that regional services and regional planning are quite incompatible as the COG is currently structured (Mogulof, 1971). That argument is probably less true today only because COGs are involved in far less planning and increasingly more service delivery programs.

The direct service delivery and management support service roles, however, put COGs directly in competition with several other types of organizations, a situation that rarely existed or exists for planning programs. There is direct competition from the private sector, universities, state "local affairs" agencies, state municipal leagues, county associations, and various public interest groups. This situation, in metropolitan areas, has been characterized as an "administrative supermarket" for service delivery (Yates, 1974:219). Maintaining these new service relationships in the midst of this "supermarket" will be extremely difficult as the political wind drifts away from regionalism. One forecast states that "the future requires both regionalism and decentralization. But if there should be a pattern, it will be in the direction of decentralization of local services and programs. For decades, the doctrine among urbanists was that local government should be regionalized. That consensus has broken down" (Rutter, 1981:25). So what appears as newly evolved service delivery and management support roles for COGs may actually represent a shift in emphasis from planning to anything "relevant."

Although there is increasing use of nontraditional service delivery and management support arrangements, use of COGs is not emerging as the natural or popular new option. Various regional or interjurisdictional strategies include informal agreements for pooling and exchange of equipment and other resources, interjurisdictional contracting, annexation, mutual assistance compacts and shared obligations, transfer of functions, joint powers agreements, and creation of new special purpose agencies. Consequently, even where an interest in regionalizing services exists, COGs are not necessarily the preferred institutional choice.

Two other emerging patterns are having the practical effect of narrowing the appeal and role of COGs. One is the new emphasis on decentralization and focus on neighborhoods as the target service area, and the other is the more prominent role of states in local affairs. The reemergence of neighborhood organizations is leading to a reassessment of service delivery arrangements. Instead of embracing the argument that economies-of-scale are realized through larger service delivery arrangements, particularly in this era of cost-saving initiatives, more and more local jurisdictions are rejecting it in favor of other financing methods. User fees and new taxing arrangements are proving more popular methods to support services and, in the process, eliminating the appeal of the economies-of-scale argument often advanced by COGs. Support for small service delivery areas has come from a growing number of studies, such as the works of Ostrom, Parks and Whitaker (1973), that document greater efficiency and citizen preference for such arrangements. This new interest in neighborhoods generally works against COGs.

A more significant challenge to COGs, however, comes from state local affairs agencies. The state role is the pivotal one constitutionally under the New Federalism. Consolidation of many categorical grant programs into a few block grant programs administered by states has changed the focus of relations within states to local-state from local-regional partnerships. The block grant concept has become the key to state power under the New Federalism. COGs, which often administered federal categorical grants, used those funds and related projects to develop closer working relations with local governments. That natural advantage (i.e., control of federal funds) has shifted from COGs to state local affairs agencies. In turn, it has reduced the opportunities for COGs to participate in technical assistance associated with federally funded projects.

The increasing activism of state legislatures should lead to more visible profiles for state agencies. Whether that new activism is in the form of state land use planning and standards, housing finance authorities, or other roles, it will probably be, to some degree, at the expense of COGs. The cumulative effect will likely be to focus relations within states from local-regional to local-state. This situation poses such a serious challenge to COGs that some (Jones, 1981) fear it may result in the extinction of many regional associations.

In summary, the new service efforts by COGs generally represent a concerned attempt to preserve a legitimate relationship with local governments. The struggle to preserve these relationships will likely meet with varying success throughout the country because of differences in regional size, jurisdictional complexity, political attitudes, individual history, and service problems. Given the clear departure from the original planning purpose of COGs and their unclear future, it is timely to reexamine the broader issue of metropolitan governance and the role COGs might play in that process.

EXPECTATIONS AND SHORTCOMINGS OF COUNCILS OF GOVERNMENTS

Two sets of expectations about COGs need to be identified. First, among most local officials they represented an alternative to city-county consolidation, annexation, or metropolitan government. As such, COGs were often accorded at least unenthusiastic support in hopes of avoiding something "worse." By contrast, several federal agencies, particularly ACIR, and advocates of metropolitan reform had genuinely positive expectations. To them, COGs represented vehicles for redistributive policy and institutional arrangements for meaningful comprehensive planning for regional growth and development. One proponent of COGs (Wikstrom, 1977:xiii) claimed that "massive, governmental, structural reform is neither needed nor desired in the American metropolis, since councils provide an ideal, responsible, democratic mechanism for program coordination, policy direction, and management." A handbook prepared by the National Association of Regional Councils (NARC, 1977) states "within their regional councils, local officials are able to define and direct the proper course for the solution of area-wide problems that cannot be solved within a single jurisdiction."

As an early advocate of regionalism, the ACIR, in the mid-1960s, described COGs as "being a useful means of stimulating greater cooperation among governmental officials, creating public awareness of metropolitan problems, and developing an areawide consensus on more effective use of handling these problems" (ACIR, 1966). . . . By the mid-1970s, however, it was describing COGs as having a limited ability to link planning with implementation and produce authoritative regional decision-making (ACIR; 1977b). That COGs have served as vehicles of "incremental" political change, both of a structural and of an attitudinal nature (Wikstrom, 1977), may be the most compelling claim made in their behalf. They have not met the more fundamental tests of equitably redistributing public resources, including attendant metropolitan financing methods, nor have they fulfilled comprehensive regional planning needs.

Most significantly, COGs, with few exceptions, have failed to develop effective political strategies for state support, relevant legislation, and reform policies. Two and a half decades of search for relevance, legitimacy, and authority have yielded only crumbs and tokens. This history is creating the preface for a new book on regional or metropolitan governance. It is one in which the COG will be replaced by some structure for regional governance, a structure less dependent on local government and more involved with state government.

AN UPDATED LOOK AT REGIONAL GOVERNANCE

How the governance of metropolitan areas can be improved remains the dominant and fundamental problem associated with any new effort for reform. Central to this problem is structural reform, an issue that has been sidetracked for a decade or more. COGs have inadvertently diverted us from this issue by achieving varying degrees of visibility on selected policy issues. Continued legislative, academic, and editorial proposals for improved metropolitan governance represent an ongoing process, however retarded, in search of a more effective relationship between a political ideal and current realities.

It is time to render a judgment on what COGs have contributed to metropolitan governance. Even if one concedes that the "incremental" success argument is valid, it is generally limited to matters of public education and awareness of regional and metropolitan problems, not substantive achievement on operational policy issues. COGs have tended to "intergovernmentalize" everything and, in the process, cloud our vision of the metropolitan forest by dealing with too many small trees. Unfortunately, since COGs have largely failed to produce the desired areawide change, they offer little guidance for new decision choices on the future of metropolitan areas. The failure of COGs is only in part of their own making. Local governments have expected COGs to serve as a collective voice for them, which is often not the same as a regional voice. State governments have assiduously avoided the fundamental issues of structural reform in metropolitan areas, and the federal government, through its various programs, has often subverted local agendas by promoting federal ones.

Under the New Federalism, states will increasingly determine the character of metropolitan areas. The rapid growth of metropolitan areas occurred during an era of weak state government, a time when states were probably intimidated by federal efforts in behalf of metropolitan government. Today, however, "most states have modernized their constitutions and their legislatures, strengthened the Governor's role, and achieved fiscal muscle" (Becker, 1981:5). This modernization and strength provide new opportunity for states to exercise their responsibility in a renewed examination of metropolitan governance.

Although it is too difficult to forecast the precise timetable of state actions, we will soon approach a new cycle for addressing the problems of governing metropolitan areas. Among the options available to states as alternatives to COGs are regionalizations of state bureaucracies, development of enabling legislation for home-rule urban or metropolitan counties, continued establishment of single-purpose special districts, or the two-tiered concept (i.e., separation of metropolitan wide and local functions) of regional government. Any serious study of structural reform must include the latter option. Both ACIR (1977a) and the Committee for Economic Development (CED, 1970) have given us a head start. It is time to dust off their respective proposals developed in the 1970s.

The record of COGs and metropolitan reform over the past two decades needs to be documented before state legislatures. COGs have not been successful in linking planning to implementation, in achieving compromise or negotiated solutions to major metropolitan problems, in converting themselves into authoritative regionwide decision makers, or in becoming viable alternatives to local institutions. Additionally, single-purpose special districts continue to proliferate. In brief, federal and state efforts to develop coordinated regional policy through COGs have failed from lack of initiative in some cases and weak commitment in other cases. Over two decades of experimentation with COGs have not produced functionally effective metropolitan federations but have preserved local governments as "republics in miniature" (Wood, 1958:153). Nothing could be more antithetical to modern metropolitan governance.

REFERENCES

Advisory Commission on Intergovernmental Relations. 1966. *Metropolitan Councils of Government* (Washington, D.C.: Government Printing Office).

_____. 1976. *Improving Urban America: A Challenge to Federalism* (Washington, D.C.: Government Printing Office).

_____. 1977a. *Regionalism Revisited: Recent Areawide and Local Responses* (Washington, D.C.: Government Printing Office).

Advisory Commission on Intergovernmental Relations. 1977b. *State Legislative Program: 2. Local Government Modernization* (Washington, D.C.: Government Printing Office).

Becker, Stephanie. 1981. "1980 Spotlights Rebalancing Federalism," *Intergovernmental Perspective* (Winter): 4–5.

Atkins, Patricia S. 1983. "Substate Regionalism: The Nether Regions of Government," paper associated with doctoral dissertation research (College Park: University of Maryland).

Bender, Lewis G. 1982. "The Regionalism Alternative in Rural Areas," *Policy Studies Review* 2:89–96.

Committee for Economic Development. 1970. *Reshaping Government in Metropolitan Areas* (New York: Committee for Economic Development).

Hanson, Royce. 1974. "Land Development and Metropolitan Reform," in Lowden Wingo (ed.), *Reform as Reorganization: The Governance of Metropolitan Regions* (Washington, D.C.: Resources for the Future, Inc.).

Hartman, Richard C. 1983. "Where Regional Councils are Heading," presented to the Southwestern Pennsylvania Regional Planning Commission, September 8–10.

Hawley, Amos H., and Basil G. Zimmer. 1970. *The Metropolitan Community: Its People and Government* (Beverly Hills, Calif.: Sage Publications).

Jones, Victor. 1981. "Regional Councils and Regional Governments," paper presented at the American Society for Public Administration National Conference, April.

Mogulof, Melvin B. 1971. *Governing Metropolitan Areas: A Critical Review of Councils of Governments and the Federal Role* (Washington, D.C.: The Urban Institute).

National Association of Regional Councils. 1977. "Welcome to Your Regional Council: A Handbook for COG Board Members," unpublished.

Ostrom, Elinor, Roger B. Parks, and Gordon P. Whitaker, 1973. "Do We Really Want to Consolidate Urban Police Forces? A Reappraisal of Some Old Assertions," *Public Administration Review* 33: 423–32.

Rutter, Lawrence. 1981. "Strategies for the Essential Community: Local Government in the Year 2000" *The Futurist* 15:19–21.

Wikstrom, Nelson. 1977. *Councils of Government: A Study of Political Incrementalism* (Chicago: Nelson-Hall).

Wood, Robert C. 1958. *Suburbia: Its People and Their Politics* (Boston: Houghton Mifflin).

Yates, Douglas. 1974. "Service Delivery and the Urban Political Order," in Willis Hawley and David Rogers (eds.), *Improving the Quality of Urban Management* (Beverly Hills: Sage Publications): 213–40.

6

Financing Local Governments in the German Federal System

Arthur B. Gunlicks

In a book containing essays on various aspects of federalism in the United States, it is not inappropriate to remind the reader that there are other federal systems that function in ways that are both similar and different from American patterns.[1] A basic similarity exists, of course, in the territorial distribution of power and organization of administrative relationships in federal systems, although even here important differences may be found under the surface. In spite of basic similarities, one might expect also to find differences among federal systems in certain aspects of administrative behavior and practices resulting from historical traditions unique to each individual federal system. When one looks carefully at other federal systems, one finds, indeed, that such differences not only exist but that they can represent alternative ways of thinking about politics and administration. Such findings may be not only interesting in and of themselves but also useful and instructive to outside observers who are seeking ideas to deal with certain shortcomings in their own systems.

One of the most important questions facing all political systems concerns the financing of public services, facilities, and activities. Studies and reports dealing with fiscal crises of national governments in all parts of the world have been commonplace for many years. More recently, studies have appeared concerning local governments and problems associated with the financing of the growing number of public services at that level (e.g., ACIR, 1985; Sharpe, 1981). While local governments everywhere are apparently experiencing varying degrees of difficulties, there is no reason to believe that the means of financing one system of local government should not be of interest to outside observers either as a positive model to investigate further or as a negative example to avoid. The purpose of this chapter is to provide the reader with a description of a system of local government finance that is very different from American practices, not only in the means by which revenues are collected and distributed among the different levels of government but also in the detailed attention given to questions of fiscal equalization among state and local governments. The issue at this point is not so much whether Americans should or—given the political and institutional obstacles that tend to resist experimentation—even could adopt any of the German measures; rather, it is whether a more than casual awareness of certain foreign practices might not induce some scholars and practitioners in this country to think in terms of alternative schemes of incremental change in the financing of those public policies that they see threatened under current pressures for greater governmental decentralization and program reductions.

AN OVERVIEW OF GERMAN AND AMERICAN FEDERALISM

One is probably familiar with the distinction between federal and unitary systems of territorial organization of political and administrative authority but may not be aware of a second dimension of the division of power and responsibility that is an important factor in understanding German and American federalism. This dimension is areal or spatial versus functional administrative organization.

Functional administration is a major characteristic of American government. First and foremost, we accept as self-evident the concept of functional duality, that is, the traditional concept of dual federalism which assumes that the federal government is responsible for certain functions, the states for others. If there is a conflict, federal law prevails. In terms of public administration, we see functional principles applied in the form of dozens of federal independent agencies and regulatory commissions or in the field offices of federal departments or agencies that have little or no overlap with state and local governments. At the local level, and in metropolitan areas in particular, we have a veritable "jungle" of fragmented local units of administration in the form of special districts, including school districts, as well as numerous general-purpose governments, each of which is responsible for only a limited part of the whole area.

The spatial model, in contrast, calls for policymaking by the central authorities and policy-implementation by regional and/or local general-purpose authorities. In this case, "dualism" lies essentially in a division of responsibility for administration, not for policymaking. The central level provides rules and regulations for those functions that it delegates to the regional levels. Some of these functions are implemented by the regional units; however, most are passed on with or without refinements in the rules to the local authorities for implementation. Each regional and local general-purpose unit of administration below the central level is responsible for all of the governmental functions within its territory, whether these are higher level functions delegated to the lower levels or self-government functions either mandated by higher levels or self-determined by local councils. Administrative responsibility—as opposed to political responsibility, which, however, is not always easily separable from administration—rests with a chief administrative officer at each level (in France, for example, the prefect at the department level and the mayor at the local level). Each chief administrative officer is also responsible for supervising lower levels within his unit's area in their implementation of delegated functions. The concentration of responsibility for all public functions—delegated, mandated, and self-determined—in one area is called "unity of command" or "unity of administration" (*Einheit der Verwaltung*). Sometimes it is referred to in the United States as the "classic" administrative model.

The spatial and functional models can each be subdivided into unitary and federal systems. Both nineteenth-century France and Prussia were classic examples of unitary systems with spatial administration, although Prussia was considerably more decentralized than France (Gunlicks, 1984). Later, of course, Prussia joined with 24 other German states in forming a new federal German state characterized by an administrative rather than by a policymaking dualism. Both Britain and the United States are characterized by their functional administrative traditions, yet Britain is a unitary state, while the United States has been a federation since 1789.

The distinction between the spatial and functional models of administration is important to anyone who wishes to grasp some of the fundamental differences in the political-administrative traditions of the two federal systems, the United States and the Federal Republic. On the other hand, it would not be correct to focus too much attention on the distinctiveness of the separate traditions from which they evolved. In the first place, each system has been described as a kind of ideal type, when in fact there have always been a number of exceptions to the general rules of distinction. In the second place, developments have taken place in both countries that have blurred the distinctiveness of each system. The most obvious of these developments has been the change in the United States from dual (functional) federalism to cooperative federalism and then to what is now called intergovernmental relations. Hundreds of programs have been passed by Congress since the New Deal that involve federal, state, and local cooperation in the financing and administration of federal policies. Fragmentation of administration in a wide variety of functional patterns continues to exist, but the old dual division of policymaking powers has been severely undermined, with few activities left for the states or local governments to deal with exclusively.

In spite of the system of spatial administration in Germany, state (*Land*) governments do have traditional powers in certain areas such as culture in general and education in particular. And German local governments, in contrast to local governments in the United States, enjoy a long tradition of general competence (*Allzuständigkeit*), according to which they may perform any activity not already regulated by the laws of higher levels. In the meantime, a form of cooperative federalism has come to Germany also, especially since the Finance Reform of 1969. As a result of this reform and other developments, criticism is growing in the Federal Republic that the central government is interfering in the few areas of policymaking reserved to the states (*Länder*) and undermining the traditionally important general competence of the local governments. The strong similarities in the critical reactions to intergovernmental relations in both systems suggest that while significant differences may still exist between American and German federalism, there has been a convergence in recent decades that makes the two systems more comparable than before.

FINANCING LOCAL GOVERNMENT

General

In addition to the historically different administrative traditions of American and German federalism, there are two important legal-institutional differences that should be noted in any comparison of local government financing in the two systems. First, in contrast to the silence of the American Constitution, the German Basic Law contains an entire section (Section X) on the financing of the three basic levels of general purpose government.[2] The detailed provisions of this section, which incorporate the important Finance Reform of 1969, will be outlined below. Second, unlike the American Senate, the popularly elected members of which represent state and local governments only indirectly at best, the German Bundesrat consists of delegates who represent directly and are even sent to Bonn by the 11 *Land* governments. This gives the *Länder* and the local governments for which the *Länder* are legally responsible a direct voice in the political bargaining that produces the compromises that make up the system of *Land* and local government financing.

The Distribution of Tax Resources

In the United States, there is a system of financing in which more or less separate tax sources can be identified for each level of government. The federal level is identified with income taxes, the states with sales taxes, and the local governments with property taxes; however, this does not preclude other levels from applying the same tax; for example, most states have some form of income tax. In Germany, the rule is that any one revenue source may be taxed by only one level of government. Instead of different levels of government competing for revenues from the same source, the German alternative has been for one level to collect the taxes and then to share the revenues with another level.

Separate Taxes

The federal government has reserved to it the government monopolies for matches and brandy; customs duties, most of which are transferred to the European Common Market; most consumer taxes, such as tobacco, liquor, and gasoline taxes; and a variety of other relatively minor taxes. The *Länder* may place taxes on wealth and inheritance, automobiles, land acquisition, betting on races, gambling casinos, and beer. They may tax for the purpose of fire protection and secure additional revenues through lotteries. Local governments have few tax resources of their own. The most important tax traditionally has been the business tax (*Gewerbesteuer*). Since the Finance Reform of 1969, 40 percent of the revenues from this tax have been shared with the *Land* and federal governments. Since the yield from this tax depends on the amount of business activity in the community, significant differences exist among local governments in their dependence on the business tax. It accounts on the average for about 40 percent of all local revenues. Other municipal taxes include the real estate tax on urban (*Grundsteuer* B) and rural[3] (*Grundsteuer* A) property; local consumer or user taxes, for example, entertainment, nonalcholic beverages, dogs, hunting and fishing, and licenses for the sale of beer. Together, these taxes account for only about 3–5 percent of all municipal tax revenues. In spite of the general competence of local governments (*Allzuständigkeit*), they do not have the power to tax without the authority of higher law (Rosenschon, 1980).

Common Taxes

While the federal government has exclusive jurisdiction over monopolies and customs duties, it has concurrent powers over all other taxes. In keeping with the German federal tradition, however, the *Land* govern-ments are responsible for the laws concerning traditional local taxes. Taxes shared by the different levels of government are regulated at the federal level, but the political process at this level includes the participa-tion of the *Bundesrat*, which represents the *Land* governments.

The shared taxes in Germany are those placed on income, corpora-tions, and sales of services and products, which together are called the *Gemeinschaftssteuern*. These account for two-thirds of all tax revenues in the Federal Republic. Since 1980 the municipalities have received 15 percent of the income taxes derived from the payments of local citizens. The remaining 85 percent of the income tax and all of the revenues from the corporation tax are divided equally between the *Land* and federal governments. The value-added sales tax (VAT), which is less sensitive to economic conditions than the income and corporation taxes, was added to the shared taxes by the finance reform of 1969. In 1983 it was raised to 14 percent of the sale price; in order to help pay for the added costs to the Common Market resulting from the admission of Spain and Portugal in January 1986, it was raised to 15 percent. The proportion of the value added tax given to the *Länder* was set at 33.5 percent in 1983, and it will be raised to 35 percent in 1986. Although the business tax (*Gewerbesteur*) is not technically a shared tax, the sharing of 40 percent of its proceeds with the federal and *Land* governments since 1969 has had the effect of making it a part of the system of shared taxes.

FEDERAL AID TO THE *LÄNDER*

Joint Tasks

One of the most important changes made in the Basic Law as a result of the Finance Reform of 1969 was the insertion of a new section (VIIIa) and two new articles (Articles 91a and 91b) concerning "joint tasks" (*Gemeinschaftsaufgaben*) involving both the federal and *Land* govern-ments. This new section on joint tasks has legally formalized the system of "cooperative federalism" that now exists in the Federal Republic.

Article 91a provides for federal participation in the execution of certain *Land*-level functions, when these are important to the public at large and when federal assistance is required in order to make improvements in living conditions. Such functions include the expansion of old and the construction of new institutions of higher education (not just univer-sities) and university medical clinics, improvements in agriculture, and improvements in coastal protection measures. Provision is also made for common framework planning regarding the joint tasks. Federal law calls for planning commissions representing federal and *Land* executives. Plans are implemented by the *Länder*, which must approve any project carried out within their territory. The federal government assumes responsibility for 50 percent of the expenditures for the construction of institutions of advanced education, university clinics, and improvements in the regional economic structure; it assumes at least half of the costs for agricultural and coastal improvements.

Article 91b, the second of the two articles that deals with joint tasks, authorizes the federal and *Land* governments to cooperate in the promotion of facilities and activities involving scientific research. Unlike the provisions of Article 91a, the proportionate share of costs between the two levels for scientific research is not regulated in Article 91b.

Grants for Delegated Functions

According to Article 104a of the Basic Law, the federal and *Land* governments are financially responsible for their respective public tasks; however, the federal government is obligated by Article 106 to provide the *Länder* with financial grants to compensate them for any loss of revenue or increase in expenditure that results from the implementation of a federal law. The same article requires the federal government to compensate the *Länder* and local governments for any special activities, such as a census or facilities—for example, a military base—that impose an unusual burden on these units. These special grants are different from the compensation of the *Länder* for the nonadministrative costs of administering functions delegated by the federal government. Such functions include rent subsidies, home construction assistance, individual savings account subsidies, support for vocational training, gasoline subsidies for agriculture, and compensation for military maneuver damage. Where the *Länder* carry more than 25–50 percent of the financial burden, approval by the *Bundesrat* is required. If the federal government pays for more than half of the costs, the activity becomes a delegated function of the federal government.

Federal Aid for Investments

Since the *Land* and local governments are responsible for about 80 percent of all public investments, these can have considerable impact on the economy of the Federal Republic. Therefore, the Finance Reform of 1969 gave the federal government the right to give aid to the *Land* governments for investment projects that are designed to counter disturbances in the economic balance, to contribute to an equalization of economic differences in the federal territory, or to promote economic growth. Federal grants for investment purposes are program oriented, and they are directed especially at important investment initiatives, which are considered essential by the federal government but which could probably not be completed without federal assistance. The federal government may not itself assume responsibility for the program; it and all costs that follow after completion remain the responsibility of the *Land* or local government. Federal support for investments by local governments is given to these units through the *Länder*, not directly (von Münch, 1978:637–39; Blümel, 1981:229). The American practice of direct aid to local governments is seen as a violation of *Land* autonomy.

The right of the federal government to provide grants for investments that promote economic growth is a virtually open-ended authorization, since almost any investment can be interpreted as contributing to economic growth. In sharp contrast to the United States, however, federal grants for these various investment purposes have been focused on only a handful of areas. Throughout the 1970s the most important of these were urban development projects; municipal transportation; and hospital, public housing, and student dormitory construction (von Münch, 1978; for a discussion in English of federal grant policies and developments to the mid-1970s, see Reissert, 1980).

FISCAL EQUALIZATION AMONG THE *LÄNDER*

The separate taxes, shared or common taxes, and federal grants to the *Länder* are all a part of what is called in Germany "vertical tax equalization." In order to provide a more equitable distribution of tax revenues than vertical equalization alone can produce, a "horizontal tax equalization" among the *Länder* and municipalities has been added as an important feature of the *Land* and local tax systems.

As noted above, the local governments, that is, municipalities, receive 15 percent of the income tax revenue, while the federal and *Land* governments receive an equal share of the remaining 85 percent. The federal and *Land* governments also share equally two-thirds of the value-added tax (VAT) and 40 percent of the business tax. Excepting the VAT, the *Länder* retain their share of the common taxes from revenues collected within their boundaries. Three-fourths of the VAT is distributed on the basis of population, one-fourth on the basis of need. The latter funds are provided only up to the point at which the receiving *Land* has reached 92 percent of the average *Land* revenue per inhabitant. *Länder* that still need financial aid are assisted by additional grants from the federal share of the VAT.

Given the relatively large population of the eight territorial *Länder* in the Federal Republic and the virtually uniform tax system, differences among the *Länder* in tax potential are small in comparison to the United States. In 1978 the range in the ratio of tax potential was only 1.24 to 1 (Zimmermann, 1981:38). Nevertheless, the Basic Law prescribes federal measures to promote uniform living conditions (Article 72 and Article

106), and one of these measures is the Fiscal Equalization Law of 1969, as revised in 1977. This law provides for a calculation of *Land* fiscal potential, including the fiscal potential of its municipalities, together with the tax needs of the *Land* and local governments (Zimmermann, 1981:35–38).

The first goal of the fiscal equalization procedures among the *Länder* is to increase the tax need indicator of the deficit *Länder* to 92 percent of the average for all of the *Länder*. The remaining deficit of 8 percent is supplemented only up to 37.5 percent. This brings the revenues of deficit *Länder* up to at least 95 percent of the average tax revenue for all *Länder*. *Länder* with above average revenues may retain their surpluses up to 102 percent; thereafter, 70 percent of the surplus between 102 and 110 percent and all of the surplus above 110 percent is contributed to the equalization fund. In 1978 the result of this equalization process was that the 1.24 to 1 range in the tax revenue potential was reduced to 1:1.07, which is a remarkable degree of equality in per capita revenue by American standards (Zimmermann, 1981:38).

FISCAL EQUALIZATION WITHIN THE *LÄNDER*

Goals and Methods

Horizontal fiscal equalization takes place not only among the *Länder* but between the *Land* and its local governments. The concerns of the *Länder* in their equalization policies include the maintenance and strengthening of local self-government, the supplementation of local resources, the equalization of fiscal differences among municipalities, the consideration of structurally conditioned needs, and the activation of the local government budgets for economic stabilization policies (Voigt, 1980).

While all of these goals are important, most attention in recent years has probably been focused on structural differences and needs within the *Länder*. The provisions of the Basic Law concerning "unity of living conditions" have been used by all of the *Länder* as an authorization for creating a system of "central places," that is, larger towns or cities that serve other municipalities in the area as centers of social services, economic activity, recreation, culture, and general public administration. These central places can be categorized further by size and importance. Both *Land* categorical grants for infrastructure investments and the more general formula grants have been important sources of income for central places in recent years (Voigt, 1980). As can be seen from the discussion so far, the emphasis on equality in the provision of public services in Germany makes very difficult an application or acceptance of American public choice theories.

Fiscal Equalization between *Land* and Local Governments

According to Article 106, paragraph 7, of the Basic Law, the *Länder* are to provide their local governments with a certain percentage of their revenue from the common taxes. *Land* laws are also to determine whether and to what extent the *Land* taxes are to be shared with the localities. From 1970 to 1977 the *Länder* made available to their local governments one-third of their tax revenues for local government fiscal equalization (*kommunaler Finanzausgleich*). Since this equalization is a *Land* function, differences can and do exist concerning the amounts of *Land* revenues that are shared with local governments. In 1977, for example, Lower Saxony shared 37.8 percent of its tax revenue with its local governments, while the figure for the Saarland was only 27.7 percent. The per capita average for the fiscally stronger group of *Länder* was 506 DM, for the fiscally weaker group 490 DM (Voigt, 1980).

Forms of *Land* Aid to Local Governments

In most of the *Länder*, a distinction is made between two forms of aid: general purpose formula grants and special categorical or project grants. Since the terms are not the same in all of the *Länder*, Voigt has suggested that aid be divided into three general categories: general purpose grants (*allgemeine Finanzzuweisungen*); special purpose grants; and infrastructure investment grants (Voigt, 1980; but for a different categorization scheme, see Elsner, 1979).

Most general purpose grants are provided in the form of formula grants—distributed primarily on the basis of population—however, some general purpose grants are provided on the basis of need. Formula grant proportions vary among the *Länder* and ranged in 1977 from about 55 percent of total aid in the Saarland to about 28 percent in Bavaria. The formula grants have the double purpose of providing all local governments with additional revenues—and in this way are similar to American revenue sharing and bloc grants—and of helping further to equalize revenues. Calculation formulae for meeting these twin purposes vary among the *Länder*, but the similarities are strong. In all the *Länder* the tax potential of the municipalities is determined by adding the property tax for urban and rural real estate, 60 percent of the business tax on profits and capital, and the municipal share of the income tax. The relatively insignificant municipal taxes on beverages, dogs, and so forth are not considered in the calculations. Differences, on the other hand, can be found among the *Länder* in terms of the rates applied to various taxes for the measurement of tax potential.

The calculation of need for the formula grants to the local governments consists of adding population size (*Hauptsatz*) and special needs not met by population (*Nebensätze*), for example, compensation for being a "central place," for serving as a base for foreign troops, or for being a health spa. Educational or social service needs may also be considered. It is interesting to note that the population factor in the formula is affected by municipal size in such a way that additional weight is given to larger municipalities. Thus a municipality in Bavaria, for example, receives a weight of 100 percent for 3,000 inhabitants, 110 percent for 10,000 inhabitants, 125 percent for 25,000 inhabitants, and so forth, up to 150 percent for 500,000 inhabitants. The reasoning behind these progressive rates lies in the experience that the larger the municipality, the higher the costs of government per person. For the counties, on the other hand, a progressive increase is given on the basis of the number of small villages, since administrative costs in small units are also higher. The final calculation consists of combining the *Hauptsatz* and the *Nebensatz* into the *Gesamtsteur*, which then is multiplied by a basic sum (*Grundbetrag*) set annually by the *Land* parliament (Voigt, 1980:72–78; Elsner, 1979:161). Given the acceptance for decades in Germany that larger size leads to higher costs per capita, it seems unfortunate that the typically parochial debates in the United States over economies of scale could not have been better informed by checking some foreign experiences.

Special purpose grants are designed to finance all or part of certain functions. Special purpose grants include grants that compensate the local government for carrying out delegated tasks; grants for direct transfer payments, for example, rent subsidies; and grants for certain functional areas, such as schools, welfare payments for those who do not qualify for unemployment compensation, war burden sharing, streets and especially commuter transportation (Voigt, 1980:67–68).

The general grant category is oriented toward financing infrastructure investments at the local level. Grants for this purpose, like project grants in the United States, are awarded on the basis of applications from the local units of government. They do not normally cover all of the costs of government. They are frequently criticized for distorting the priorities of local governments and thus limiting to some extent local autonomy (Voigt, 1980:69).

Fiscal Equalization within the Counties

While the municipalities have the business tax, the property tax, and a variety of other modest taxes, only about 3 percent of the revenues received by counties comes from their own tax sources (Wandhoff, 1982:75). Nor do they receive a share of the income tax or the VAT. On the other hand, the *Länder* are required by the Basic Law (Article 106, par. 7) to provide their municipalities and counties with a proportion of their income from the common taxes, the percentage to be determined by the *Land* parliaments. Since they do not have their own tax resources, the counties are dependent on formula grants, project grants, and infrastructure investment grants from the *Land* and on the county assessment (*Kreisumlage*). The county assessment, which accounts for about one-third of county revenues on the average (Meichsner, 1983:70) is the assessment by the county councils on all municipalities within the area of the county for a proportion of their income from their real estate and business taxes, formula grants, and the income tax. The assessment rate, which must be approved by the administrative district authorities, depends on the needs and capacities of the county and its municipal units. Larger municipalities generally pay a larger assessment than they receive in benefits, and smaller towns and villages generally receive more in benefits, thus contributing further to an equalization of finance (Wagener, 1982:27–30).

As a general rule, the county assessment may not exceed 50 percent of municipal tax revenues, on the grounds that a higher proportion would undermine municipal autonomy. While the methods used to calculate the average county assessment vary, the municipalities paid an average nationally of about one-third of their tax income to the counties in 1978. The counties, in turn, are required to pay an assessment to the administrative districts (Wagener, 1982:37–38).

CONTROVERSIES IN GERMAN LOCAL GOVERNMENT FINANCE

The Finance Reform of 1969 created a system of financing that contained even more tax sharing features than had existed before, thus making local governments less dependent on any one tax source and providing more stable and reliable income flows. In addition, measures providing for more equalization among the *Länder* and among local governments within the *Länder* were included in the constitutional and legislative changes brought about by the reform. A third element of the reform was a clarification and rationalization of the system of financial grants that had grown up since the 1950s without a clear constitutional basis. These changes were to make possible more and better financial planning for all levels of government, including counter-cyclical measures that would, for example, increase investments in periods of economic stagnation or decline. In the most general sense, of course, the finance reform of 1969 was supposed to meet the demands of the various associations representing local governments for a fair and efficient system of local government financing that would provide adequate revenues for active and progressive councils and administrations.

As is usually the case with reforms that generated great expectations, the numerous goals of the Finance Reform of 1969 have not been met in full. Revenues for local governments increased, but expenses increased to an even greater extent. The issue of local government autonomy, however, has become central in the debate over the principles behind the Finance Reform of 1969 and their impact on German federalism.

The right of local governments to determine their own budgets is one of the "core" areas protected by the Basic Law and *Land* constitutions. On the other hand, local governments are financed in a national system in which they share important tax revenues with other levels. Local governments have no major taxes over which they exercise complete control. Even the business tax, the rates of which are set by the municipalities, is now shared with the *Land* and federal governments.

More problematic is the responsibility of the *Länder* for the fiscal equalization that takes place within their borders. Thus the *Länder* determine the total amount to be distributed and the distribution scheme among the county-free or independent cities, counties, and municipalities that belong to the counties. They determine the range within which rates for property and business taxes may be set, and they provide the funds for activities and services that they delegate to the local governments (Wandhoff, 1982:71–74).

Most troublesome, in the view of some critics, is the effect on local government autonomy of the federal "joint task" financing and *Land* special purpose grants. The Finance Reform of 1969 was supposed to help clarify responsibility for certain grant programs and to limit their effects on local autonomy. Instead, "mixed financing" (*Mischfinanzierung*) programs grew to the point that there are now very few functions for which some funds from a special grant are not available (Pappermann, 1984:247–48). This increased sharing of responsibility for functions at the local level was promoted even more by the local government reforms of the 1960s and 1970s, which were oriented strongly toward considerations of efficiency in the creation of larger units of local government (for a discussion in English of local government reforms in Germany, see Gunlicks, 1977 and 1981). In the 1970s the view seemed to prevail that all levels should cooperate in implementing activities of common concern. *Land* legislatures also tended to interpret—some would say thoroughly misinterpret—those provisions of the Basic Law that called for maintaining the equivalency of living conditions by introducing numerous programs for which the *Land* and local governments could share the costs (Pappermann, 1984:249–50). By the end of the 1970s more than 10 percent of the federal budget was designated for "joint task" financing, a proportion very close to the 11.5 percent of total 1984 federal outlays for federal grants-in-aid in the United States (Lawson and Benker, 1985:21).

Just as problematic—or perhaps even more problematic than the federal grants—are the special purpose grants of the *Länder*. In 1981 in

North Rhine-Westphalia, for example, there were 134 grant funds available to local governments on the basis of mixed financing. Even the funds with small amounts of money carried with them provisions and regulations that interfered seriously with local autonomy. By the end of the 1970s, *Land* grants of all kinds provided on a national average 30 percent of the revenues of local governments. One-half of these funds were from special purpose grants, which provide detailed instructions for their use. Special purpose grants for investment have become so important that by the end of the 1970s North Rhine-Westphalia was able to control to some degree 60 percent of all local investments made within its borders (Pappermann, 1984:250).

Criticism of the system of "mixed financing" is based on a variety of arguments. The Basic Law provisions according to which each level of government is independent of the other in financial matters are weakened; local government autonomy is undermined, in part through the common interests of functional authorities to strengthen their relations at varying levels at the expense of the spatial administrative organization of *Land* and local governments; decision making is made less transparent; decision making is made unnecessarily complicated and lengthy; establishing political responsibility is made difficult; maintenance costs for investments are not covered by grant assistance, thus placing a sometimes unanticipated burden on local governments; local priorities are manipulated by the availability of grant funds; and administrative and personnel costs are increased significantly by the red tape inherent in mixed financing schemes (Pappermann, 1984:254–60).

The Finance Reform of 1969 that called for more cooperation between the federal and *Land* governments and between these and their local governments in an effort to provide a more secure financial base for the various levels and promote more equality in living conditions now is seen as having had some unanticipated consequences. According to critics, these have undermined the German spatial-federal system in such a manner that the traditionally clear division in administrative responsibilities among the levels of government has been seriously eroded. The replacement during the past 50 years of the old dual (functional) federalism in the United States by what is now called intergovernmental relations is criticized on strikingly similar grounds. It is too complex, too bureaucratic, too centralized, too expensive, and too much lacking in accountability. It appears, then, that both federations have moved in the direction of a new and different system of more shared responsibility—or, depending on one's perspective, no responsibility—which has narrowed to a considerable extent the traditional distinctions between the two. Whether President Reagan's New Federalism or efforts by critics of German cooperative federalism to resist any further undermining of *Land* and local autonomy can be successful under the impact of the modern welfare state and the centralizing trends associated with it remain to be seen.

NOTES

1. The author wishes to thank the Faculty Research Committee of the University of Richmond and the Hochschule für Verwaltungswissenschaften in Speyer for the financial and administrative support, respectively, that made this study possible.

2. Highly detailed discussions of this section can be found in the numerous commentaries on the Basic Law. See, for example, von Münch (1978).

3. German cities, towns, and villages may receive revenues from rural property because they include within their municipal limits virtually the entire land area of the Federal Republic; that is, there is very little unincorporated territory. Legally, then, a German county is a territorial corporation (*Gebietsverband*) that contains the combined area of a number of smaller territorial corporations called cities, towns, and villages (*Gemeinden*). Larger cities, usually with populations in excess of 100,000, may form city-counties or county-free cities (*Stadtkreise* or *kreisfreie Städte*). In the United States, only Virginia has city-county separation on a statewide basis.

REFERENCES

Advisory Commission on Intergovernmental Relations. 1985. *The States and Distressed Communities* (Washington, D.C.: Government Printing Office).

Blümel, Willi. 1981. "Die Rechtsgrundlagen der Tätigkeit der kommunalen Selbstverwaltungskörperschaften," in Günter Püttner, *Handbuch für kommunale Wissenschaft und Praxis*, Bd 1, *Grundlagen* (New York, Berlin, and Heidelberg: Springer-Verlag):229–64.

Elsner, Hermann. 1979. *Das Gemeindefinanzsystem* (Cologne: Verlag W. Kohlhammer).

Gunlicks, Arthur B. 1977. "Restructuring Service Delivery Systems in West Germany" in Vincent Ostrom and Robert P. Bish (eds.), *Comparing Urban Service Delivery Systems: Structure and Performance* (Beverly Hills, Calif.: Sage Publications, 1977): 173–96.

——. 1981. "The Reorganization of Local Governments in the Federal Republic of Germany," in Arthur B. Gunlicks (ed.), *Local Government Reform and Reorganization: An International Perspective* (Port Washington, N.Y.: Kennikat Press): 169–81.

——. 1984. "Administrative Centralization and Decentralization in the Making and Remaking of Modern Germany," *The Review of Politics* 46: 323–45.

——. 1986. *Local Government in the German Federal System* (Durham, N.C.: Duke University Press).

Lawson, Michael W., and Karen M. Benker. 1985. *Significant Features of Fiscal Federalism: 1984 Edition* (Washington, D.C.: U.S. Government Printing Office).

Meichsner, Erhard. 1983. "Kreis und Gemeindefinanzen 1983," *Der Landkreis* (February): 62–71.

Pappermann, Ernst. 1984. "Mischfinanzierung als Hemnis der Haushaltskonsolidierung?" in Hans Herbert v. Armin und Konrad Littmann (eds.), *Schriftenreihe der Hochschule Speyer*, Bd 92 (Berlin: Duncker & Humblot): 247–60.

Reissert, Bernd. 1980. "Federal and State Transfers to Local Government in the Federal Republic of Germany," in Douglas E. Ashford (ed.), *Financing Urban Government in the Welfare State* (London: Croom Helm): 158–78.

Rosenschon, Jürgen E. 1980. *Gemeindefinanzsystem und Selbstverwaltungsgarantie* (Cologne: Verlag W. Kohlhammer und Deutscher Gemeindeverlag).

Sharpe, L. T. (ed.). 1981. *The Local Fiscal Crisis in Western Europe* (Beverly Hills, Calif.: Sage Publications).

Voigt, Rüdiger. 1980. *Das System des kommunalen Ausgleichs in der Bundesrepublik Deutschland*, Helft 5/6, *Kommunalforschung für die Praxis* (Stuttgart: Richard Boorberg Verlag).

von Münch, Ingo. 1978. *Grundgesetz-Kommentar*, Bd 3 (Munich: C. H. Beck'sche Verlagsbuchhandlung): 615–832.

Wagener, Frido. 1982. "Landkreise und Kreisfinanzen," in Frido Wagener (ed.), *Kreisfinanzen*, Bd 1 (Göttingen: Verlag Otto Schwartz & Co.): 1–46.

Wandhoff, Rolf. 1982. "Staat und Finanzen," in Frido Wagener (ed.), *Kreisfinanzen*, Bd 1 (Göttingen: Verlag Otto Schwartz): 71–100.

Zimmermann, H. 1981. *Studies in Comparative Federalism: West Germany* (Washington, D.C.: Advisory Commission on Intergovernmental Relations).

Part 3
Federal-State Relations

7

OSHA, the States, and Gresham's Law: From Carter to Reagan

Frank J. Thompson and
Michael J. Scicchitano

In July 1981, Senator David Durenberger convened a subcommittee hearing to explore an aspect of intergovernmental relations that in his view had "received very little attention." Specifically, the subcommittee set out to investigate the role of the states in implementing major federal regulatory policies (U.S. Senate Committee on Governmental Affairs, 1982: 2). These policies included the Clean Air Amendments of 1970, the Occupational Safety and Health Act of 1970, and the Resource Conservation and Recovery Act of 1976.

By 1985, state enforcement of federal regulatory policy was no longer a lost world to students of intergovernmental relations. Government reports as well as scholarly studies had explored important dimensions of the subject (e.g., see Eads and Fix, 1984; Lester et al., 1983; Marvel, 1982; Menzel, 1983; U.S. Advisory Commission on Intergovernmental Relations, 1984; and Williams and Matheny, 1984). While these analyses resulted in important gains, gaps in understanding persist. This essay takes a further step toward expanding knowledge of the subject by examining enforcement vigor under the Occupational Safety and Health Act (OSHA).

Enforcement vigor must be distinguished from the promulgation of safety and health standards by the bureaucracy (e.g., requirements that exposure to hazardous substances not exceed certain levels). Enforcement vigor denotes the intensity of agency actions aimed at monitoring targeted enterprises to determine their compliance with standards as well as the propensity of the agency to punish violations.

By examining data on enforcement vigor related to one federal program, this essay broaches two major questions. First, do the states
achieve higher or lower levels of enforcement vigor than the federal
bureaucracy in implementing Washington's regulatory programs? Because the occupational safety and health program features a substitution
approach to intergovernmental relations, the analyst can address this
question within the context of a single program. Under the substitution
approach, federal laws establish the basic policies and states choose
whether to assume administrative responsibilities. If a state decides not
to participate or cannot meet Washington's expectations, the federal
government marshals its own bureaucracy to implement the law directly. In the case of occupational safety and health, one can compare
the level of enforcement vigor achieved by state-operated programs with
that sustained by the federal bureaucracy in the nonparticipating states
where it holds direct jurisdiction.

A second question central to this study concerns the responses of state
programs to a shift in Washington's orientation toward regulation and
intergovernmental relations. To the extent that policymakers in the nation's capital reduce the enforcement vigor of the federal bureaucracy
and give states more discretion to run their programs, will participating
states pursue enforcement deregulation or resist it? A movement by the
states to deregulate would provide support for Gresham's Law of state
participation in regulatory programs. Rowland and Marz (1982:572) define this law as the tendency for "lax regulation to drive out stringent
regulation." States presumably compete to attract and retain businesses
by reducing their regulation to whatever floor the federal government
will tolerate; in essence, they bid down to the lowest common de-
nominator. Given this dynamic, granting the states more freedom in the
implementation process presumably invites a downward spiral in enforcement. Deregulation of the private sector and state discretion march
hand in hand. This essay explores whether this version of Gresham's
Law applies to the occupational safety and health program.

In focusing on these issues, the authors: (a) provide background information about the program as well as the measurement of enforcement
vigor; (b) compare the enforcement vigor achieved by the states with
that of the federal bureaucracy; (c) examine changes in state enforcement from the Carter to the Reagan years as well as some potential
sources of variation in state responses; and (d) speculate about some
more general implications of the case.

THE MEASUREMENT OF ENFORCEMENT VIGOR

The Occupational Safety and Health Act purports to reduce injury and
illness in the work place through research into occupational hazards as

well as the promulgation and enforcement of protective standards. While the statute envisioned that a new federal agency, the Occupational Safety and Health Administration (OSHA), would lead this initiative, it also encouraged states to "assume the fullest responsibility" for worker well-being. In support of this aim, the law authorized OSHA to pay up to 90 percent of a state's cost in developing a plan for occupational safety and health. Once OSHA officials found a state plan acceptable, they could fund up to half of the cost of that program. The statute required OSHA to monitor a state agency to assure that its safety and health rules were at least as effective as those issued by OSHA and that it had qualified personnel and adequate funds. If the state program failed to meet these and related standards or a state chose not to participate, OSHA could claim jurisdiction and take over implementation with its own personnel. By 1977, 23 states continued to operate their own programs, and by the early 1980s this number had shrunk to 21.

This study draws on data collected from OSHA and the states, which tap various aspects of enforcement over the seven-year period from fiscal 1977 through fiscal 1983. One measure is a program input, the mean number of occupational safety and health inspectors employed by a state program annually per 100,000 civilian employees in its jurisdiction. Three other indicators of enforcement vigor deal with basic program outputs at the street level—the number of inspections, citations, and serious citations assessed on business by a regulatory agency per 100,000 members of the civilian work force. Serious cited violations deserve attention because they tend to carry heavy monetary penalties.[1] The enforcement indicators cannot be treated as summary measures of agency effectiveness in promoting compliance with standards and, ultimately, health in the work place. Nonetheless, they capture important aspects of enforcement vigor and program performance.

A COMPARISON OF STATE AND FEDERAL ENFORCEMENT VIGOR

The considerable variation among states on the four enforcement indicators (see table 7.1) reaffirms the more general proposition that states possess substantial discretion and react quite differently when implementing federal policy. The data in table 7.1 also testify to the relative vigor of state enforcement. Eleven of 23 states employed more compliance officers per 100,000 civilian employees than OSHA, while nine employed less. Twenty-two of 23 states had higher inspection and citation rates than OSHA. Only serious citations point toward greater enforcement vigor by the federal bureaucracy. While the ratio for all states surpasses OSHA's rate of 56 serious citations per 100,000 civilian employees, OSHA's rate exceeds that of 14 states. Most state agencies are

Table 7.1 State and OSHA Enforcement Vigor, Annual Average, FY 1977–1983

Program	Compliance Officers	Inspections	Citations	Serious Citations
	(Per 100,000 Members of Civilian Labor Force in Area Served)			
Alaska	8.6	569	1520	117
Arizona	1.3	231	246	23
California	1.7	168	414	39
Colorado[a]	1.6	174	588	18
Connecticut[a]	2.0	239	676	12
Hawaii	5.1	786	1954	172
Indiana[b]	2.6	209	551	148
Iowa[c]	1.8	120	245	79
Kentucky[b]	2.3	195	524	22
Maryland	3.2	274	349	35
Michigan	2.0	542	1408	84
Minnesota[b]	2.0	216	540	55
Nevada[b]	3.8	543	1106	45
New Mexico[e]	1.6	79	188	33
North Carolina	1.7	188	559	39
Oregon[b]	5.3	747	1451	180
South Carolina[b d]	1.9	144	525	47
Tennessee	1.7	145	337	40
Utah[b]	2.8	332	709	30
Vermont	3.9	284	1191	79
Virginia	1.9	112	276	28
Washington[c]	4.3	860	1811	112
Wyoming	4.5	277	787	44
All States	2.3	279	658	61
OSHA	2.0	99	208	56

SOURCE: OSHA; state survey conducted by the authors; U.S. Bureau of Labor Statistics (1980).

[a] State dropped out of the program in 1978.

[b] The data input for FY 1982 for the state is an estimate based on two quarters of data.

[c] The data input for FY 1983 for this state is an estimate based on three quarters of data plus additional data from FY 1984.

[d] The data input for this state for FY 1983 is an estimate based on three quarters of data.

[e] Does not include data from FY 1983.

busier conducting more inspections and citing more violations but are less inclined to issue citations that have a big financial penalty.

ENFORCEMENT UNDER CARTER AND REAGAN

Do changes in presidential administrations produce shifts in the enforcement of regulatory policies? Conventional wisdom and several studies suggest that this often occurs (e.g., Menzel, 1983; Moe, 1982). Whether state implementation of federal regulatory policy facilitates or impedes this development has received less attention.

The Reagan administration brought a perspective to the occupational safety and health program that differed markedly from that dominant during the Carter years. First, the Reagan administration put a greater emphasis on deregulation of the private sector. This emphasis included weakening certain health and safety standards; it stressed a less punitive orientation toward businesses that broke the rules. In the words of Thorne Auchter, Mr. Reagan's appointee to head the agency, "OSHA's real concern is not crime and punishment." (U.S. House Committee on Appropriations, 1983:644). Rather, Auchter viewed OSHA as a consultant working in cooperation with business to remedy health and safety problems.

This commitment to a consultative rather than punitive mode went beyond rhetoric. For instance, the agency revised its field manual for inspectors to emphasize their responsibilities as consultants (Wines, 1983:2010). This represented a sharp departure from the legalistic approach of the Carter administration, which ordered inspectors to cite any violations they unearthed. OSHA also instituted new informal conferences with employers to settle citations; these often led to reductions in proposed penalties. In addition, OSHA devised various strategies for exempting firms with strong safety records from in-depth inspections. As a result of these and other changes, OSHA declined on three of four measures of enforcement vigor from the Carter years to the first three years of the Reagan administration.

Second, the Reagan administration differed from the Carter administration in stressing the importance of state discretion in the implementation process. Throughout the 1970s, OSHA carefully monitored and issued countless directives to state programs. Top Reagan appointees promised to pursue a less intrusive approach. Claiming that OSHA compliance offices had "devoted an inordinate amount of time to monitoring state programs," Auchter closed many of these offices and announced that the agency would depend largely on a "paper review" of state programs (U.S. House Committee on Appropriations, 1981:493–94, 517). Whereas OSHA officials under Carter threatened to withdraw approval of certain state programs for failing to meet enforcement requirements, Reagan officials quickly renounced these threats. OSHA under Reagan also worked to reduce court pressures on the states to hire more inspectors. In these and other ways, OSHA conveyed a more permissive orientation toward state enforcement of regulatory standards. (It deserves note that OSHA proved far less permissive in dealing with the promulgation of safety and health rules by the states. Corporate lobbies expressed fears that allowing the states excessive freedom would unleash "regulatory balkanization" with various states adopting different standards. Gottlieb, 1982.)

Gresham's Law?

Did the joint emphasis on enforcement deregulation and greater state discretion by the Reagan administration lead to the triumph of Gresham's Law? In sum, did it spawn a movement among state programs to reduce enforcement? If so, did the states cut enforcement more than OSHA did in nonparticipating states? Table 7.2 provides some clues by comparing the mean annual values of the four enforcement indicators during the Carter years to those in evidence during the Reagan period.[2]

In general, the states did not cut enforcement to the same degree as OSHA. To be sure, states declined more than OSHA on one of the measures, inspections per 100,000 civilian workers. OSHA demonstrated a tiny increase on this indicator, while 16 of 21 states moved in the opposite direction. When comparing performance along this dimension, however, it is important to note that OSHA introduced a new standard operating procedure for federal safety inspectors during the Reagan years. This procedure called upon the OSHA safety officer to start an inspection by reviewing the logs of recordable injuries suffered by workers at a given site. If the firm's lost workday injury rate fell below the latest national average for manufacturing injuries, the compliance officer would generally terminate the inspection without a further search for infractions of OSHA rules. This effort at targeting meant that OSHA's personnel engaged in many paper inspections, a departure from practices under the Carter administration.

The other indicators of enforcement vigor do not reveal the same pattern as inspections. OSHA's ratio of inspectors to 100,000 civilian workers declined by 17 percent from the Carter to the Reagan period. Only two states receded at a more rapid rate. Thirteen of 21 states increased their ratios albeit by modest amounts. The pattern with respect to citations is similar in part. OSHA's overall citation rate dropped by 27 percent from the Carter to the Reagan years; the serious citation rate slipped downward by the same amount. This trend was far less evident in the states. Granted, 13 of 21 states revealed a greater percentage decline

Table 7.2 Changes in State and OSHA Annual Enforcement Vigor from the Carter (FY 1977–80) to the Reagan Years (FY 1981–83)

Program	Compliance Officers change	Compliance Officers % change (Per 100,000	Inspections change Civilian	Inspections % change Employees	Citations change in Area	Citations % change Served)	Serious Citations change	Serious Citations % change
Alaska	-2.3	-25%	-181	-28%	-896	-47%	66	74%
Arizona	.1	11	89	46	-129	-43	9	45
California	.1	11	- 13	- 7	- 95	-21	20	66
Hawaii	.4	8	261	39	-199	-10	-61	-31
Indiana	.4	17	42	22	69	13	37	28
Iowa	- .1	- 7	- 76	-50	-207	-62	- 5	- 7
Kentucky	.1	6	- 7	- 4	-343	-51	8	44
Maryland	- .4	-12	- 83	-27	-257	-56	4	11
Michigan	- .2	- 8	-126	-21	-154	-10	13	17
Minnesota	- .4	-20	- 44	-19	-199	-32	14	29
Nevada	.5	15	229	51	143	14	13	34
New Mexico	.3	19	- 11	-13	- 95	-43	6	20
North Carolina	- .1	- 7	- 42	-21	-288	-42	5	15
Oregon	- .6	-11	-417	-45	-564	-33	28	17
South Carolina	- .1	- 3	- 70	-40	-429	-61	- 7	-14
Tennessee	0	1	- 07	- 5	-160	-39	22	73
Utah	.1	5	- 79	-21	-367	-42	1	3
Vermont	.4	11	- 49	-16	-415	-30	36	56
Virginia	.4	21	- 3	- 3	5	2	16	75
Washington	.3	6	36	4	71	4	2	1
Wyoming	2.0	54	- 60	-20	106	14	15	41
All States	.1	3%	- 33	-11%	-149	-21%	14	25%
OSHA	- .4	-17%	4	4%	- 63	-27%	-17	-27%

in the overall citation rate than OSHA. Five states, however, increased their citations per 100,000 civilian employees from the Carter to the Reagan years. Furthermore, only one state receded more than OSHA in terms of serious citations, with 18 of 21 states showing increased rates on this dimension. During the Reagan period, states appeared more willing to use consultative means to deal with minor infractions but were more vigorous in ferreting out and citing serious infractions.

The degree to which states facilitated or resisted enforcement deregulation can be assessed further by sorting them into three categories—reflectors, resisters, and straddlers. Reflectors are those states that experienced decline on at least three indicators of enforcement vigor from the Carter to the Reagan years, thereby matching or exceeding OSHA (which declined on three of four measures). Resisters are states that showed increases in enforcement vigor on at least three of the indicators. Straddlers are states that increased on two indicators but declined on two others, thereby sending mixed signals about their orientations toward enforcement deregulation.

Slightly over one-third of the states are reflectors. Two of them, Iowa and South Carolina, outpaced OSHA by receding on all four measures of enforcement while the remaining six reflectors (Alaska, Maryland, Michigan, Minnesota, North Carolina, and Oregon) featured reductions on three of four enforcement indicators. Most of the states did not follow OSHA's lead so clearly. Six resisters (Arizona, Indiana, Nevada, Virginia, Washington, and Wyoming) bucked the trend. The remaining seven (California, Hawaii, Kentucky, New Mexico, Tennessee, Utah, and Vermont) proved to be straddlers.

Potential Sources of State Variation

What accounts for the three basic types of responses to federal deregulation among the states? At least on the surface, several explanations seem possible. One emphasizes *convergence;* perhaps, resisters are states that ranked relatively low on measures of enforcement during the Carter years while reflectors ranked high. Such a pattern seems partly consistent with Gresham's law. Resisters may be more able to swim against the federal stream because even with greater enforcement they will still have very competitive business climates. In contrast, reflectors are presumably eager to become more competitive by floating with the currents of deregulation.

An explanation based on *wealth* may perhaps prove potent. Richer states may be under less pressure to create favorable business climates by reducing enforcement than their less affluent counterparts. Wealthier states may more readily be able to provide the resources the state agency needs to operate an occupational safety and health program. If the explanation based on wealth possesses merit, one would expect resisters to be more affluent than reflectors.

Pressure group theories may also contribute to understanding. Proregulatory pressures emanating from society are probably more intense in some states than others. In the case of occupational safety and health, unions comprise the major group fighting for strict protective standards and energetic enforcement of them. If these proregulatory groups are assertive or workers themselves complain vigorously about hazards, state agencies may be more likely to resist deregulation initiatives from Washington. Of course, businesses often apply pressure in the opposite direction. Manufacturing industries tend to house more safety and health threats than businesses in the service sector. They probably stand to lose more financially from vigorous enforcement. Consequently, states where these industries play a larger role in the economy may well be more inclined to become reflectors.

Problem severity may also account for variation. Policymakers in states with higher occupational injury and illness rates may be more reluctant to become reflectors for fear that it will exacerbate the threat to worker well-being. States with relatively low rates may more readily imitate OSHA's move toward deregulation.

Table 7.3 presents data on reflectors, straddlers, and resisters designed to provide at least a preliminary test of each of the four explanations. First, the table provides mean scores of the different types of states on selected variables. Second, it presents two Pearson correlation coefficients derived by using the state typology to create two dummy variables. One variable represents resister states versus all others; the other, reflector states compared to all others. The computation of Pearson r's provides a further check on the conclusions suggested by differences among the means. It offers a parsimonious measure of the strength of the relationship between a given independent variable and a certain type of state.

Overall, the data provide very limited support for the sundry hypotheses. When one applies F and t tests, none of the differences among means achieves statistical significance at the .05 level or less. Nor do any of the correlation coefficients prove statistically significant at this level. However, the small number of cases involved as well as the exploratory nature of this analysis justify an examination of the data for patterns consistent with the four explanations.

A slight tendency exists for states to follow the pattern suggested by the convergence hypothesis. Reflectors were marginally more likely to feature greater enforcement during the Carter years. The relationship is so slight, however, that rejection of the hypothesis at this point seems prudent. The data provide even less support for the proposition that affluent states will more readily resist trends in Washington aimed at deregulation. If anything, wealthier states revealed a somewhat greater proclivity to become reflectors. Again, however, a comparison of mean values as well as an examination of the correlation coefficients reveal inconsistent and weak trends. The proposition that states with more acute occupational safety and health problems will more readily join the ranks of resisters also enjoys little support.

Ultimately, only the group pressure variables seem suggestive in accounting for a state's propensity to be a resister, straddler, or reflector. To be sure, the two variables designed to measure the presence of pro-regulatory pressures in a state, complaint rate and percentage of the work force that is unionized, possess very limited predictive power. However, a consistent tendency exists for states with economies more

Table 7.3 Relationship between State Type and Selected Variables

Independent Variables	Mean Values[a]			Pearson r	
	Reflectors N=8	Straddlers N=7	Resisters N=6	Reflector Vs. All Other	Resister Vs. All Other
	(Standard Deviations in Parentheses)			(Dummy Variables)	
Convergence					
	(State annual means 1977-80)[b]				
Compliance Officers	3.5 (2.8)	2.7 (1.3)	2.8 (1.2)	.20	-.07
Inspections	405.7 (283.1)	270.3 (199.1)	340.1 (269.7)	.19	.00
Citations	911.8 (578.8)	803.5 (585.7)	717.3 (548.0)	.13	-.12
Serious Citations	73.0 (43.5)	57.3 (63.6)	60.1 (48.9)	.4	-.05
Wealth					
% Unemployed, 1982	10.4% (2.7)	9.1% (2.0)	9.7% (2.3)	.21	-.03
Per capita income, 1980	$9856 (1682)	$8527 (1385)	$9842 (921)	.15	.24
Government Revenue Per capita, 1981	$1636 (1830)	$973 (236)	$1026 (293)	.28	-.13
Increase in Revenue Per capita, 1977-81	$802 (1519)	$279 (124)	$291 (177)	.27	-.13
Group Pressure					
% Union, 1978	20% (9)	20% (7)	21% (9)	-.02	.07
Annual Complaints 1977-81[b]	43 (36)	31 (20)	35 (18)	.20	-.05
% Work Force in Manufacturing, 1982	17% (8)	15% (7)	13% (7)	.24	-.22

Table 7.3 *(continued)*

Independent Variables	Mean Values[a]			Pearson r	
	Reflectors N=8	Straddlers N=7	Resisters N=6	Reflector Vs. All Other	Resister Vs. All Other
	(Standard Deviations in Parentheses)			(Dummy Variables)	
Manufacturing Estab- lishments, 1977[b]	317 (88)	311 (83)	265 (59)	.17	-.29
Manufacturing Estab- lishments, 200 or more employees, 1977[b]	106 (30)	92 (32)	74 (31)	.35[e]	-.37[d]
Manufacturing Value, 1977[c]	$5464 (1906)	$4086 (1946)	$4014 (2670)	.32[e]	-.17
Problem Severity					
Injury and Illness Rates, 1979-1980, Per 100 Full-time Workers	9.1 (1.7)	9.9 (1.0)	9.8 (1.4)	.12	-.27

SOURCES: U.S. Occupational Safety and Health Administration; U.S. Department of Commerce, 1983; U.S. Advisory Commission on Intergovernmental Relations, 1983.

[a]These are computed by adding the values for each state and dividing by the number of states. F tests and T tests comparing reflectors to straddlers and resisters unearthed no relationships that were statistically significant at the .05 level or less.

[b]Rate per 100,000 civilian employees.

[c]Rate per civilian worker.

[d]Statistically significant at the .10 level.

[e]Statistically significant at the .15 level.

dominated by the manufacturing sector to follow Washington in the move toward enforcement deregulation. In the case of each of four manufacturing variables, reflectors tend to have the highest scores followed in order by straddlers and then resisters. The correlations between being a resister and having heavy concentrations of manufacturing consistently runs in a negative direction; the correlational pattern for reflectors is the opposite. All but one of the coefficients exceed .2 and three are greater than .3. The consistent (if modest) relationship between a state's economic dependence on manufacturing and its propensity to reflect Washington's pursuit of deregulation provides some support for a business-dominance thesis concerning deregulation. States that house industries more likely to gain from lax enforcement may manifest more intense lobbying by business on behalf of this objective. Elected officials and state occupational safety and health administrators may respond by reducing enforcement.[3]

It deserves emphasis, however, that table 7.3 in general provides limited support for the four hypotheses. Much variance remains unexplained. Other modes of statistically analyzing the data seem unlikely to alter this conclusion.[4] Hence, more thorough explanations may depend on either uncovering more valid measures of the various concepts already explored or, more likely, developing explanations that focus on other qualities of a state (such as characteristics of the state occupational safety and health agency).

IMPLICATIONS

The experience under the Occupational Safety and Health Act suggests certain lessons for those who seek to comprehend the role of the states in implementing federal regulatory programs. First, this case challenges the view that the states will sabotage or, minimally, lag behind the commitment of the federal government in enforcing federal regulatory policy. This pessimistic perspective in part springs from the implementation literature, which often portrays states as potential veto points in the implementation process (e.g., Ingram, 1977). It also emanates from the traditional justification for a new federal regulatory program, namely, that the states have failed to deal with the problem. A corollary of this justification holds that state involvement in implementing federal regulatory policy will breed weaker enforcement. The occupational safety and health program has certainly not been immune to this perception. The leadership of the American Federation of Labor-Congress of Industrial Organizations (AFL-CIO), for instance, persistently voiced suspicions of the states and urged that enforcement be turned over to the federal bureaucracy. During both the Carter and

Reagan years, however, the enforcement vigor of most states exceeded that achieved by OSHA itself.

Some observers may claim that the relatively favorable impression of state performance conveyed by this study is an artifact of the particular measures used. Perhaps; states lag far behind Washington on other dimensions of enforcement. For example, state agencies may prove inferior to OSHA in devising an effective strategy for targeting specific firms for inspections. Or state compliance officers may conduct lower quality inspections at work sites than their federal counterparts. On balance, however, no compelling reason emerges as to why this should be the case. During the 1970s and 1980s, the gap between federal and state administrative capacity narrowed. The U.S. Advisory Commission on Intergovernmental Relations comes close to the mark in pointing to a "profound restructuring of the state governmental landscape" whereby state agencies became "more professional in their operations than they ever have been" (1985:364). Simultaneously, austerity, personnel cuts, bash-the-bureaucrat rhetoric, and other factors have probably reduced the cost-effectiveness of many federal agencies (e.g., Rubin, 1985). Hence, it seems improbable that the particular performance measures employed paint an excessively sanguine picture of state performance relative to OSHA's.

Second, the study points to a tension between Washington's desire to ease regulatory pressures on the private sector and to enlarge state discretion in the implementation process. In this regard, it challenges the applicability of Gresham's Law of state participation in regulatory programs. Faced with open support for deregulation of the private sector in Washington and greater tolerance for state discretion (at least with respect to enforcement), a minority of the states followed OSHA's lead and became reflectors. Nearly as many states, increasing enforcement, became resisters, while another third straddled the issue.

Efforts to account for state variations in their response to enforcement deregulation by OSHA met with limited success. A convergence dynamic, whereby states that have ranked high on enforcement reduce their effort in order to compete with less vigorous states, does not appear to be operating. Nor can one find much support for the view that affluent states, those with more acute occupational safety and health problems, or those featuring greater proregulatory pressure (union strength, high complaint rate) more readily resist Washington's invitation to deregulate. A modest tendency does exist for states with proportionately larger manufacturing sectors to become reflectors. This could imply that Gresham's Law becomes more germane when industries particularly sensitive to the potential costs of safety and health regulation play a more dominant role in a state's economy. Fear that manufacturing firms may depart for other states may be a modest stimulus to reduced enforcement of occupational safety and health standards.

Several factors probably account for the limited applicability of Gresham's Law. In some instances, state officials may not be willing to sacrifice health goals for the sake of economic development. Or they may view other policies and implementation strategies, such as those affecting corporate taxation, as far more critical in competing for business.[5] Whatever the precise dynamics, the inapplicability of Gresham's Law raises the specter of trade-offs between deregulating the private sector and granting states more discretion in the implementation process.

The propositions suggested by the occupational safety and health program need to be examined in the context of other federal regulatory initiatives. It may be that the pattern of enforcement evident in this case primarily characterizes programs that feature a substitution approach. State participation under this approach is highly voluntary both in a legal and moral sense. Legally, state governments have the clear option to decide whether they wish to play the implementation game. The fact that OSHA assumes jurisdiction if a state withdraws provides a kind of moral freedom to make this choice. State policymakers can opt out of the occupational safety and health program without seeming callous or morally irresponsible; they can give the problem to the federal government. Other regulatory programs make state participation much less voluntary in either the legal or moral sense of the term. The Clean Air Act, for instance, virtually conscripts state governments into an implementation role.

In cases where state participation is highly voluntary, states committed to regulatory objectives may outnumber those that get involved in order to create a hospitable business climate by softening the impact of federal policy. If such a selection process is at work, this study probably exaggerates the number of resisters and straddlers that will emerge in the face of pressure for deregulation and a more permissive orientation toward state discretion in Washington. Until future research addresses this issue, however, assertions that state implementing agents comprise the weak link in the enforcement chain need to be treated with skepticism.

NOTES

1. Data on both serious citations and assessed penalties for each state were available for the period from fiscal 1977 through 1981. During this period, correlation coefficients (Pearson r) between the two variables for each year ranged from .60 to .91 with a mean correlation of .73.

2. Would the results of this analysis be the same if the transition years between presidential administrations, 1977 and 1981, were excluded? In general, yes. In the case of serious citations, however, state increases from the Carter to the Reagan years are somewhat inflated by low scores on this dimension in 1977. But even if data from 1977 are deleted, the basic point about state performance relative to OSHA's remains the same.

3. The construction industry typically has a high accident rate. It therefore seemed pertinent to examine whether states with a large percentage of economic activity devoted to construction were more likely to become reflectors. The data provide no support for this proposition. Two potentially pertinent factors, among others, need to be taken into account in considering this finding. The construction industry persistently constitutes a smaller sector of a state's economy than manufacturing. Furthermore, unlike manufacturing or high-tech industries, it tends not to be the focus of competition among the states.

4. The small number of cases inhibit application of sophisticated statistical techniques. The authors did, however, experiment with several methods of measuring and accounting for change from the Carter to the Reagan years. These efforts employed regression analyses; they did not produce findings that substantially differ from those reported in the text.

5. Court intervention may have also played a role in shaping state performance. In 1978, a federal court of appeals ordered OSHA to establish specific personnel benchmarks for state programs (*AFL-CIO v. Marshall*). OSHA did not, however, set final benchmarks during the period under examination. The Reagan administration persistently expressed opposition to the court order and attempted to circumvent it by obtaining changes in the statute. Thus, it seems unlikely that the court decision weighed heavily as a causal factor shaping state behavior.

REFERENCES

Advisory Commission on Intergovernmental Relations. 1983. *1981 Tax Capacity of the Fifty States* (Washington, D.C.: Government Printing Office).
———. 1984. *Regulatory Federalism: Policy, Process, Impact and Reform* (Washington, D.C.: Government Printing Office).
———. 1985. *The Question of State Government Capability* (Washington, D.C.: Government Printing Office).
Eads, George C., and Michael Fix (eds.). 1984. *The Reagan Regulatory Strategy: An Assessment* (Washington, D.C.: Urban Institute).
Gottlieb, Daniel W. 1982. "Business Mobilizes as States Begin to Move Into the Regulatory Vacuum," *National Journal* 14: 1340–43.
Ingram, Helen. 1977. "Policy Implementation Through Bargaining: The Case of Federal Grants-in-Aid," *Public Policy* 25: 499–526.
Lester, James D., James L. Franke, Ann O'M. Bowman, and Kenneth W. Kramer. 1983. "Hazardous Wastes, Politics and Public Policy: A Comparative State Analysis," *Western Political Quarterly* 3: 257–85.
Marvel, Mary. 1982. "Implementation and Safety Regulation: Variations in

Federal and State Administration under OSHA," *Administration and Society* 14: 15–33.

Menzel, Donald C. 1983. "Redirecting the Implementation of a Law: The Reagan Administration and Coal Surface Mining Regulation," *Public Administration Review* 43: 411–20.

Moe, Terry M. 1982. "Regulatory Performance and Presidential Administration," *American Journal of Political Science* 26: 197–224.

Rowland, C. K., and Roger Marz. 1982. "Gresham's Law: The Regulatory Analogy," *Policy Studies Review* 1: 572–80.

Rubin, Irene. 1985. *Shrinking the Federal Government* (New York: Longman).

U.S. Department of Commerce. 1983. *Statistical Abstract of the United States: 1984* (Washington, D.C.: Government Printing Office).

U.S. House Committee on Appropriations. 1981. *Departments of Labor, Health and Human Services, Education, and Related Agencies Appropriations for 1982, Part 1* (Washington, D.C.: Government Printing Office).

_____. 1983. *Departments of Labor, Health and Human Services, and Related Agencies Appropriations for 1984, Part 1* (Washington, D.C.: Government Printing Office).

U.S. Senate Committee on Governmental Affairs. 1982. *State Implementation of Federal Standards, Part 1* (Washington, D.C.: Government Printing Office).

Williams, Bruce A., and Albert R. Matheny. 1984. "Testing Theories of Social Regulation: Hazardous Waste Regulation in the American States," *Journal of Politics* 46: 428–58.

Wines, Michael. 1983. "Auchter's Record at OSHA Leaves Labor Outraged, Business Satisfied," *National Journal* 14: 2008–13.

8
Reshaping the Regulatory Partnership: The Case of Surface Mining
David M. Hedge and Donald C. Menzel

Immediately upon taking office, the Reagan administration initiated a series of steps intended to reshape the character of regulation in the United States. These steps included requiring greater OMB clearance of new rules and regulations, reducing the rate of federal enforcement, mandating cost-benefit analysis for all "major" regulations, cutting the budgets and personnel levels of many regulatory agencies, and substantially reducing the rate of new rules and regulations (Eads and Fix, 1982; Fix 1984).

Equally important, and perhaps more enduring, the administration has attempted to achieve deregulation through the devolution of regulatory authority to the states. While a framework of joint state-federal regulation still exists, reduced federal oversight, the acceleration of formal delegation, and more flexible federal standards have enhanced significantly the states' regulatory role (Fix, 1983). From an intergovernmental perspective, regulatory relief thus represents an attempt to fashion a new partnership in federal-state regulation—one in which the states assume greater responsibility for day-to-day enforcement within their borders and where, ideally, federal and state authorities work in greater harmony.

Yet despite considerable federal initiative and congressional and public support, a series of obstacles—administrative, legal, and political—stand in the way of regulatory change (see, e.g., DeLeon, 1978; Mitnick, 1980; Samuels and Shaffer, 1982; Bardach and Kagan, 1982). Where deregulation entails devolution to the states, additional constraints emerge. Some have questioned, for example, whether the states have the requisite technical and fiscal resources to assume greater regulatory responsibility, particularly in the face of cuts in federal aid (see Fix, 1984). Still others challenge the notion that the states will necessarily pursue deregulation when given the choice (see Mashaw and Rose-Ackerman, 1984; Thompson and Scicchitano, this volume).

Further constraints exist at the micro- or field level. Students of regulation and implementation have long understood that those on the front line of delivering a public service enjoy considerable discretion and often determine through their daily actions what policy is—independent of congressional intent, agency rules and regulations, or the express desires of their administrative superiors (Kaufman, 1967; Lipsky, 1980; and Bardach and Kagan, 1982). Accordingly, effecting regulatory relief frequently demands reshaping the attitudes and actions of those responsible for day-to-day implementation. More particularly, where deregulation entails changes in the character of enforcement and takes place within a system of joint federal-state regulation, two sets of changes are often necessary for successful regulatory relief.

First, the attitudes and behavior of federal line personnel need to be altered to conform to the current goals of regulatory reform. In many instances, this requires shifting from the command-and-control values, perceptions, and enforcement styles developed in earlier administrations to a more flexible, balanced approach reflected in Bardach and Kagan's (1982) notion of the "good inspector." Second, for regulatory relief to succeed, federal-state field relationships have to improve. In the 1970s, joint federal-state regulation was characterized by considerable conflict and, as a result, a lack of coordination, delay, and an uneven pattern of enforcement. To achieve both regulatory relief and the spirit of the president's New Federalism, state and federal officials need to develop more positive attitudes toward one another, interact in a more cooperative manner, and exhibit greater attitude congruence. Neither change will come easily; the attitudes and behaviors of line personnel are difficult to control, much less change, and state-federal conflict is practically a historical constant.

Our ongoing study of field-level changes in federal and state enforcement of surface mining regulations can provide insight into these concerns. Specifically, federal enforcement data and surveys of federal and state officials conducted in 1980 and 1982 are used to examine changes at the field level during the Carter-Reagan administrations. Two sets of questions guide that analysis:

1. Have the enforcement behaviors of Office of Surface Mining (OSM) inspectors changed as a result of the Reagan administration's efforts at deregulation? Have field-level personnel developed attitudes consistent with admin-

istration regulatory objectives? To what extent is attitude change necessary for regulatory relief?

2. Have state-federal relations improved as a result of changes at OSM? Do state and federal officials find themselves more in agreement on issues of the environment, regulation, and coal operators? Have federal officials developed a more positive set of attitudes toward state counterparts?

BACKGROUND

Implementation of the Federal Surface Mining Control and Reclamation Act (PL 95-87) provides a useful setting for examining these questions. Under the authorizing legislation and subsequent regulations, the federal government established a series of standards designed to improve the quality of surface mining and to ensure greater uniformity in regulation across the 28 coal-producing states. Operating within a framework of partial preemption, the states are required to adopt laws and regulations consistent with the federal law as a condition for assuming and maintaining primacy over enforcement of the act within their borders. Until state programs were approved (which in most cases did not occur until 1982), parallel federal-state implementation prevailed.

Under the Carter administration, OSM moved aggressively in establishing and enforcing the new surface mining standards. At the field level, efforts were made to (a) recruit an inspector corps sympathetic to the new agency's goals and operating style, (b) minimize inspector discretion, and (c) encourage and reward ticket writing. In dealing with the states, OSM pursued a similar strategy by insisting that the states strictly comply with federal standards in fashioning their own rules and regulations and by using grants-in-aid to coerce state compliance (see Menzel, 1981). Not surprisingly, considerable federal-state conflict and tension emerged, and implementation of the act moved slowly and fitfully. By the end of its term in office, the Carter OSM had granted full program approval to only two states, while an additional 15 states had received conditional approval.[1]

In contrast to the Carter era, the Reagan OSM has adopted a more flexible, bargaining based approach in its enforcement and has shifted much of the responsibility for day-to-day enforcement of the surface mining act to the states. At OSM, this has translated into a reduction in agency personnel levels and reviewing and, in some cases, has eliminated what are felt to be burdensome regulations and led to substantial reorganization of the regional field offices (see Menzel, 1983). With respect to the states, OSM accelerated the rate of program approval so that by the end of FY 83, 12 states had gained full approval for their programs and an additional 13 states had been granted conditional approval. As the states gained full primacy, OSM's enforcement role shifted to one of providing technical assistance and conducting oversight inspections in each of the states.[2]

METHOD

Our study focuses on field-level changes over the interim phase (1977–82) of the surface mining program—a period during which the states were still seeking primacy, while responsibility for enforcement rested with *both* federal and state authorities. Surveys of OSM and state (West Virginia) inspectors in 1980 (n = 128) and 1982 (n = 114) together with aggregate level statistics on OSM enforcement activities serve as the data base for examining three sets of changes over the Carter-Reagan administrations.

First, aggregate level data (1979–82) on federal inspections and ticket writing are used to describe field-level behavioral shifts before and after the Reagan administration assumed control of OSM. Second, we analyze changes (1980-82) in a series of general orientations that the literature and our observations indicate are important in site level regulation. Included are inspector perceptions toward surface mining regulations, energy and environment, coal operators, and enforcement style (what we have labeled rule orientations).[3] Third, survey data are used to discover whether the quality of federal-state field-level relations has improved under the current administration. Initially that analysis examines changes in the attitudes of our OSM sample toward their state counterparts and perceptions of the quality and importance of federal-state relations. In addition, we compare, within West Virginia, federal and state attitudes in 1980 and again in 1982 to discover whether the attitude gap we observed earlier has closed under the Reagan administration.

FINDINGS

Behavioral Changes

Tables 8.1 and 8.2 demonstrate that OSM officials have been successful in altering enforcement behaviors among field level personnel. According to the values in table 8.1, from 1980 to 1981 OSM inspectors made fewer inspections and issued fewer notices of violations (NOVs) and cessation orders (COs). The decrease in ticket writing is especially dramatic; the 1981 levels represent a yearly decline of roughly 67% for both NOVs and COs. Similar conclusions are warranted when the rate of NOVs and COs per inspector are compared. While the typical inspector in 1980 issued 39 NOVs and 9 COs, by 1982 these figures had dropped to 9 and 2.5 respectively.

Further insight into changes in OSM's enforcement style can be ob-

Table 8.1 Changes in OSM Enforcement Behavior: 1979–1982

	1979	1980	1981	1982[a]
# of inspections	20,306	34,987	27,070	9,739
Inspections per # of inspectors	100	198	222	117
# of Notices of Violations (NOVs)	4,461	6,924	2,368	742
# of Cessation Orders (COs)	815	1,627	594	208
Citation Ratio[b]	25.9	48.3	24.3	11.4
NOV Ratio[c]	21.9	39.1	19.4	8.9
CO Ratio[d]	4.0	9.2	4.9	2.5

SOURCE: U.S. Office of Surface Mining.

[a] as of August 1982.

[b] ratio = (NOVs + COs)/# of Inspectors.

[c] ratio = NOVs/# of Inspectors.

[d] ratio = COs/# of Inspectors.

tained by examining the perceptions of state personnel. As part of our 1980 and 1982 surveys, we asked state inspectors in West Virginia how they perceived their OSM counterparts. Those responses, reported in table 8.2, indicate that OSM inspectors (at least those in West Virginia) did, indeed, become slightly more flexible, less strict, more cooperative, and less environmentally minded.

Table 8.2 State (West Virginia) Perceptions of Federal Inspectors, 1980–1982

Trait	1980 (n=44)	1982 (n=53)
Flexible	5.5	5.0
Strict	2.1	2.8
NonCooperative	4.5	5.5
Environmentally Minded	1.8	2.2

Entries are median responses. R's asked to evaluate OSM inspectors along seven-point semantic differential anchored at the low end by the traits identified above. A higher value indicates less of the trait.

Changes in General Orientations

OSM's success in redirecting inspector behavior, however, is not matched in terms of changing the general orientations of field personnel. A glance at table 8.3 indicates that senior officials have not been able to reorient inspectors in a manner consistent with the goals of regulatory relief at OSM. Given OSM's current emphasis on a bargaining style of enforcement, we expected, for instance, field personnel to exhibit more flexible attitudes toward rule enforcement. That did not happen. OSM inspectors in 1982 prove just as likely to take the position that regulations should be literally enforced.

Similar findings emerge when we compare our inspectors' attitudes

Table 8.3 Changes in OSM General Orientations, 1980–1982 (National OSM Sample)

Attitudes	1980 (n=74)	1982 (n=61)
Attitudes toward coal operators[a]	2.4	2.4
Rule orientation[b]	2.3	2.4
Support for regulations[c]	5.1	4.8
Environmental attitudes		
Importance of coal production[d]	68%	40%
Surface mining as environmental threat[e]	46%	53%
Energy-environment tradeoff[f]	4.8	4.7

[a]Entries are means from summated scale. Higher values indicate more favorable view of the operators.

[b]Entries are means of summated scale. Higher values indicate greater rule rigidity.

[c]Entries are means of summated scale. Higher values indicate more favorable view of regulations.

[d]Percent who report that coal production is _very_ important.

[e]Percent who view surface mining as a _major_ environmental threat.

[f]Respondents asked to place themselves on seven point energy v. environment scale, 1 = pro-energy and 7 = pro-environment. Table entries are median responses.

toward the coal operators across the two administrations. In 1980, the operators were perceived as primarily concerned with making a profit, lacking the expertise to comply, and not interested in protecting the environment (see Hedge and Menzel, 1985). Generally, the summary scores reported in table 8.3 indicate those views have not changed.

In only two instances—support for the regulations and attitudes toward energy and the environment—is there a major shift in orientations but in each case that development is not consistent with the larger aims of regulatory relief at OSM. In 1980 we discovered moderate support for the federal program; regulations were perceived as fair, consistent, effective, and enforceable (see Hedge and Menzel, 1985). That changed in 1982 as OSM inspectors found themselves enforcing what are essentially the states' regulations or the so-called permanent program. Overall (see table 8.3) field personnel viewed the regulations less favorably in 1982. In a parallel fashion, table 8.3 indicates that federal inspectors have become less supportive of energy production and more protective toward the environment despite current efforts at OSM to shift from the proenvironment stance of the Carter era. Part of that, no doubt, reflects the larger public's current position on issues of energy and environment. Nonetheless, OSM inspectors do find themselves at odds with their superiors on this issue.

Changes in Intergovernmental Attitudes and Behaviors

While OSM officials have not been successful in reshaping general orientations, the evidence in tables 8.4 and 8.5 indicates that field-level personnel have developed a set of intergovernmental attitudes and behaviors consistent, at times, with existing regulatory goals and the president's New Federalism. The data in table 8.4, for example, suggest that federal-state relations at the field level have improved under the Reagan administration; by 1982, there appears to be less OSM-state conflict, the amount of state-federal contact increases, and a significantly larger percentage of OSM personnel report enjoying at least good relationships with their state counterparts. That reorientation is also seen in the importance attached by federal personnel to a good working relationship with state officials. In 1980, slightly less than half of our respondents felt that a cordial intergovernmental setting was crucial to doing their job properly. By 1982, nearly three inspectors in five had adopted that perspective.

At the same time, the remaining evidence indicates that improvements in federal-state relations are not complete. In 1980, OSM officials took a rather dim view of their state counterparts. State officials were seen as only moderately effective, environmentally minded, and technically informed (see Hedge and Menzel, 1983). According to the scale

Table 8.4 Changes in OSM Intergovernmental Attitudes and Behaviors, 1980–1982 (National OSM Sample)

	1980	1982
Evaluation of state counterparts[a]	4.6	4.7
Perceived conflict[b]	46%	24%
Reported state-federal contacts[c]	31%	50%
Perceived dependency[d]	46%	57%
Evaluation of relationship state officials [e]	68%	81%

[a] Entries are means from a summated scale. Higher values mean more favorable view of counterpart.

[b] Percent of respondents who see conflict with state officials as somewhat or serious problem.

[c] Percent who report 2–3 contacts with state officials in a typical week.

[d] Percent who feel that a good working relationship with state officials is very necessary for effective job performance.

[e] Percent who rate relations with state officials as good or excellent.

Table 8.5 Value Congruence between State and Federal Inspectors, 1980–1982 (West Virginia Sample)

	1980		1982	
Attitudes[a]	OSM (n=17)	DNR (n=44)	DNR (n=8)	OSM (n=53)
Support for the regulations	5.4	4.3	5.0	4.8
Rule orientations	2.5	1.9	2.5	1.7
Attitudes toward coal operators	2.7	2.8	2.7	2.5
Environmental attitudes				
Importance of coal production	82%	71%	50%	47%
Surface mining as environmental threat	18%	14%	38%	31%
Energy-environment tradeoff	4.7	5.2	4.3	5.4

[a] See Table 3 and footnote 3 for description of scales/items.

values in table 8.4, those and other views have not changed. Similarly, examination of table 8.5 suggests that, at least in West Virginia, state and federal officials are no closer today in terms of how they view enforcement, the coal operators, and the environment than they were in earlier years. And, while federal-state attitudes toward the regulations are more aligned in 1982, that convergence comes at the expense of federal field-level support for surface mining rules (see table 8.3). In short, while there is reason to believe that intergovernmental field relations have improved under the Reagan administration, *basic value differences still persist.*

DISCUSSION

The experiences of federal and state surface mining inspectors suggest two principal conclusions concerning field-level changes in surface mining enforcement. First, the Reagan administration has been quite successful in altering the behaviors of field-level regulators. Both the rate of enforcement and ticket writing dropped substantially in 1981–1982. Moreover, the evidence indicates that field-level intergovernmental interactions today fit nicely with the administration's desire for a more balanced and cooperative regulatory partnership. Second, field-level attitudes did not change to any appreciable extent between 1980 and 1982. OSM inspectors remained surprisingly resilient in their views toward the coal industry, state counterparts, and how regulations should be enforced. What attitude change did take place was not consistent with larger goals of regulatory reform. Equally important, we found little evidence that the basic orientations of federal and state officials have converged in the 1980s. For all practical purposes, the OSM inspector corps has not embraced regulatory reform, despite the fact that their behavior has been dramatically altered under the new administration. What implications can be drawn from these conclusions?

One important implication is that the behaviors of front-line personnel are not as unchangeable or as difficult to control as students of street-level bureaucracy imply. Certainly the surface mining experience supports the notion that agency leaders can induce desired behaviors by relying on the formal authority and sanctions available to them, even in the face of informal line tendencies to the contrary. There is little evidence in our study, for example, to suggest that lower level bureaucrats sought to stymie the sweeping set of reforms put in motion at OSM. Apparently, OSM field-level personnel had little difficulty responding (behaviorally) to the desires of their superiors for regulatory relief in the coal fields.[4]

This leads to another implication—namely, the adaptability of street-level bureaucrats. In general, two pictures are presented. One suggests that they are not very adaptable at all and, in the case of regulators, are more inclined to go by the book. A second outlook suggests that they are adaptable, but it is an adaptability based on coping with the situation. Our findings are more in line with the latter notion of adaptability. OSM inspectors probably altered their behaviors while maintaining their previously held attitudes in order to cope with the change taking place around them.

Another lesson that can be drawn from our analysis is that creating a corps of good inspectors is neither necessary nor desirable for achieving regulatory relief. OSM officials experienced little difficulty in achieving more flexible enforcement at the field level despite their failure to reshape their inspectors' attitudes toward regulatory goals, enforcement styles, and the objects of regulation (i.e., to create good inspector attitudes). Further, the OSM experience suggests that site-level regulatory reform can be achieved without giving inspectors substantial discretion (as some reformers argue is necessary). Rather, it requires a successful strategy of managed discretion. We suspect that OSM inspectors today are no less monitored, controlled, and cajoled than they were under the Carter administration—automatic ticket writing has been replaced by automatic nonticket writing. Indeed, had the new OSM officials simply granted their inspectors greater discretionary authority, the substantial behavioral changes we observed probably would not have occurred as field-level personnel simply acted on their moderately rule-rigid, proenvironmental, and anticoal industry attitudes and values.

Finally, the surface mining case provides some basis for being cautiously optimistic about the ability of state and federal officials to recast their regulatory partnership into a more balanced, cooperative federalism. More particularly, our findings suggest that federal and state officials need not like each other or hold similar views to work cooperatively together in regulating the private sector.

NOTES

1. Of these, 12 received conditional approval only in the last three months of the Carter administration.

2. OSM's goal, not yet fully realized, is to conduct oversight inspections in 17 percent of each state's inspectable units.

3. Unrotated factor loadings were used to create summary scales for inspector rule orientations, attitudes toward the operators and state counterparts, and evaluations of the regulations. See Hedge and Menzel (1985) for a description of the items used in each of those scales.

4. An alternative interpretation of the data might also be justified. Given the gap between behaviors and attitudes at OSM, one could also argue that a lack of attitudinal change has acted as a drag on OSM efforts to achieve regulatory reform. While ticket writing clearly declined under Secretary of the Interior James Watt's leadership, one can only speculate how much further it would

have decreased had inspector attitudes moved in a direction consistent with broader agency goals.

REFERENCES

Bardach, Eugene, and Robert A. Kagan. 1982. *Going by the Book: The Problem of Regulatory Unreasonableness* (Philadelphia: Temple University Press).

DeLeon, Peter. 1978. "A Theory of Policy Termination," in Judith V. May and Aaron Wildavsky (eds.), *The Policy Cycle* (Beverly Hills: Sage): 279–300.

Eads, George C., and Michael Fix. 1982. "Regulatory Policy," in John Palmer and Isabel Sawhill (eds.), *The Reagan Experiment* (Washington, D.C.: The Urban Institute): 129–56.

Fix, Michael. 1984. "Transferring Regulatory Authority to the States," in George C. Eads and Michael Fix (eds.), *The Reagan Regulatory Strategy: An Assessment* (Washington, D.C.: The Urban Institute Press).

Hedge, David, and Donald C. Menzel. 1983. "Loosening the Regulatory Ratchet: A Field Level View of Environmental Deregulation," paper presented at the 1983 meeting of the American Political Science Association, September 1–3, Chicago.

_____. 1985. "Loosening the Regulatory Ratchet: A Grassroots View of Environmental Deregulation," *Policy Studies Journal* 13: 599–606.

Kaufman, Herbert. 1967. *The Forest Ranger* (Baltimore: Johns Hopkins Press).

Lipsky, Michael. 1980. *Street-Level Bureaucracy* (New York: Russell Sage Foundation).

Mashaw, Jerry, and Susan Rose-Ackerman. 1984. "Federalism and Regulation," in George C. Eads and Michael Fix (eds.), *The Reagan Regulatory Strategy: An Assessment* (Washington, D.C.: Urban Institute Press).

Menzel, Donald C. 1981. "Implementation of the Federal Surface Mining Control and Reclamation Act of 1977," *Public Administration Review* 41: 212–19.

_____. 1983. "Redirecting the Implementation of a Law: The Reagan Administration and Coal Surface Mining Regulation," *Public Administration Review* 43: 411–20.

Mitnick, Barry M. 1980. *The Political Economy of Regulation* (New York: Columbia University Press).

Samuels, Warren J., and James D. Shaffer. 1982. "De-regulation: The Principle Inconclusive Arguments," *Policy Studies Review* 1: 463–69.

9

Implementation of Intergovernmental Regulatory Programs: A Cost-Benefit Perspective

Pinky S. Wassenberg

A multitude of federal programs offer financial and technical assistance to state and local governments willing to implement federal policies according to federal specifications. Most of the literature dealing with these intergovernmental programs focuses on programs designed to provide public works projects or social services (e.g., Wright, 1978; Howitt, 1984). Relatively little attention has been paid to those intergovernmental programs that are designed to involve state governments in the implementation of federal regulations.

This study will propose a framework to study the extent to which states have become involved in these intergovernmental regulatory policies. The framework will be used to examine the implementation of the National Pollution Discharge Elimination System (NPDES) program under the Federal Water Pollution Control Act (FWPCA) Amendments of 1972. Under that statute, the federal government is responsible for establishing the regulatory standards applicable to point-source polluters (P.L. 92-500, §402). State governments may apply for authority to implement these regulations within their boundaries (P.L. 92-500, §402[a]).

This pattern, permitting states to apply for the authority to implement federal regulatory standards, has been used in other areas of regulation, including occupational health and safety, pure food and drugs, air pollution control, and toxic wastes (Lester et al., 1983; Lieber, 1975; Lowi, 1979; Game, 1979). Although these studies indicate a great deal of variation in state involvement in the implementation of these programs, there is no intergovernmental regulatory program in which all 50 states have chosen to participate.[1] The question to be explored in this study is suggested by the variation in state involvement in these programs. Why do some states have implementation authority while others do not?

Two things must occur for a state to have program authority. First, the state must apply for that authority. Second, the federal government must grant the state's application. Therefore, there are two reasons why a state may not have program authority—they may not have applied for it or, alternatively, their application may have been denied.

Identifying the reason for variation in state participation in these programs is relevant to the understanding of intergovernmental relations, policy implementation, and comparative state policy analysis. The practice of delegating implementation authority to state governments is widely used in federal regulatory policies and an increase in the practice is central to the Reagan administration's New Federalism proposals (Hanus, 1981; Hawkins, 1981). Advocates of intergovernmental delegation appear to assume that states want the added authority and that federal agencies are willing to reduce their control over programs for which they are responsible by delegating implementation to the states. However, little attention has been paid to the circumstances under which states seek to participate in these intergovernmental programs and how successful state applicants for program authority are in obtaining it from the federal agencies in charge of individual programs.

An analysis of state involvement in these programs could also contribute to the literature on policy implementation by determining what factors influence the implementation of statutory mandates requiring intergovernmental delegation. From a comparative policy analysis perspective, this study may add to the understanding of the correlates of state regulatory policy output and response to federal policy initiatives. These questions will be explored through the analysis of state participation in the implementation of the NPDES program.

THE NPDES PROGRAM

The NPDES program was established in Section 402 of the 1972 Federal Water Pollution Control Act Amendments. NPDES is a permit program. It makes it unlawful to discharge pollutants into the nation's waters without first obtaining a permit from either the U.S. Environmental Protection Agency (EPA) or designated state permitting agency (P.L. 92-500, §402[a][1], 1972). These permits set out the requirements a discharger must meet. A discharger who does not have a permit or who violates the conditions of a permit is subject to civil and criminal penalties. This requirement is aimed primarily at industrial dischargers and municipal waste treatment plants, the two major sources of point-source pollution (U.S. Senate, 1972:3736).

Since NPDES is administered by the EPA, a state wishing to participate in the program may apply to the administrator of the EPA for the authority to implement the program within state boundaries (§402[a][5] and 40 C.F.R. §§123.21-123.29 [1984]). The administrator is instructed by the statute to grant a state application if the state can demonstrate that it has the capacity to implement the program and ensure enforcement of federal requirements.

A state program may be broader in scope than the federal NPDES program, and it may require more stringent effluent limitations and water quality standards. However, it may not require less than existing federal standards or be narrower in scope. If the EPA administrator suspects that a state is not complying with the requirements of the act, he/she may revoke state program authority. Section 106 of the 1972 amendments establishes grants to states with programs to offset the reasonable costs of the state program.

Table 9.1 States with and without National Pollution Discharge Elimination System Program Authority (1972–1984)

States With Authority

Alabama	Nebraska
California	Nevada
Colorado	New Jersey
Connecticut	New York
Delaware	North Carolina
Georgia	North Dakota
Hawaii	Ohio
Illinois	Oregon
Indiana	Pennsylvania
Iowa	South Carolina
Kansas	Tennessee
Kentucky	Vermont
Maryland	Virginia
Michigan	Washington
Minnesota	West Virginia
Mississippi	Wisconsin
Missouri	Wyoming
Montana	

States Without Authority

Alaska	New Hampshire
Arizona	New Mexico
Arkansas	Oklahoma
Florida	Rhode Island
Idaho	South Dakota
Louisiana	Texas
Maine	Utah
Massachusetts	

When a state applies for NPDES authority, the application is published in the *Federal Register*. If the application is approved by the EPA, notice of approval is published in the *Federal Register*. Based on these published notices, it was determined that 35 states applied for NPDES authority from 1972 through 1984. All states' applications were granted by the EPA. Table 9.1 lists the states in each category.

Since all state applicants were successful, one cannot explain the variation in state involvement as a function of decision making by the federal agency. The answer must lie with the states. Therefore, the balance of this essay will focus on trying to discover why some states applied for authority while others did not.

ANALYTIC FRAMEWORK AND HYPOTHESES

Both the comparative state policy analysis and policy implementation literature have been criticized for lacking explicit theoretical underpinnings (Van Horn and Van Meter, 1976; Dye, 1979; Edwards, 1980). Mazmanian and Sabatier (1983) provide one of the few frameworks for the analysis of policy implementation explicitly tied to a theoretical base. Their model will be relied upon in the development of the framework presented here for the analysis of state involvement in the NPDES program. Mazmanian and Sabatier's model is tied to two theoretical traditions—rational choice theory and organization theory (1983:19). They assume that the actors in the implementation process are rational actors who direct their actions toward the maximization of a combination of goals—power, security, and well-being. Similarly, in this analysis, it is assumed that state decision makers examine the choice to participate in the implementation of intergovernmental regulatory programs in terms of how such participation will influence their power, security, and well-being. In other words, they weigh the costs and benefits of state participation. Those states that perceive the benefits of applying to outweigh the costs would apply, while those states that perceive the costs to be greater than the benefits would not.

One benefit available to states that gain program authority is the discretion inherent in the implementation of any policy. The literature on implementation supports the conclusion that at least some discretion accompanies the authority to implement (Thomas, 1976; Lowi, 1979). Mazmanian and Sabatier (1983:25) include the extent to which the statute limits this discretion as a variable related to the likelihood of successful implementation of a policy. Since only one program will be examined in this study, it is reasonable to assume that the amount of discretion comprising this benefit is a constant across states.

The dependent variable in this analysis is state application for NPDES program authority. It is a dichotomous variable. If a state has applied for program authority, it is given a score of 1; if it has not applied, it receives a 0. Determination of state status was made based on reports published in the *Federal Register*.

The factors that potentially may be considered by states in their decisions regarding application for program authority are too numerous for comprehensive enumeration. This study will focus on four factors: 1) the political influence of the regulated group, 2) the seriousness of the target problem in the state, 3) Republican party dominance in the state government, and 4) the economic health of the state.

Strength of the Regulated Group

Ripley and Franklin (1983:72–73) observe that the implementation of regulatory policies differs from the implementation of other types of policy. Implementors of regulatory policy are imposing specifically identifiable (usually monetary) costs on a specific target group being regulated in the name of achieving less concrete benefits for the public at large. This gives the regulated group an issue around which to organize. An organized target group can put pressure on an implementing agency directly or indirectly through the legislature to which the agency is responsible for its authority and appropriations. This pressure can be directed at the agency to get it to use administrative discretion to reduce the costs being imposed on the regulated groups or individuals.

The diffuse nature of the public interest justification for regulation makes it more difficult for a public interest group to form and place pressure on the agency to encourage aggressive implementation of the regulations over the objections of the regulated group. For this reason, Mazmanian and Sabatier (1983:23–25) consider the influence of the private target group as a factor of major importance under the category of problem tractability. They hypothesize that successful implementation is more likely if the target group is small in relation to the rest of the population. One would expect the probability of successful implementation of a regulatory program to increase as the potential political influence of the target group decreases.

The influence available to the regulated group could be used against implementors of a policy imposing costs on that group. If a federal entity is implementing policy, it would be the target of the pressure. It is reasonable to assume that a state gaining program authority would also gain the attention of the target group. This represents a cost to be considered by state decisionmakers in weighing the benefits and costs of program authority. The magnitude of the cost would depend on the extent of the regulated group's political influence within the state.

An indicator of the strength of the regulated group is the per capita value added by manufacture in the state. It represents manufacturing industries' contribution to the state economy. Economically important industries probably present major political influences in state decision making. Manufacturing industries are a primary target of the NPDES program, and the EPA has acknowledged that compliance with the program will impose significant costs on this target group (CEQ, 1980:127).

The use of an independent variable measured yearly, a single-point variable, presents difficulties when the dependent variable is measured over a period of several years. In this case the dependent variable, state program application, is measured from 1973 through 1984. Tucker (1982) has documented the potential difficulties of combining single-point measurements and periodic measurements in comparative state policy research. Many socioeconomic single-point measurements of state characteristics vary over time sufficiently to effect the analysis of their relationship to policy outcome variables.

To deal with this problem, averages of indicators have been used where possible. The last major revision of the FWPCA prior to 1972 occurred in 1965. The programs created under the 1965 amendments were in place until 1972. This period represents the status quo from which the states had to make decisions about program application. When possible, measures of the independent variables are averages taken from this time period. Using this period also avoids the possibility of having measures of independent variables that postdate the dependent variable. For example, the indicator per capita value added by manufacture is an average of the figures published for 1967, 1971, and 1972 in the *Book of the States*. It is hypothesized that the larger the per capita value added by manufacture is in a state, the less likely the state will be to apply for NPDES program authority.

Seriousness of the Target Problem

State decision makers may be more willing to risk incurring the displeasure of a regulated group if the general public within the state is strongly supportive of the regulation. The extent of public support for a policy is a factor also included in the Mazmanian and Sabatier (1983:23–25) model under the heading of tractability. A factor that arguably can be related to both the extent of public support for a regulatory policy and, consequently, to the potential willingness of an agency to resist target group pressure is the extent to which objective evidence is available indicating that the regulated activity presents a problem within the state (Clarke, 1979; Dye and Davidson, 1981; Lester et al., 1983; Thompson and Scicchitano, 1983).

It is hypothesized that a state is more likely to apply for program authority if water pollution presents a serious problem in that state. The most straightforward way to measure this variable would be a measurement of the amount of pollution present in state waterways. Unfortunately, those data do not exist. Prior to 1971, there were no systematic reporting practices of water pollution data. The reporting system put in place by EPA in 1971 reports the prevalence, duration, and intensity of water pollution in major drainage basins (CEQ 1972:11). It is not possible to translate basin-based data into state figures. Therefore, alternative indicators must be used.

Estimated Treatment Costs

EPA provides data on the estimated annual costs in states for the treatment of industrial discharges (EPA, 1972:2:103). These figures are provided by the states and will be used as an indicator of the severity of a state's water pollution problem. The dollar figures represent EPA's estimate of the average per-plant cost to manufacturers in a given state of treating industrial discharges to bring them into compliance with FWPCA discharge and water quality requirements. The dollar amounts given are in 1967 dollars, based on discharge measurements and flow conditions in 1968. It is assumed that the costs of treatment are proportionate to the severity of the pollution problem within a state. It is hypothesized that the higher these costs are, the more likely a state will apply for program authority.

State Population Characteristics

Although industrial water use accounts for most point-source water pollution, it is not the sole cause. Municipal waste treatment works account for the balance of point-source pollution (CEQ, 1976:15). The contribution of population concentration to the severity of the target problem was measured by two indicators, the percent of the population living in urban areas and population density as published for 1970 in the *U. S. Statistical Abstract*. It is hypothesized that a state will be more likely to apply for program authority if it has a higher score on these two indicators.

Pre-Existing State Regulation

State commitment to water pollution control may also be evidenced by the existence of state regulations in the area prior to the creation of the federal program. Wenner (1971) provides the date each state first adopted a water pollution control program and the funding level of that program in 1969. It is hypothesized that the older a state water pollution control law, the more likely the state will be to apply for NPDES program authority. Also, it is hypothesized that the higher a state's water quality control expenditures in 1969, the more likely the state will be to apply for program authority.

Republican Party Dominance

The relationship between Republican party dominance in a state and state application for program authority can be expressed within the cost/benefit framework of this analysis if one accepts the idea that symbolic factors should be included. The Republican party's stand on the issue of the proper division of power between the states and the federal government has gained such symbolic status. It is not just a question of being in favor of the dual federalist model of the allocation of power between two levels of government, it is a question of "states' rights" and supporting the transfer of power to the level "closest to the people."

The dominance of one political party or the other in state politics is frequently measured using the Ranney Index of interparty competition (Ranney, 1976). Possible values on the index range from 0, which equals total Republican control, to 1 representing total Democratic control. Bibby et al. (1983:67) have computed the values for all 50 states for the period 1974–1980. Most state applications occurred during the 1973–1980 period. It is hypothesized that the smaller the state score on the Ranney Index (more Republican), the more likely the state will be to apply for program authority.

State Economic Health

The final measure to be considered in this analysis is categorized in the comparative state policy literature as the economic or fiscal health of the states. This variable has been found to be related to state regulatory policy outputs (Clarke, 1979; Dye and Davidson, 1981; Lester et al., 1983).

One would expect a state in economic trouble to be less willing than an economically healthy state to assume the added regulatory responsibility of implementing a federal program. In addition, the revenue available to state governments should decline as economic productivity declines, and a state government facing reduced revenues may be unwilling to seek further regulatory responsibilities. This should be the case even though most intergovernmental regulatory programs provide economic assistance to states with program authority. The federal funds are often late in arriving, and the amount can sometimes be less than that promised, leaving the states to absorb the additional costs (Thomas, 1976). Therefore, a state with a healthy economy should be more likely to apply for program authority. Two indicators were used: 1) per capita income, and 2) rate of unemployment.[2]

It is hypothesized that 1) the higher a state's per capita income, the more likely the state is to apply for NPDES authority; and, 2) the lower the state's rate of unemployment, the more likely the state is to apply for NPDES authority.

ANALYSIS AND RESULTS

Given that the dependent variable in this study is nominal, the statistical procedures available are limited. Discriminant analysis is used (see generally, Klecka, 1980; Aldrich and Cnudde, 1984). The procedure involves identifying the set of discriminating variables that best describes the differences between groups represented by the dependent variable. In this analysis, the groups are applicant and nonapplicant states. The discriminating variables are the independent variables described above.

Discriminant analysis assumes that the discriminating variables are normally distributed. Klecka (1980:60–63) argues that discriminant analysis is sufficiently robust to tolerate some violation of this assumption. Since the population analyzed includes only 50 cases, it is unlikely that all the independent variables are normally distributed. The violation has impact primarily on tests of significance and the assessment of probabilities of group membership. With regard to tests of significance, the violation should have limited impact on this analysis since the cases analyzed (all 50 states) represent the entire population rather than a sample.

The strong likelihood of abnormally distributed discriminating variables does limit the type of discriminant analysis used, however. Analysis of the characteristics differentiating applicant from nonapplicant states begins with nine potential discriminating variables—a fairly large number for only 50 cases. A common way of reducing that number would be to use one of the stepwise methods of discriminant analysis. However, the stepwise methods arrive at a final set of discriminating variables by determining whether inclusion of a particular variable will make a statistically significant addition to the explanatory power of the discriminant function (Klecka, 1980:52–60). Reliance on statistical significance to define the components of the discriminant function would be unwise given the violation of the normality assumption. Therefore, alternative criteria for selecting particular discriminating variables have been used. Those with very small standardized discriminant function coefficients were excluded.[3] Consideration was given also to finding the combination of discriminating variables that maximizes the percentage of cases correctly classified by the discriminant function.

Since it is known that 35 states have applied for NPDES program authority, the discriminant analysis was based on the prior specification of a .70 probability that a case will fall into the applicant group and a .30

probability that it will fall into the nonapplicant group (Klecka, 1980:46–47; Aldrich and Cnudde, 1984:287–90).

Based on the small size of their standardized discriminant function coefficients, population density and the age of the state's water pollution control statute were excluded from the analysis. Table 9.2 presents the results of the discriminant analysis of the remaining independent variables. The figure in parentheses following the variable is the standardized discriminant function coefficient for the variable.

The indicator of the influence of the target group, average per capita value added by manufacture (−.77), was related to state application in the expected direction. The higher this figure, the less likely the state was to apply. Of the seven variables included in the analysis, this indicator proved to be the third most powerful variable in explaining the differences between applicant and nonapplicant states. This finding differs from that reported in Thompson and Scicchitano's study (1983) of

Table 9.2 Results of Discriminant Analysis of State Characteristics Related to State Application for Program Authority

Variables[a]	Indicators	Expected Relation to Application	Discriminant Function Coefficient
Influence of target group	Average per capita value added by manufacturing	Inverse	−.77
Seriousness of target problem	Average per-plant cost of pollution control	Direct	.54
	Percent of population in urban areas	Direct	.78
	State pollution control expenditures 1969	Direct	.43
Republican party dominance	Average Ranney index of interparty competition	Inverse	−.33
State economic well-being	Average percent unemployed	Inverse	.49
	Average per capita income	Direct	−.87

Canonical Correlation = .59
Wilks Lambda = .66
p = .0006
Percent of cases correctly classified = 80%.

[a] An attempt was made to reduce the multiple-indicator variables to factors. The factors were obtained and used in a discriminant analysis. A very low Wilks Lambda was achieved (.85).

the correlates of state participation in federal occupational health and safety programs. They found no relationship between target group strength and state participation.

Three indicators of the seriousness of the target problem were included: the percent of population living in urban areas (.78), the average per-plant cost of pollution control (.54), and state water pollution control expenditures for 1969 (.43). The data confirmed the hypotheses that all three would be directly related to state application. That is, the higher the state scores on each of the three indicators of severity of the target problem, the more likely the state is to be an applicant rather than nonapplicant state. The percent of population in urban areas was the second most powerful contributor to the discriminant function coefficient; average per-plant costs and 1969 expenditures were the fourth and sixth most powerful, respectively.

The finding that the severity of the target problem is related to state application in the expected direction concurs with the results reported in the comparative state policy literature. Lester et al. (1983) found that the seriousness of the target problem was related to the strength of state regulations of toxic waste. Game (1979) reported that population density was directly related to the stringency of state air pollution programs, and Clarke (1979) showed that states with growth management problems tended to have the strictest growth management regulations.

As hypothesized, the analysis indicated that the lower the state's score on the Ranney Index of interparty competition (−.33), the more likely the state was to apply. However, this variable made the smallest contribution to the discriminant function. This weak relationship between Republican party domination and state application for program authority agrees with a similar finding by Thompson and Scicchitano (1983), who found a weak relationship between Republican party domination of a state government and the state's participation in federal occupational safety and health programs.

Two indicators of state economic health were included in the final analysis, average per capita income (−.87) and the average percent unemployed (.49). However, the relationship between these variables and application was not in the direction hypothesized. The higher a state's average percent unemployment, the more likely the state is to be an applicant state. Also, states with lower per capita income are more likely to be applicant states. In fact, per capita income is the most powerful of the variables included. Unemployment is the fifth most powerful.

Based on these two indicators, the data suggest that economically healthy states are less likely to apply for program authority. Perhaps the availability of federal funds to offset program costs is more desirable than has been assumed (cf. Thomas, 1976). It may be that states with economic problems are accustomed to seeking aid from the federal government for programs and, therefore, are less resistant to becoming involved in intergovernmental programs than are states whose economic health permits greater independence.

The discriminant function coefficient composed of these seven variables correctly classifies 80 percent of the states. Of the 35 applicant states, 30 (85.7 percent) were correctly classified as applicants based on their scores on the discriminating variables. Ten of the 15 nonapplicant states (66.7 percent) were correctly classified. This suggests that while these discriminant variables do a good job of explaining why states apply for program authority, they do not do as well in explaining why states do not apply. It may be that there are factors not included that discourage states from applying for program authority when those states would otherwise be applicants, based on the characteristics they share with applicant states. A comparison of states' responses to several programs may help discover these characteristics, since they may be program-specific rather than state characteristics.

CONCLUSIONS

This study differs from much of the comparative state policy and intergovernmental relations literature because it proceeded from an explicit theoretical basis. It began by assuming that the state decision makers weighed the alternatives regarding application for program authority in terms of their costs and benefits. The results of the application of that perspective to the question of why some states apply and other do not are encouraging but not conclusive. Five of the seven hypotheses were confirmed. Further work is required to determine if this set of factors apply to other intergovernmental regulatory programs.

The findings of this analysis are not encouraging, should the national government desire to find ways of increasing state participation in these intergovernmental programs. The seven characteristics that explain most of the variation in state application are not manipulable factors. For example, the national government cannot increase the severity of the target problem or decrease the influence of a target group in a state to encourage that state to participate in the implementation of a federal program. The fact that states with economic problems seem more interested in the program than economically healthy states does suggest that the financial incentives of involvement in these programs should not be underestimated and can, perhaps, be enhanced to encourage broader state participation.

Finally, at least within this one program, the federal agency seems extraordinarily willing to delegate power to the states. It is possible that all state applicants were successful because only those which had reached an informal understanding with the EPA prior to formal application actually filed applications. This determination would require an in-depth study of the review process used by the agency. The overall success of state applicants suggests that the transfer of power may happen more quickly if the possession of the power is made more attractive to the states than it currently appears to be.

NOTES

1. Ripley and Franklin (1982:72–73) divide regulatory policies into two types—competitive regulatory policies and protective regulatory policies. Competitive regulatory policies grant specific goods and services to a few designated individuals or groups selected from a large number of competitors. These goods and services are assumed to be related to the public interest and thus the government has the right to be involved in their allocation. Protective regulatory policies "are designed to protect the public by setting the conditions under which various private activities can occur." The regulatory policies referred to in this study are protective regulatory policies. The framework set out in this study should not be applied to competitive regulatory policies without modifications reflecting the difference in the relationship between the regulator and regulated under the two types of policies.

2. The figures for per capita income and the percent unemployed were taken from *Statistical Abstract of the United States.* Per capita income was given for 1966, 1968, 1970, and 1972. The percent unemployed was given for 1968 through 1972. An average for each indicator was computed.

3. Standardized discriminant function coefficients can be interpreted as one would interpret standardized regression coefficients. An arbitrary point of .20 was chosen as the minimum size discriminant function coefficient for retention of a variable. Any variable with a standardized discriminant function coefficient below this level was deleted from the analysis.

REFERENCES

Aldrich, John, and Charles F. Cnudde. 1984. "Probing the Bounds of Conventional Wisdom: A Comparison of Regression, Probit, and Discriminant Analysis," in H. Asher, H. Weisberg, J. Kessell, and W. Shively (eds.), *Theory Building and Data Analysis in the Social Sciences* (Knoxville: University of Tennessee Press): 263–300.

Bibby, John F., Cornelius P. Cotter, James L. Gibson, and Robert Huckshorn. 1983. "Parties in State Politics," in Virginia Gray, Herbert Jacob, and Kenneth Vines (eds.), *Politics in the American States: A Comparative Analysis* (Boston: Little, Brown and Co.): 59–95.

Clarke, Susan E. 1979. "Determinants of State Growth Management Policies," *Policy Studies Journal* 7: 753–62.

Council on Environmental Quality. 1972. *Environmental Quality: Third Annual Report of the Council on Environmental Quality* (Washington, D.C.: Government Printing Office).

————. 1976. *Environmental Quality: Seventh Annual Report of the Council on Environmental Quality* (Washington, D.C.: Government Printing Office).

————1980. *Environmental Quality: Eleventh Annual Report of the Council on Environmental Quality* (Washington,D.C.: Government Printing Office).

Dye, Thomas R. 1979. "Politics Versus Economics: The Development of the Literature on Policy Determination," *Policy Studies Journal* 7: 652–62.

Dye, Thomas R., and Dorothy K. Davidson. 1981. "State Energy Policies: Federal Funds for Paper Programs," *Policy Studies Review* 1: 255–62.

Edwards, George C., III. 1980. *Implementing Public Policy* (Washington, D.C.: Congressional Quarterly Press).

Environmental Protection Agency. 1972. *The Economics of Clean Water—1972.* Vols. 1 and 2 (Washington, D.C.: Government Printing Office).

Game, Kingsley W. 1979. "Controlling Air Pollution: Why Some States Try Harder," *Policy Studies Journal* 7: 728–38.

Hanus, Jerome J. (ed.). 1981. *The Nationalization of State Government* (Lexington, Mass.: D. C. Heath and Co.).

Hawkins, Robert B. (ed.). 1981. *American Federalism: A New Partnership for the Republic* (San Francisco: Institute for Contemporary Studies).

Howitt, Arnold M. 1984. *Managing Federalism: Studies in Intergovernmental Relations* (Washington, D.C.: Congressional Quarterly Press).

Klecka, William R. 1980. *Discriminant Analysis* (Beverly Hills: Sage Publications).

Lester, James P., James Franke, Ann O'M. Bowman, and Kenneth Kramer. 1983. "Hazardous Wastes, Politics, and Public Policy: A Comparative State Analysis," *Western Political Quarterly* 36: 257–85.

Lieber, Harvey. 1975. *Federalism and Clean Waters: The 1972 Water Pollution Control Act* (Lexington, Mass.: Lexington Books).

Lowi, Theodore. 1979. *The End of Liberalism: the Second Republic of the United States.* 2d ed. (New York: W. W. Norton and Co.).

Mazmanian, Daniel A., and Paul A. Sabatier. 1983. *Implementation and Public Policy* (Glenview, Ill.: Scott, Foresman and Co.).

Ranney, Austin. 1976. "Parties in State Politics," in Herbert Jacob and Kenneth Vines (eds.), *Politics in the American States: A Comparative Analysis* (Boston: Little, Brown and Co.): 51–92.

Ripley, Randall, and Grace Franklin. 1982. *Bureaucracy and Policy Implementation* (Homewood, Ill.: The Dorsey Press).

Thomas, Robert D. 1976. "Intergovernmental Coordination in the Implementation of National Air and Water Pollution Policies," in Charles O. Jones and Robert D. Thomas (eds.), *Public Policy Making in a Federal System* (Beverly Hills: Sage Publications): 129–48.

Thompson, Frank J., and Michael J. Scicchitano. 1983. "State Implementation of Federal Regulatory Policy: The Case of Occupational Safety and Health," presented at the Southern Political Science Association, November, Birmingham, Alabama.

Tucker, Harvey J. 1982. "Its About Time: the Use of Time in Cross-Sectional State Policy Research," *American Journal of Political Science* 26: 176–95.

U.S. Senate. 1972. Senate Report No. 92-414. *U.S. Congressional and Administrative News:* 3668–3739.

Van Horn, Carl E., and Donald S. Van Meter. 1976. "The Implementation of

Intergovernmental Policy," in Charles O. Jones and Robert D. Thomas (eds.), *Public Policy Making in a Federal System* (Beverly Hills, Calif.: Sage Publications): 39–62.

Wenner, Lettie M. 1971. "Enforcement of Water Pollution Laws in the U.S." Ph.D. Diss., University of Wisconsin.

Wright, Deil S. 1978. *Understanding Intergovernmental Relations* (North Scituate, Mass.: Duxbury Press).

Part 4
Federal-Local Relations

10

Deregulation of State and Local Governments: The Reagan Years

Catherine H. Lovell

The first three years of the Reagan administration's efforts to "deregulate" in the intergovernmental sphere showed mixed results in providing more flexibility for state and local governments and in helping beneficiaries of programs. Because the results have been so varied in different functional areas, the Reagan administration's deregulation efforts appear to have been more ideologically inspired than based in a theoretical framework or on careful consideration of some of the very real problems of unhealthy overregulation and how they might be solved. The administration's efforts were expressed in "getting-the-government-off-our-backs" rhetoric and set in a context of domestic program budget cuts. Sorting the implementing actions from the rhetoric and identifying deregulation actions as distinct from budget cuts have been difficult but informing.

The intergovernmental regulatory relationship is one of the most difficult of practical day-to-day federalist relationships. Over the last decade complaints from state and local governments have increased as the national role has grown bigger, broader, and deeper, and more and more programs have been financed by the federal government and conducted jointly by two or more governmental spheres. Some state and local officials had increasingly claimed, in the decade prior to the Reagan administration, that growing numbers of nationally imposed requirements had skewed local priorities, added to the costs of operating their governments, and unnecessarily limited their flexibility and effectiveness in delivering programs to respond to the needs of the majority of their residents. It is in this context that the Reagan administration made deregulation of intergovernmental programs a major announced aim.

When the Reagan administration proclaimed its assault on regulations, however, various public interest groups expressed concern about possible deregulatory consequences. They feared that reduction or relaxation of federal requirements would greatly erode the process that had been made in such areas as civil rights and environmental protection, labor standards, and programs for the poor. These groups felt that national guidelines and specific enforcing procedures were important—without them, they contended, the short-sighted and status quo-oriented views of state and local elites would prevail (Roberts, 1982).

Since over 80 percent of all federal rules affecting states and local governments are attached as conditions of financial aid, the administration's deregulation efforts would need to focus on grant relationships. This study analyzes the administration's first three years of deregulatory activity in four functional areas of intergovernmental grants.

The complete regulatory process may be thought of as having three dimensions: statutory, administrative, and behavioral. A thorough examination of deregulatory activity must consider all three dimensions. Since regulations in large part are statutorily based, examination of regulatory changes must include a study of changes in enabling legislation. In order to detect changes in administratively based rules, those rules that go beyond the language of the statute and provide implementation guidelines must be examined. Data on these first two dimensions were obtained from enabling statutes and the *Federal Register*.

Deregulation on the behavioral dimension is more difficult to identify. It manifests itself by relaxation of compliance attitudes and mechanisms—by reductions in the intensity with which rules are enforced by agencies. For the research discussed here only the findings on the first two dimensions are reported.[1]

CRITERIA FOR EVALUATION OF REGULATORY CHANGES

Three criteria were developed for evaluating the administration's changes in regulations. The first criterion was whether the change increased or decreased the quantity and complexity of rules. A repeated criticism of federal rules had been that they were growing ever more numerous and that they were increasingly specific, often redundant, and overly complex (Lovell, 1979; Lovell and Tobin, 1981; ACIR, 1984; Bush, 1981). The second criterion was whether the change expanded or reduced flexibility for the grantee government in managing the program. A general criticism of federal rules had been that they unnecessarily constrained local autonomy and local management capabilities, leaving little scope for management of programs in ways that were responsive to local situations. The third criterion was whether the change would enlarge or restrict benefits to the affected client population or to the intended policy. Many observers had feared that relaxation of federal rules and devolution of management to the states would result in less benefits for intended clients and policies.

Each rule change was judged on the direction of the change when compared with the previous rule. On the first criterion, a rule change was considered as decreasing quantity and complexity if the change shortened the rule by deleting provisions or by rewording it in a simpler version. The change was considered as increasing quantity and complexity if provisions were added or language in an existing provision was expanded. If a new rule was simply substituted for another of approximately the same length, the change was considered as having no effect.

On the second criterion, flexibility, a rule change was considered to expand flexibility for the grantee government if it provided fewer constraints on the decision making of the grantee government, either in programs or procedures, by being less explicit or by clearly stating that certain decisions are the purview of the grantee government. Flexibility is reduced if formerly allowed grantee actions are circumscribed or if new prohibitions are added that reduce grantee autonomy.

Evaluation of rule changes on the third criterion, benefit effects, required a clear yet sometimes arbitrary determination of "beneficiary" group or policy. In some programs the beneficiaries are clients to be served (such as low-income children in a school lunch program), while in others it is a policy to be advanced (such as the improvement of air quality in an environmental program). In some cases benefit effects could not be assigned in the absence of further longitudinal research because how the states or local governments use their expanded flexibility must be documented over time.

RULE CHANGES IN FOUR INTERGOVERNMENTAL GRANT AREAS DURING THE FIRST THREE YEARS OF THE REAGAN ADMINISTRATION

Rule changes in some 50 programs in four functional areas were identified and evaluated against the three criteria described above. In two of the areas—the community development entitlement program and income maintenance—the design of grants made to states or local governments remained essentially as before the Reagan administration took office. In the other two areas—community services and education—many categorical programs formerly given largely to local governments and nonprofit agencies were block granted to the states. Also, the community development program for small cities was turned over to the states to manage, and funds were block granted to the states for that purpose.

For the community development entitlement program and the income maintenance cluster of programs where no changes were made in the structure of the programs, the rules that governed them at the conclusion of the Carter administration, January 1981, were compared with changes made in those rules by the Reagan administration up to the end of 1983.[2] Before-after comparisons for the grant programs in these two functional areas are summarized below. Local government managers' perceptions about the changes as they affected the largest cities of 14 states were obtained by interview in the summer and fall of 1983.[3] These findings are summarized also.

In three other grant areas—community services, education, and small cities community development—major structural changes were made by block granting to the states. For programs in these three areas, before-after *Federal Register* comparisons were not applicable. Instead, the rules that had applied to the categorical programs under the Carter administration, before combination into block grants under the Reagan administration, were compared with the new rules that the states developed to replace federal regulations. Perceptions of local government program managers in two of the three new block grant areas are provided.[4]

COMMUNITY DEVELOPMENT PROGRAMS

The Community Development Entitlement Program that provides block grants from the Department of Housing and Urban Development (HUD) directly to local governments was amended under the Reagan administration in 1981. Appropriations were reduced, application procedures were simplified, some new and eligible activities were added, and citizen participation requirements were reduced.

The final rules for the amended program incorporated six statutorily based rule changes and eight administratively based changes. The changes had little effect on the quantity and complexity of the rules (the first criterion); the number of rules and their complexity remained essentially the same. The changes expanded flexibility for recipient governments (the second criterion) in both administrative procedures and program design.

Two of the statutory changes (reductions in citizen participation requirements and limitations on allowable spending for social services) and two of the administrative changes (changes in definitions of slum or blighted areas and changes in the criteria for interpreting the meaning of "principally benefiting low and moderate income families") were

Table 10.1   Local Manager Perceptions of Grant Rule Changes

	Community Development[a]	Income Maintenance[b]	Community Service[c]	Education[d]
SIMPLICITY				
Procedures				
more	14	0	6	12
no change	3	2	2	2
less	1	5	4	0
Programs				
more	11	0	4	12
no change	7	2	2	2
less	2	5	6	0
FLEXIBILITY				
Procedures				
more	9	2	1	12
no change	7	3	4	2
less	2	2	7	0
Programs				
more	11	2	1	13
no change	3	2	3	1
less	4	3	8	0
BENEFITS				
more	3	0	2	8
no change	11	0	1	5
less	4	7	9	1

[a]Represents responses of eighteen local managers in fourteen states.

[b]Represents response of seven local managers in six states.   In the other eight states income maintenance is managed directly by the states.

[c]Represents responses of twelve local managers in twelve states.

[d]Represents responses of fourteen local managers in fourteen states.

judged to reduce benefits to low and moderate income people. Two of the rule changes potentially provided for more benefits (specific inclusion of mobile homes in real property that can be aided by grant funds and relaxation of Davis Bacon requirements). The other changes either had no effect on benefits for low and moderate income people or it was too soon to determine effects that may result from the increased decision-making flexibility given to the local governments.

The final rules issued by HUD and summarized above were, however, quite different from the interim rule changes originally proposed by the administration—public and congressional pressure forced HUD to restore, at least partially, more strict interpretations requiring targeting to low income persons.

The Urban Development Action Grant Program (UDAG) was also amended in 1981. There were five major statutorily based rule changes and no major administrative changes. The changes made no essential difference in the quantity of rules, slightly expanded grantee flexibility in three of the five changes, and, in the two changes where benefit effects could be determined, provided fewer benefits.

Perceptions of local community development managers about the effects of the changes differed somewhat from the before-after comparisons discussed above. A majority of the 18 managers in 14 states found the new rules to be simpler than the old—a dimension on which they agreed with the researchers (see table 10.1). Although the number of rules was not reduced, application procedures and community participation requirements were simplified. A majority found the rules on both program and procedure dimensions to be more flexible, a finding consistent with the research team's before-after comparison.

A majority of the local managers felt that there would be no change in the benefits of the program, although four of the eighteen thought that benefits for low-income people would be less, since targeting to the poor was not as carefully prescribed under the new rules. Three respondents felt that benefits would be greater. A careful examination of the responses of these three respondents showed that they did not accept the researcher's definition of the beneficiaries as low-income clients but rather were thinking of the beneficiaries as "the community as a whole."

INCOME MAINTENANCE PROGRAMS

Changes in requirements governing the income maintenance or welfare cluster of programs were made in 1981. Four programs within the cluster were examined: child nutrition, summer food services, Aid to Families with Dependent Children (AFDC), and food stamps. In all the programs there were extensive changes—in general, directed to tightening eligibility and cutting fraud possibilities.

In the child nutrition programs, there were nineteen statutory changes and six major administrative rule changes. In the summer food service program there were seven statutory and six administrative changes. In the food stamp program the number of changes were thirteen and three, respectively, and in AFDC, thirteen and three. The pattern of changes in all four programs showed that the quantity of rules was increased, and that, in general, flexibility for the states in managing the programs was reduced (except in the two nutrition programs, where flexibility was somewhat expanded in types of meals that can be served and in plan submission requirements). An overwhelming majority of the rule changes in the four programs where benefit effects could be assigned resulted in less benefits for low-income clients.

Perceptions of local income maintenance managers were obtained in six states.[5] In general, the perceptions of the local managers about the changes agreed with the before-after comparisons of the researchers (see table 10.1). Most of the managers found the new rules to be more complex, less flexible, or unchanged, and benefits for targeted clients were found to be fewer across the board.

FUNCTIONAL AREAS BLOCK GRANTED TO THE STATES

For the programs studied in the three functional areas discussed in the following summary, federal agencies have withdrawn from direct relationships with local governments and now serve as agents to pass funds to the states, which now manage the programs. From the point of view of local governments and beneficiaries, what is now pertinent are the rules that the states make to replace federal regulations.[6]

The incorporation of formerly categorical programs into the new block grants and their management now by the states provides an unusual opportunity to test various theories about the consequences of state rather than federal management. One theory, dominant in political science literature, suggests that redistribution is more difficult to achieve as decision-making arenas are narrowed (Schattschneider, 1960; Riker, 1964; Caputo and Cole, 1974; Dommel, 1975; Peterson, 1981; Morgan and England, 1984). Although not necessarily theoretically grounded, many public interest groups hold similar opinions that states are more "conservative" than the national government and that programs are less likely to benefit the relatively disadvantaged when run by the states. On the two other criteria (rule quantity and rule flexibility) not directly related to the benefits dimension, many observers of state-local interactions predicted, when the block grants were enacted, that, under state control, regulations applied to local governments would be as numerous and complex as they were under the federal government and that flexibility for local governments might actually be less than it was when federal regulations controlled local grant programs directly.

The findings discussed here, although limited to comparisons between the former federal regulations and those issued in only seven or eight states, begin to supply data to confirm or refute these contentions.

The data reported here are based on comparisons between former federal rules and new state rules. Seven states were observed for community development and community services rules, and eight, for education.[7] Perceptions of local government program managers about the changes in the two programs are also reported.

The State Community Development Block Grant (Small Cities Program)

In the seven states where the new state rules for the Small Cities Community Development Block Grant were examined, a wide range of program designs and program emphases were found. The majority of the seven states kept the number and complexity of rules about the same as they had been under HUD management. All seven states expanded small city program flexibility by providing more options and less rigorous project criteria, although four of the states added new specific requirements regarding targeting. Nearly all of the states expanded reporting, fiscal, and record-keeping requirements. On the benefits criterion, one state's regulations appear to lead to more low/moderate income benefits, three states to less, and three cannot yet be determined because evaluation depends on what project decisions the small cities make.

The State Community Services Block Grant

The State Community Services Block Grant rules were examined in the same seven states and compared with the rules that the federal Community Services Agency had used to manage the program before it was block granted. Programs in each of the seven states were different. All used the flexibility given to them by the block grant generally to decrease the number of rules for local Community Action Program (CAP) agencies.

Although the structure of CAP agencies was protected by the block grant language, CAPs in six of the states now have less flexibility in some types of rules and slightly more flexibility in others. Most of the states made some adjustments to advisory board compositions, and several changed the mix and priorities of activities and restricted definitions of client eligibility. Benefit effects of the states' changes in rules are mixed. In one state the new rules appeared to provide for more benefits to poor people. In three states benefits are expected to be fewer because of more restrictive definitions of program eligibility, prohibitions against an advocacy role for CAP employees, and deemphasis of participation of the poor in CAP processes. The benefit effects in two other states were mixed.

Perceptions of local CAP agency managers were obtained in 12 states.[8] As Table 10.1 shows, the perception of a majority of the local CAP agency administrators was that the states have imposed more complex rules on them and less flexible program and procedural rules than the federal government required of them. The most pervasive perception was that benefits for poor people would be less. Respondents mentioned in particular that state program regulations were less flexible because of the strict designation of fundable projects and more specific guidelines for advisory councils and for state approvals for expenditures. Respondents as a group were primarily concerned about cuts in funding levels and attributed some part of the expected decrease in benefits to "interference and disruptive influence" of the states' new oversight responsibility.

The Education Block Grant

Chapter 2 of the Elementary and Secondary Education Block Grant incorporated 28 of some 40 previously categorical educational programs. Three programs that previously had been direct federal to local education agency programs were studied.[9]

In the education block grant, Congress decreased the number of applicable federal regulations, allocated funds to states on a formula basis, and restricted the states' abilities to impose rules on local education agencies. Since Congress drastically cut regulations and prohibited the states from adding new regulations, the quantity and complexity of rules affecting local school agencies were reduced and their flexibility was expanded. Local education agencies can now determine where to allocate their Chapter 2 block grant funds among a list of programs within each of the subchapters and can design combinations of these programs to meet their individual needs. Since there are so many programs with varying client groups and so much flexibility is given to local agencies, the benefit effects of the rule changes are impossible to assign at this time.

The pattern of local education agency administrator perceptions about the changes is clear. As Table 10.1 shows, 13 of the 14 managers interviewed felt that both procedural and program regulations are now less complex. Moreover, 12 and 13 managers, respectively, believed that there is more flexibility in both procedural and program options. The one administrator who saw no change across the board was in a state which, by the time of the interview in the fall of 1983, had not yet implemented the new regulations. The eight administrators who thought that benefits would be increased felt that, because of decentralization of decision making to local education agencies, programs could now be better tailored to the specific needs of the district. The five managers who predicted no change based their opinions on reductions in the amount of money available to implement the new flexibility. The one administrator who thought that benefits are likely to be reduced felt that fewer funds will be targeted to the needy.

CONCLUSIONS

The biggest deregulatory success of the Reagan administration was in the new block grants to the states. Compared with the categorical grants they replaced, Congress and the administering agencies attached far fewer programmatic and procedural conditions. Under the new block grants (education excepted, where local education agencies instead of states gained flexibility), states were given greater authority to set priorities on uses of funds and were given flexibility to design their own implementing rules. The findings show, however, that the new block grants to the states do not necessarily mean less regulation or more flexibility for local governments (except in education), since state regulations have replaced federal requirements. In fact, some observers might argue that compliance mechanisms at the state level may be more rigorous than those local governments have experienced from the federal government. Some evidence exists that enforcement of regulations by federal agencies in the past has been variable and often less than rigorous (Massey and Straussman, 1985).

In contrast to the reduced federal regulation of the states through the block grants, the findings show that more complex and restrictive federal requirements have been applied in the categorical public assistance programs. In these cases, the administration's major substantive goals, such as reducing welfare costs and diminishing welfare dependency, took precedence over its deregulatory goals. Since over 80 percent of federal aid remains in categorical programs, the finding that regulations in categorical programs were little changed or even made more restrictive means that less deregulation has taken place than might have been expected as a result of the administration's rhetoric.

The data reported here also show that in all programs studied, where benefit effects could be assigned, the majority of federal deregulatory changes were accompanied by reductions in program benefits to those groups or policies targeted by the legislation. The picture of the benefit effects of deregulation through block granting to the states cannot be known fully until state and local actions have been implemented long enough to allow an evaluative study of consequences. Where benefit effects could be assigned, however, state rules generally reduced benefits for targeted clients. Although the sample of states studied was small, the states included are from different regions and are of different sizes and state-local structures.[10] If the results of decision making in most states on community development and community services are similar to those found in the seven states of this study, the theories of the political scientists and the fears of some of the interest groups who predict less redistributive actions as decision arenas are narrowed would be substantiated.

Although the administration did not "thin the thicket of federal regulations" in most intergovernmental programs, as far as the states are concerned, the deregulatory changes in the new block grants represent some reversal of what had been a basic direction in American federalism for several decades. Whether the current period represents more than a modest pendulum swing, motivated primarily by federal budget considerations and temporary ideologies, will depend partly on the eventual benefit consequences of federal devolution and partly on further reassessments of what the federal role should be. Reexamining the intergovernmental regulatory relationship will be part of the process. In particular, as domestic programs are reconstructed in coming years, a careful evaluation must be made of where the line should be drawn between necessary federal policy guidelines and unhealthy overregulation of state and local governments. The administration has made no effort to date to advance a coherent theory on this subject or to encourage widespread consultation on the subject with Congress, affected public interest groups, or state and local governments. The administration's actions to increase federal requirements in some areas while devolving responsibilities in other program areas begs the question.

NOTES

1. The findings reported here are based on two years of research by the author, done with the support of the National Science Foundation, Program Grant No. SES 8205159, and completed in June 1984.

2. The *Federal Register* was the principal source for both new and old rules. Agency officials were interviewed where clarification was necessary.

3. The interviewers were associates on the team that did the evaluation study of the Reagan domestic program conducted by the Princeton Urban and Regional Research Center, Woodrow Wilson School of Public and International Affairs, directed by Richard Nathan and Fred Doolittle. The localities and the associates were: Arizona, Phoenix (Maricopa County), John S. Hall; California, Los Angeles (Los Angeles County), Ruth Ross; Florida, Orlando (Orange County), Lance deHaven-Smith; Illinois, Chicago (Cook County), Charles J. Orlebeke; Massachusetts, Boston (Suffolk County), Arn Howitt; Mississippi, Jackson (Hinds County), Lewis H. Smith; Missouri, St. Louis (St. Louis County), George D. Wendel; New Jersey, Newark (Essex County), Richard W. Roper; New York, Rochester (Monroe County), Sarah F. Liebschutz; Ohio, Cleveland (Cuyahoga County), Charles F. Adams, Jr.; Oklahoma, Tulsa (Tulsa County), R. Lynn Rittenoure; South Dakota, Sioux Falls (Minnehaha County), William O. Farber; Texas, Houston (Harris County), Susan A. MacManus; Washington, Seattle (King County), Betty Jane Narver.

4. Since only large city local managers were interviewed, the small cities community development program was not included.

5. In eight of the fourteen states, income maintenance is managed directly by the states so local perspectives are not applicable.

6. Data were obtained from the *Federal Register* for the federal regulations and from various state documents and interviews for the state regulations.

7. The seven states included for community development and community services were Arizona, California, Illinois, Massachusetts, Oklahoma, Texas, and Washington. Mississippi was added for the other three functions. The eight states were chosen from among the fourteen states in the Princeton study (see note 2 above) so as to obtain geographic and sectional variety and close-to-average position on the Stephens State-Local Centralization Scale. For discussion of this index, see Stephens, 1974, and Stephens and Olson, 1977.

8. Interviews were conducted in only 12 of the 14 localities because the locality in Mississippi does not have a CAP agency, and the locality in South Dakota was denied funding by the governor.

9. Those selected were all programs that had been directed in whole or in part by local education agencies. They were The Basic Skills Improvement Program from Subchapter A, the Magnet Schools Program of the Emergency School Aid Act from Subchapter B, and the Community Education Program from Subchapter C.

10. Making generalizations is always a problem with samples of states, since there is so much variety among states; therefore, the findings are suggestive rather than generalizable.

REFERENCES

Advisory Commission on Intergovernmental Relations. 1984. *Regulatory Federalism: Policy, Process, Impact and Report* (Washington, D.C.: Government Printing Office).

Bush, George. 1981. *Year-End Summary of Actions Taken by the Presidential Task Force on Regulatory Relief* (Washington, D.C.: Office of the Vice President).

Caputo, David A., and Richard Cole. 1974. *Urban Politics and Decentralization* (Lexington, Mass.: D.C. Heath).

Dommel, Paul, 1975. "Urban Policy and Federal Aid: Redistribution Issues," in Robert L. Lineberry and Louis H. Masotti (eds.), *Urban Policy Problems* (Lexington, Mass.: D.C. Heath).

Lovell, Catherine H. 1979. "Coordinating Federal Grants From Below," *Public Administration Review*, 39: 432–39.

Lovell, Catherine H., and Charles Tobin. 1981. "The Mandate Issue," *Public Administration Review* 41: 318–31.

Massey, Jane, and Jeffrey D. Straussman. 1985. "Another Look at the Mandate Issue: Are Conditions of Aid Really So Burdensome?" *Public Administration Review* 45: 292–300.

Morgan, David R., and Robert E. England. 1984. "The Small Cities Block Grant Program: An Assessment of Programmatic Change Under State Control," *Public Administration Review* 44: 477–82.

Peterson, Paul E. 1981. *City Limits* (Chicago: University of Chicago Press).

Riker, William H. 1964. *Federalism, Origin, Operation, Significance* (Boston: Little, Brown).

Roberts, Paula. 1982. "New Federalism or Old Hoax?" (Washington, D.C.: Center for Law and Social Policy).

Schattschneider, E. E. 1960. *The Semi-Sovereign People* (New York: Holt, Rinehart, and Winston).

Stephens, G. Ross. 1974. "State Centralization and the Erosion of Local Autonomy," *Journal of Politics* 36: 44–76.

Stephens, G. Ross and Gerald W. Olson. 1977. "Pass-through Federal Aid and Interlevel Finance in the American Federal System 1957 to 1977," *A Report to the National Science Foundation* (Kansas City: University of Missouri), Vol. 1.

Part 5
State-Local Relations

11

State-Local Administration of Redistributive Federal Programs: A Study of Community Development Grants

Osbin L. Ervin and Mary H. Watson

A common conclusion in the recent literature on intergovernmental relations is that the New Federalism of the 1970s, with its block grant and revenue sharing programs, significantly increased the number and strength of direct federal-local programmatic relationships. In specific reference to the 1974 Community Development Block Grant (CDBG) program, Lovell (1983:95) observed that it "in effect, enticed a whole new group of general purpose local governments, who had had minimal relationships with the federal government before, into *direct federal-local partnerships* [emphasis added] and made the local governments active *implementors of nationally determined policies* [emphasis added]."

If new federal-local partnerships were indeed formed by the CDBG program (and it appears they were), they were in part replaced by state-local partnerships with the passage of the 1981 amendments to the program. These amendments allow states to assume administration of the Small Cities portion of the program from the Department of Housing and Urban Development (HUD), and 46 states had assumed administrative responsibility by fiscal year 1984. Under this new intergovernmental arrangement, each participating state receives a single block grant, which it further distributes to constituent local governments.

This new arrangement for allocation of CDBG monies is mirrored by eight other such new arrangements—in the policy areas of health services, social services, and education. Thus, direct federal-local relationships in implementing national domestic policy have to an important degree given way to state-local relationships, and research on the post-1981 CDBG program may hold implications for other areas of public policy.

The issue examined in this essay is the degree to which state community development priorities differ from those of HUD and, relatedly, the degree to which these priorities address the national objectives of the CDBG legislation. The issue is examined by using information on grant awards across the three major CDBG funding categories of housing, public facilities, and economic development. Both aggregate and separate data on state grant awards are studied. The first question addressed in the analysis is that of general state orientations and priorities and the second question is that of differences in priorities across the various states. Lastly, an attempt is made toward a partial explanation of state differences.

The matter of congruence between state-local priorities and national objectives appears important to both the viability of the new state-local partnership and the implementation of national community development policy. The 1981 amendments allow states wide discretion in administrative procedures and in choosing among eligible local projects. It is clear, though, the amendments intended that this discretion be exercised within the boundaries of program purposes. If state CDBG priorities are different from and less clearly directed toward program objectives than those of HUD, then questions about state capability to implement national urban policies will likely be raised, and state discretion may indeed be threatened.

Before turning to the data on Small Cities awards, it is important to 1) briefly review the purposes and eligible activities of the CDBG program, 2) deal with the question of why these purposes might be less well addressed by the states than by HUD, and 3) posit a relationship between funding categories and satisfaction of national objectives.

PURPOSES OF THE CDBG PROGRAM

The primary objective of the CDBG legislation (*U.S. Statutes,* PL 93-383:634) is "the development of viable urban communities by providing decent housing and a suitable living environment and expanding economic opportunities, primarily for persons of low and moderate income." This objective has remained constant through the ten years of the program. Beyond this primary objective, the original legislation contained seven specific national objectives (including elimination of slums and blight) and six eligible activities, all of which remain in place today. An additional specific objective and eligible activity relating to economic development was contained in amendments passed in 1977, and a further eligible activity providing for assistance to for-profit entities was added in the amendments of 1981. As was indicated earlier, the various eligible activities are conventionally collapsed into the categories of housing, public facilities, and economic development for purposes of tabulation and analysis.[1]

Three aspects of the CDBG legislation are of special importance to this essay. First, the primary objective appears to clearly establish a social targeting intent of the Congress. Funding for the various specific objectives and eligible activities is to be primarily for persons of low and moderate income. A study by Dommel et al. (1980:11–12) indicates that the social targeting issue occupied a prominent place in the congressional debate accompanying CDBG passage.[2] Second, the specific objective of eliminating slums and blight appears especially prominent in the CDBG legislation and related HUD regulations. The Dommel study (p. 13) indicates that this objective "remained legislatively a coequal" of social targeting. Third, it is important to note that the legislation did not contain a specific economic development objective or related eligible activities until passage of the 1977 amendments. The 1981 amendments then built on the economic development provisions of 1977 by authorizing assistance to private, for-profit entities, when necessary to an economic development project.

HUD rules for state administration of the post-1981 Small Cities program (*Federal Register*, 1982) appear to allow states wide discretion in grant award decisions. However, state decisions as to which specific projects and purposes are to be funded are constrained by repeated HUD references to "the primary objectives of the Act" and to the intent that the monies be used "principally for persons of low and moderate income." For example, the rules indicate that "each state may develop a definition of 'low and moderate income families' for purposes of assuring compliance with the primary objectives of the Act" (p. 15297); and, they refer to the secretary's "obligation to enforce compliance with the manifest intent of Congress as declared in the Act" (p. 15297).

The 1981 amendments and related HUD rules then alter neither the primary nor secondary objectives of the act. The major change included in the amendments, in addition to that allowing state administration, is the provision for assistance to private-for-profit organizations.[3]

THE STATES AND SOCIAL TARGETING

There is reason to expect that state Small Cities grant priorities may be somewhat different from those of HUD, and there is reason to hypothesize that they may, in fact, not address the national program objectives as well as those of HUD. The major objectives of the CDBG program are redistributive in nature. Monies are to be appropriated from the national treasury and targeted to the benefit of low and moderate income persons, and relatedly, to neighborhoods experiencing blighted and slum conditions. Two recent papers and a book provide support for the argument that states may not be as likely as HUD to target Small Cities monies to the national objectives.

In *City Limits*, Peterson (1981) argues that cities cannot be expected to pursue redistributive policies and that states are less likely than the national government to pursue such policies. According to Peterson, the objectives of governmental programs can be separated into three categories—allocational, developmental, and redistributive—with any particular program being largely oriented toward one or the other of these purposes. The interests of local government, Peterson writes, require that it "concentrate on development as against redistributive objectives" (p. 69). The major interest of the local community is, according to this thesis, in enhancing its tax base and protecting its economic well-being, an interest that in most cases is not well served by transfer of wealth from the more to less affluent. Peterson's theme is well supported in the earlier work of Schattschneider (1960) and Caputo and Cole (1974), and it offers strong support for the expectation that state and local governments are less likely than the national government to target CDBG benefits to low-income persons.

Morgan and England (1984:4) have shown that a great deal of the theoretical literature in American politics "supports the position that the greater the degree of decentralization, the less likely the community will pursue redistributive policies." And they argue further that "new federalism proponents have misjudged national influence and underestimated the capacity of subnational officials to shape domestic welfare policy to local ends." The basic argument of Morgan and England and much of the literature they cite is that the narrower the scope of political conflict, the less likely are redistributive policies to be pursued.

Morgan and England's thesis appears to be supported by their case study of Oklahoma. They studied Oklahoma's FY 82 funding decisions across the three categories of housing, public facilities, and economic development. In comparing the 1982 allocations with HUD's FY 81 decisions, they found a strong shift in program emphasis from housing to public facilities. In 1981, 43 percent was allocated to housing and 30 percent to public facilities, while 12 percent went to housing projects and 47 percent to public facility projects in 1982. Given the authors' assumption that public facility projects are less beneficial to low-income persons than are housing projects (an assumption that is discussed in a later section of this essay), the FY 81 to FY 82 shift is indicative of a less redistributive orientation among the states than in HUD. Morgan and England clearly see the shift as being disadvantageous to low-income Oklahomans and less oriented toward the social targeting intent of the CDBG legislation.

The second paper (Thomas, 1981) focuses on the difficulties inherent in reconciling national targeting with state involvement. The author's central thesis is that the American federal system functions in such a way that states cannot be expected to target federal urban assistance to national objectives, unless certain federal incentives and behaviors are instituted. This, he indicates, is because of the "politics of inclusion," in which subnational governments shape national programs to their own and constituent interests. "The compromises on program objectives that result from the politics of inclusion," he writes, "will have pork barrel effects if not pork barrel intentions" (p. 13).

Less systematic observation of contemporary state-local politics is further reason for hypothesizing that states may not be very effective in implementing the social targeting objective of the Small Cities program. In many states, state and local priorities converge on the theme of economic development. To a greater degree than ever before, the attention of city and village officials focuses on development of the local economy, and, in this orientation, they are strongly allied with the business and industrial leaders of the community. It is common to find the politics of even small communities dominated by the facts and figures of plant expansions or closings, retail establishments gained or lost, tourism, or jobs. At the state level, the previously modest programs and incentives for retaining or attracting business have been transformed into highly elaborate and expensive packages for business assistance (see "The Fifty Legislative Climates," 1982), and state-level politicians are even more likely than their local counterparts to base political campaigns on economic issues.

If the above assessments of state-local orientations are correct, then it can be expected that state administration of the Small Cities program will result in less funding of activities directly benefiting low-income persons and/or eliminating slums and blight than has HUD. A corollary of this expectation is that states are likely to provide increased funding for activities yielding benefits related to the general or economic development of communities. In terms of the CDBG eligible activities, states are likely to place a lower priority than HUD on housing activities and a higher priority than HUD on economic development and perhaps, public facility projects.

THE FUNDING CATEGORIES AND NATIONAL OBJECTIVES

Findings of differing funding priorities between HUD and the states may be important in their own right. But, if inferences are to be made from such priorities among eligible activities to satisfaction of national social targeting objectives, assumptions must be made about the relationships between funded activities and national objectives. The assumption of this essay is that the primary objectives of the program (i.e., benefit to low and moderate income persons and prevention of slums and blight) are better served by housing activities than by economic development and public facility projects.

There is support for such an assumption in the Third Brookings study monitoring the CDBG program (Dommel et al., 1980). The data reported in the study indicate that economic development expenditures yield lower benefits to low and moderate income groups than either housing or public facility expenditures. Housing activities, on the other hand, yield the highest low-moderate income benefits. The authors conclude that "a relationship appears to exist between the program categories funded and the income group benefits" (p. 169), and that "overall, the best way to increase the level of social targeting is to encourage increased funding for program categories that yield more benefits to lower income groups" (p. 173). Economic development projects, the authors note in reference to their data, "yield a lower level of benefits to low and moderate income groups" (p. 173).[4]

A COMPARISON OF HUD AND AGGREGATE STATE PRIORITIES

Program priorities and funding patterns for the CDBG program over the seven years of exclusive HUD administration (FY 1975–81) have been documented in annual HUD reports and analyzed in other studies. In particular, the Fifth Annual CDGB report (Department of Housing and Urban Development, 1980), and two studies by the Brookings Institution (Dommel et al., 1980; U.S. Department of Housing and Urban Development, undated) provide thorough reviews. In general, the finding of these and other reports and studies is that HUD funding heavily emphasized housing and related neighborhood conservation/revitalization activities, while, on the other hand, economic development activities were given relatively little attention.

Some of the specific observations and conclusions of the Brookings studies are helpful. Dommel et al., in referring to data in their 1980 report, note that "housing activities consistently have been the largest single program category among the sample jurisdictions" (p. 121), and that "economic development consistently has been one of the smallest CDBG categories, although it has grown more each year than any other category" (p. 137). (It should be recalled that economic development was not included among the CDBG objectives and eligible activities until 1977. However, various studies, including those by the Brookings Institute, categorized and tabulated various activities as contributing to the economic development function.) In the last Brookings study (U.S. Department of Housing and Urban Development, undated), the authors summarize funding in years five and six by writing that "housing and neighborhood conservation activities remained the dominant choices" (p. 73). With regard to economic development, they conclude that "although it remained a small category of activity, allocations for economic development continued to receive higher priority" (p. 173).

HUD's *Fifth Annual CDBG Report* (1980) reaches similar conclusions regarding housing and housing-related activities. It notes that "In the first five years of the CDBG program, cities have placed a heavy emphasis on three of the six activity groupings: acquisition, demolition, and related activities; public works; and housing rehabilitation and related activities" (p. VI-3). The data supporting this observation indicate that the funding percentages for these three groupings were 25, 27, and 23, respectively (p. VI-4). If one collapses the acquisition/demolition and rehabilitation groupings into a single "housing" category, the outcome is a 48 percent share to housing activities over the five-year period. This report also notes the relatively unimportant position of economic development activities in HUD funding patterns, but it draws attention to the 1977 amendments and indicates that city and HUD interest in such activities was on the upswing (pp. X to X-14).

The dominance of housing activities and relative unimportance of economic development activities hold through the last year of exclusive HUD administration. HUD (1983:59) reports that in FY 1981 it allocated 39 percent, 24 percent, and 4 percent of its Small Cities funds to the housing, public facilities, and economic development categories respectively. Thus, HUD Program priorities over its seven years of CDBG administration appear to have been housing, public facilities, and economic development, in that order. However, it seems that the emphasis on economic development activities increased through the years, especially in the years following the 1977 CDBG amendments.

Data from the first two years of state administration of the Small Cities program reveal a rather significant shift from earlier HUD priorities. A comparison of HUD's FY 1981 Small Cities allocations with state allocations in FY 1982 and FY 83 (table 11.1) shows heavily decreased funding for housing activities and a proportional increase in allocations to public facility and economic development projects.

In the first year of state administration (FY 82), the share of single-purpose funds allocated to housing decreased from 39 percent to 11 percent, while the share to economic development increased from 4 percent to 18 percent. Fiscal year 1983 state data are generally consistent with the figures for 1982, but they do indicate a decline in the 1982 emphasis on public facilities and an increase in the emphasis on both economic development and housing. The 1983 data yield percentages of 16, 35, and 22 for the categories of housing, public facilities, and economic development, respectively.

Table 11.1 State versus HUD Distribution of Funds across Major Program
Categories, FY 1981–1983

		Housing	Public Facilities	Economic Development	Multi-Activity and Other
HUD					
FY1981		39%	24%	4%	33%
States					
FY1982	(N=36)	11	43	18	28
FY1983	(N=24)	16	35	22	27

SOURCE: For FY1981 and 1982, U.S. Department of Housing and Urban Development (1983: 59); for FY1983, data collected via mail survey of
state community affairs agencies (Spring, 1984) and supplemented by
state reports filed with the National Clearinghouse of State Community Affairs Agencies. Data from 24 states were considered
complete and judged reliable.

As was indicated earlier, HUD continued to administer the Small
Cities program in some states during fiscal years 1982 and 1983—in
fourteen states in FY 1982 and in four states in FY 1983. Therefore, state
priorities in these first two years of state administration ought to be
compared with HUD priorities for the same two years, as well as with
pre-1982 priorities. Unfortunately, information on HUD distribution
across major program categories for these years is not available in published form. However, telephone discussions with HUD officials have

Table 11.2 State versus HUD Distribution of Funds across Major Program
Categories, FY 1983

	Housing	Public Facilities	Economic Development	Multi-Activity and Other
HUD				
FY1983	23%	32%	14%	31%
States				
FY1983 (N=24)	16	35	22	27

SOURCE: For HUD data, telephone interviews with HUD officials (Fall, 1983);
for state data, see Table 1.

yielded data for FY 1983 that are a close approximation of HUD priorities in that year.

The information indicates that for the four states (Maryland, Kansas, New Jersey, and Hawaii) in which HUD administered the FY 1983 Small Cities program, 23 percent of special purpose monies were allocated to housing, 32 percent to public facilities, and 14 percent to economic development, with the remainder being allocated to multi-activity projects. These data are compared with the 1983 state allocations in table 11.2.

The figures indicate that HUD priorities in FY 1982 and 1983 Small Cities funding may have somewhat paralleled those of the states in shifting toward economic development and away from housing. However, the HUD shift appears considerably less pronounced than that of the states.

These aggregate data indicate that states are indeed less oriented toward the redistributive intent of the CDBG program than is HUD. However, the general state lack of interest in social targeting may not be shared by all states.

INTERSTATE VARIATION IN PRIORITIES

In table 11.3 the states are rank-ordered on expenditures in each of the three funding categories (housing, public facilities, and economic development). The data indicate that aggregate state figures conceal important interstate differences in funding priorities.

The housing category is illustrative of these interstate variations. New Hampshire allocated 81 percent of its CDBG monies to projects in this category, while four states allocated none whatever to housing. As was shown in table 11.1, HUD allocated 39 percent of its Small Cities funds to housing in FY 1981 as compared to 16 percent by the states, in the aggregate, in FY 1983. And, this was interpreted as demonstrating state resistance to social targeting. This conclusion appears justified with respect to the aggregate data. But, in fact, eleven of the 43 states allocated a higher percentage to housing in 1983 than did HUD in 1981. Similar observations can be made about the other two funding categories.

In the public facilities category, it should be recalled that Morgan and England (1984) lamented the heavy allocations of Oklahoma to public facility projects and inferred that states seemed reluctant to target expenditures to low-income groups. A high level of funding for public facilities appears to indeed characterize many states (particularly in the west). On the other hand, 17 states funded this category at a lower rate in 1983 than did HUD in 1981.

Variations in economic development spending are perhaps of most interest, because it is in this category that pre-1982 HUD expenditures

Table 11.3 A Rank Order of State CDBG Spending in the Three Categories of Housing, Public Facilities, and Economic Development, FY 1983

	Housing			Public Facilities			Economic Development	
Rank	State	%	Rank	State	%	Rank	State	%
1	New Hampshire	81	1	Nevada	87	1	Illinois	48
2	California	77	2	West Virginia	73	2	Michigan	48
3	Mississippi	67	3	New Mexico	69	3	Indiana	40
4	Delaware	56	4	Utah	68	4	Maine	37
5	Washington	54	5	South Dakota	66	5	Tennessee	35
6	North Carolina	50	6	Alaska	60	6	South Dakota	34
7	Maine	48	7	Arizona	60	7	Missouri	27
8	Wyoming	47	8	Louisiana	58	8	Kentucky	23
9	Montana	46	9	Alabama	55	9	Wisconsin	23
10	North Dakota	46	10	Iowa	49	10	Pennsylvania	20
11	Colorado	40	11	Nebraska	45	11	Oregon	20
12	Vermont	38	12	Delaware	44	12	Virginia	20
13	New Mexico	29	13	Missouri	43	13	Washington	20
14	Pennsylvania	26	14	Virginia	41	14	Colorado	20
15	Missouri	24	15	Colorado	40	15	Idaho	15
16	Massachusetts	23	16	Montana	35	16	Nebraska	15
17	Nebraska	23	17	North Carolina	33	17	North Carolina	14
18	Kentucky	22	18	North Dakota	32	18	South Carolina	14
19	Michigan	18	19	Texas	31	19	Alabama	13
20	Minnesota	17	20	Oregon	30	20	Arizona	13
21	Oregon	17	21	Illinois	28	21	Iowa	12

Table 11.3 *(continued)*

22	Rhode Island	17	22	Georgia	27	22	Massachusetts	12
23	Indiana	16	23	Wisconsin	27	23	North Dakota	12
24	Wisconsin	16	24	Wyoming	27	24	Alaska	11
25	Arizona	13	25	Kentucky	26	25	Rhode Island	11
26	Connecticut	12	26	Tennessee	25	26	Minnesota	10
27	Iowa	12	27	Idaho	23	27	Texas	10
28	West Virginia	12	28	Arkansas	21	28	New Hampshire	9
29	Alabama	11	29	Rhode Island	20	29	California	7
30	Illinois	11	30	Pennsylvania	18	30	West Virginia	7
31	Alaska	9	31	Minnesota	16	31	Wyoming	7
32	Tennessee	9	32	California	14	32	Nevada	6
33	Arkansas	7	33	Maine	10	33	Louisiana	6
34	Georgia	7	34	Connecticut	9	34	Connecticut	3
35	Nevada	7	35	Indiana	9	35	Georgia	1
36	Texas	7	36	Michigan	9	36	Arkansas	0
37	Virginia	6	37	Massachusetts	7		Delaware	0
38	Louisiana	4	38	New Hampshire	6		Mississippi	0
39	Utah	2	39	Vermont	2		Montana	0
40	Idaho	0	40	Ohio	0		New Mexico	0
	Ohio	0		Mississippi	0		Ohio	0
	South Carolina	0		South Carolina	0		Utah	0
	South Dakota	0		Washington	0		Vermont	0

*The percentages for an individual state may not total 100 because of the exclusion of miscellaneous projects, multi-year projects, and administration costs. Data were available for 43 states.

Table 11.4   Rank-Order Correlation between 1981 Annualized
Unemployment Rates and FY 1983 Economic Development
Funding by States

	Unemployment			Funding	
Rank	State	%	Rank	State	%
1	Michigan	12.3	1	Illinois	48
2	Alabama	10.7	2	Michigan	48
	West Virginia	10.7	3	Indiana	40
4	Indiana	10.1	4	Maine	37
5	Oregon	9.9	5	Tennessee	35
6	Ohio	9.6	6	South Dakota	34
7	Washington	9.5	7	Missouri	27
8	Alaska	9.3	8	Kentucky	23
9	Arkansas	9.1	9	Wisconsin	23
	Tennessee	9.1	10	Pennsylvania	20
11	Illinois	8.5	11	Oregon	20
12	Kentucky	8.4	12	Virginia	20
	Louisiana	8.4	13	Washington	20
	Pennsylvania	8.4	14	Colorado	20
	South Carolina	8.4	15	Idaho	15
16	Mississippi	8.3	16	Nebraska	15
17	Delaware	7.9	17	North Carolina	14
18	Wisconsin	7.8	18	South Carolina	14
19	Missouri	7.7	19	Alabama	13
20	Idaho	7.6	20	Arizona	13
	Rhode Island	7.6	21	Iowa	12
22	California	7.4	22	Massachusetts	12

Table 11.4 *(continued)*

23	New Mexico	7.3	23	North Dakota	12
24	Maine	7.2	24	Alaska	11
25	Nevada	7.1	25	Rhode Island	11
26	⌈ Iowa	6.9	26	Minnesota	10
	⌊ Montana	6.9	27	Texas	10
28	Utah	6.7	28	New Hampshire	9
29	⌈ Georgia	6.4	29	California	7
	⊢ Massachusetts	6.4	30	West Virginia	7
	⌊ North Carolina	6.4	31	Wyoming	7
32	Connecticut	6.2	32	Nevada	6
33	⌈ Arizona	6.1	33	Louisiana	6
	⌊ Virginia	6.1	34	Connecticut	3
35	Vermont	5.7	35	Georgia	1
36	⌈ Colorado	5.5	36	⌈ Arkansas	0
	⌊ Minnesota	5.5		Delaware	0
38	Texas	5.3		Mississippi	0
39	South Dakota	5.1		Montana	0
40	⌈ New Hampshire	5.0		New Mexico	0
	⌊ North Dakota	5.0		Ohio	0
42	⌈ Nebraska	4.1		Utah	0
	⌊ Wyoming	4.1		Vermont	0

Spearman Correlation Coefficient (r_s) = .316

were least and in which states have most clearly shown a higher priority. The 1983 information indicates that Illinois and several other states continue to allocate a high percentage of their funds to economic development projects. However, eight states provided no funding for economic development. These data indicate that the aggregate figures showing state preference for the least redistributive of the three categories (economic development) fail to show the highly redistributive orientation in some states.

This information on allocations across the three CDBG funding categories confirms the expected state-by-state variation. However, given that all 43 states operate under the same federal legislation and HUD guidelines, it is surprising that the variations are so pronounced. One would not expect, for example, the 0 to 81 percent variation in the housing category and the 0 to 87 percent for public facilities.

One question remains. Why do states differ so greatly in their CDBG priorities? One possible explanation can be explored in this study—the effect that the general economic condition of the state may have on these differing priorities.[5] For purposes here, the general economic condition will be gauged by the state's unemployment rate. Following Peterson (1981), states least constrained by economic conditions should be most apt to pursue redistributive as opposed to developmental policies. Or, conversely, states feeling the strongest economic constraints would be most likely to opt for developmental as opposed to redistributive policies. In terms of the CDBG program, one would expect states having the highest unemployment rates to have been the major spenders (in percentage terms) for economic development projects, while those having the lowest unemployment rates would show little tendency to move toward economic development projects and away from the housing (redistributive) orientations of HUD.

The data in table 11.4 bear out the expected relationship between unemployment rates and funding for economic development projects. In general, the higher the unemployment rate of the state, the higher the percentage of CDBG funds allocated to the economic development category. The Spearman correlation coefficient between the two sets of rank ordered data is .316. As the correlation coefficient indicates, not all states share in the association. Ohio and Arkansas, for example, ranked among the top ten states in unemployment rate but in the bottom ten in allocations to economic development. Nonetheless, the correlation is strong enough to be more than suggestive.

This finding indicates that, in general, state and local inclinations toward the social targeting (redistributive) intent of the CDBG legislation depend on economic conditions in the particular state—the more pressing the need to create jobs and, thus, enhance the fiscal base, the more likely the state is to shape its community development program as developmental rather than redistributive policy. This finding is not surprising and, from one perspective, appears consistent with federal government intentions in allowing state assumption of CDBG administrative responsibility. The transfer of administrative responsibility was intended, in part, to allow states flexibility to develop programs consistent with their respective conditions and problems. The major point is (as argued by Thomas, 1981; and Peterson, 1981) states cannot be expected to implement redistributive federal programs in the face of state-local developmental needs. If, in such situations, the redistributive aspects of such programs appear critical, the programs are best implemented at the national level.

CONCLUSIONS AND IMPLICATIONS

The comparison of HUD and aggregate state data in administration of the Small Cities program indicates that state administration has resulted in less emphasis on housing activities and more emphasis on economic development projects, as was hypothesized. Such a shift appears to have also occurred within HUD over the same period. However, the shift appears considerably more pronounced in state funding patterns than in those of HUD. If the assumption of the relationship between program category and the incidence of benefits is valid, the findings of this chapter indicate that state program priorities, in the aggregate, address the redistributive objectives of the CDBG legislation less well than those of HUD. This finding is consistent with much of the theoretical literature, which indicates that state and local governments are not likely to be as oriented toward redistributive policies as the national government.

When state data on CDBG awards are disaggregated, it appears that state preferences for economic development as opposed to housing projects is related to the unemployment rate of the state; the higher the unemployment rate, the more likely is the state to allocate its CDBG monies to economic development projects. Thus, state propensity to reshape redistributive federal programs toward developmental objectives can be predicted, in part, on the basis of economic conditions.

There is little evidence that state and/or local discretion in spending federal grant monies can, for very long, deviate significantly from the particular national purpose without federal corrective actions. Indeed, Reagan and Sanzone's (1981:137) analysis of the Comprehensive Employment and Training Program (CETA) indicates that increased federal monitoring and more restrictive guidelines can be expected if state-local discretion results in inattention to national objectives. They conclude that, in the case of CETA, the congressional response to widespread perceptions of incongruities between local spending patterns and program objectives was "to enact restrictive conditions and to establish monitoring and auditing systems that re-create much of the paperwork that decentralization was supposed to have eliminated."

The foregoing analysis of interstate variations in CDBG funding argues for flexibility in the federal response to state CDBG priorities. States, in the aggregate, do not appear disposed toward the social targeting intent of the CDBG legislation. But, this does not hold for all states and is related to economic conditions. Federal incentives and corrective actions should take this relationship into account.

In conclusion, it seems likely that the years immediately ahead will bring increased public, congressional, and HUD attention to state-local uses of Small Cities monies. This may be an inevitable concomitant of the discretion allowed states under the 1981 amendments. If, in this event, it appears that the beneficiaries or purposes of state allocations are different from those apparently intended by the legislation, it is probable that demands for corrective action will arise and that the new state-local partnerships will be threatened with loss of discretion. If these state-local community development partnerships formed by the 1981 amendments are to be a viable replacement for the direct federal-local relationships of earlier years, the partners will have to demonstrate a willingness to address the national objectives that underlie the programs and the national government will need to exercise flexibility and imagination in responding to state-local funding patterns.[6]

NOTES

1. The housing and public facility categories are likely to be accurately understood by most readers. The kinds of activities included in the economic development category may not be as apparent to some readers. A typical economic development grant is one in which the recipient local government lends all or a portion of the funds to a private business as a contribution to new construction or expanded operations. The monies are lent at low interest and, on repayment, are considered "recaptured" for further state or local allocation. A major rationale for this approach to community development is the "leveraging" of funds (investment) from the private sector to the purpose of job creation.

2. The study by Dommel and his associates is the third of four CDBG studies conducted at the Brookings Institution. The four studies were contracted by HUD as part of an ongoing monitoring and evaluation process. Reference is made elsewhere to the first and fourth of these reports.

3. A caveat is necessary here. Goals and objectives of public programs are often more dynamic than is reflected in legislative history and agency guidelines. In some cases, they may be undergoing renegotiation and redefinition in ways not easily discernible and about which contemporary legislation and agency rules give little evidence. For a discussion of this issue, see Bardach (1977).

4. Although, as indicated, there is justification for positing these rela-

tionships, the matter is by no means settled. Determination of the beneficiaries (the income-group incidence) of CDBG expenditures in the various activities and projects is a complex methodological problem. The Dommel study (1980:155–60) acknowledges this complexity and notes limitations of the benefit measurement approach used in the study. For further discussion of the Brookings approach to assessment of income-group incidence, see the first Brookings monitoring study (Nathan et al., 1977).

5. Another possible source of influence on state allocation of Small Cities' funds lies with the nature of the administrative agency itself. Organizational characteristics, attitudes of agency administrators, and the major histor-ical/traditional function of the agency may well affect dispositions toward re-distribution. A test of this proposition lies beyond the scope of this chapter.

6. There may be two alternative assessments of CDBG funding. Both have been alluded to in earlier notes, and either would lead to a different scenario for the future of state administration. First, it may be that low and moderate income groups benefit more from economic development activities than has been as-sumed in this essay, in which case states might be viewed as innovators in implementing the social targeting objectives of the program. Second, it may be that the states, HUD, and the Congress are jointly involved in redefining CDBG purposes, in which case state funding priorities of recent years may turn out to be quite congruent with the redefined program objectives. It is not the purpose of this short essay to elaborate these other potential assessments. They do de-serve study and discussion.

REFERENCES

Bardach, Eugene. 1977. *The Implementation Game* (Cambridge, Mass.: The MIT Press).

Caputo, David A., and Richard L. Cole. 1974. *Urban Politics and Decentralization* (Lexington, Mass.: D.C. Heath).

Dommel, Paul R., Victor E. Bach, Sarah F. Liebschultz, Leonard S. Rubinowitz, and Associates. 1980. *Targeting Community Development* (Washington, D.C.: Department of Housing and Urban Development).

Federal Register. 1982. (April 8, Part IV).

"The Fifty Legislative Climates." 1982. *Industrial Development* (January/-February): 4–19.

Lovell, Catherine. 1983. "Community Development Block Grant: The Role of Federal Requirements," *Publius* 13: 85–95.

Morgan, David R., and Robert E. England. 1984. "The Small Cities Block Grant Program: An Assessment of Programmatic Change Under State Control," *Public Administration Review* 44: 477–82.

Nathan, Richard P., Paul R. Dommel, Sarah F. Liebschultz, Milton D. Morris, and Associates. 1977. *Block Grants for Community Development* (Wash-ington, D.C.: Department of Housing and Urban Development).

Peterson, Paul E. 1981. *City Limits* (Chicago: University of Chicago Press).

Reagan, Michael D., and John G. Sansone. 1981. *The New Federalism* (New York: Oxford University Press).

Schattschneider, E. E. 1960. *The Semi-Sovereign People* (New York: Holt, Rinehart, and Winston).

Thomas, Robert D. 1981. "Targeting and Federalism: Components of a Policy Dilemma," *The Urban Interest* 3:10–20.

U.S. Department of Housing and Urban Development. Undated. *Implementing Community Development* (Washington, D.C.: Government Printing Office).

_____. 1980. *Fifth Annual Community Development Block Grant Report* (Washington, D.C.: Government Printing Office).

_____. 1983. *Consolidated Annual Report to Congress on Community Development Programs* (Washington, D.C.: Government Printing Office).

U.S. Statutes at Large, Public Law 93–383, Sec. 101(c).

12

State-City Revenue Sharing Policy: Local Need versus State System Explanations

John P. Pelissero

The states have been thrust into a more pivotal role under the evolving "New Federalism." Reagan administration officials are pressuring the states to develop the capacity and willingness to be effective partners in a system of new federalism, where the federal role is reduced and state and local governments are the managers of their own problems. Specifically, the reduction in federal aid for local governments demands that states recognize the new, critical role of state assistance for urban areas and small communities, alike. Most local governments that experience a reduction in federal aid in the 1980s will seek an increase in state aid, but it will be crucial for the neediest communities, those with socioeconomic and fiscal problems that will be most adversely affected by federal aid cuts. The compelling demand that states now face is to structure state assistance to be responsive to community needs.

States provide both financial and programmatic assistance to local governments. The vast amount of state financial assistance is categorical in nature, with the largest allocations going to local governments for education and public welfare. But since 1960, noncategorical aid—state revenue sharing—has accounted for 8 to 10 percent of total intergovernmental expenditures in the 50 states. Since state revenue sharing is allocated to local governments for locally determined purposes, it presents one of the best mechanisms for aiding communities most severely affected by the loss of federal dollars.

REVENUE SHARING IN THE STATES

How extensive is revenue sharing in the states and how do states allocate these funds? The Advisory Commission on Intergovernmental

Relations (ACIR, 1980) reports that 49 states have established revenue sharing programs with their local governments, and that these funds are distributed to local governments following four popular criteria. First, returning money to the location of origin of the revenue is used when the state collects sales or income taxes that are locally imposed and then returns these to the locality. Second, reimbursing local governments for property tax exemptions authorized by state statutes is used to distribute as much as 40 percent of state-local revenue sharing (ACIR, 1980:5). Third, in 1977, 30 states allocated all or part of their revenue sharing money to local governments on a per capita basis (ACIR, 1980:6–7), which, while politically popular, does not consider the differential needs of communities and their residents. Finally, states have begun implementing revenue sharing programs that factor-in the needs of a local government. Twenty-three states have needs-based systems (Cohen, 1982:19), with need defined in terms of either local government tax capacity, tax effort, or social and economic need.

Revenue sharing has been the third largest category of state aid since the 1970s, following only aid for education and welfare. In 1982 states spent over $10 billion on local government revenue sharing, or 10 percent of total state aid. With most education and welfare funds going to other units of local government, revenue sharing is, in many states, the most important form of state aid for cities. It has grown faster than any other category of state intergovernmental spending over the past two decades, with a 1962–1982 growth rate of 1,100 percent.[1] Just how effective are the states in targeting funds to those communities most in need? The research reported here analyzes state-city revenue sharing over a 21-year period to determine the importance of city needs in the revenue sharing receipts of large U.S. cities. In addition to city need, a series of state-level factors are analyzed to assess their impact on revenue sharing.

THE RESPONSIVENESS OF STATE AID TO CITIES

The number of studies examining the responsiveness of state aid to cities has increased in recent years. Much of the research has examined either the total state financial aid program for cities or programmatic forms of assistance with most finding state aid to be responsive to some aspect of community need. For example, Dye and Hurley (1978) showed that states were responding to needs in central cities of Standard Metropolitan Statistical Areas (SMSAs) and apparently did this better than the federal government. Teitelbaum and Simon (1979), writing for the National Governors' Association, found states to be good targeters of aid, particularly when applying federal pass-through funds to cities. In a critique of Dye and Hurley's research, Ward (1981) argued that the use of per capita measures of state aid along with percentage measures of need may be misleading if such measures distort the actual relationship between need and state or federal outlays. Ward's reanalysis using total state aid (unadjusted for population) and the actual size of the city population in need (e.g., total elderly, not proportion elderly) demonstrated much stronger relationships between total aid and actual size of the need.

Subsequent research into state-city aid programs has considered this issue when analyzing the targeting of state funds. For instance, Morgan and England (1984) used total measures of state aid to examine fiscal and programmatic assistance to cities. Analyzing state programs for cities over 50,000 population, they found city distress to be an important determinant of aid allocations from 1962 to 1977. Residual state aid to cities was examined by Pelissero (1984). By regressing state aid on city population, this research examined only the nonpopulation-based portion of state aid receipts in major U.S. cities. The results supported earlier findings that state aid was responsive to city needs and further demonstrated that states became better targeters over time.

Research on the relative responsiveness of state *revenue sharing* programs is limited. One important study that has examined the effectiveness of state formula and project grants to cities (Stein, 1981) found project grants to be better targeted to social and fiscal need. One of the implications of these findings is that states with project-based revenue sharing programs can target such funds to needier communities better than with formula mechanisms, such as population-based programs. Stein also noted that the conclusions in some of the above studies must be cautiously interpreted, since each state has its own set of rules for distributing funds. He has shown that the observed responsiveness may be due to the very effective targeting of just a few states.

Given the concerns raised above, it seems appropriate to consider, in addition to need, several state system factors that may affect the distribution of state-city revenue sharing. Since state revenue sharing distribution systems are somewhat varied (ACIR, 1980), certain states will clearly be better targeters to local need than others. One of the assumptions of this research, then, is that states using a needs-based distribution system will be better targeters than states employing reimbursement, population, or formula-based systems.

More broadly, state resources in general may be hypothesized to affect state policies for urban areas. Policy scholars have shown that a state's economic resources are linked to policy outputs (see Dye, 1976); that state income is related to urban policies (LeMay, 1973); that state affluence and industrialization are positive determinants of state financial and programmatic aid to cities (Morgan and England, 1984); and that state revenue efforts are often tied to the state's disposition toward aiding local governments (Stonecash, 1981). Presumably, then, greater state resources should be positively related to state-city revenue sharing.

A third consideration revolves around the legal "service provision" relationships between states and cities. States that have become more central providers of local services (Stephens and Olson, 1979) are also found to give less aid to local governments (Morgan and England, 1984). In addition, states have been shown to give larger aid amounts to cities with heavier financial burdens, those who fund education and welfare services from the municipal budget (Morgan and England, 1984). Further research into state categorical aid to cities for welfare and education supports the proposition that state aid for these two functions is targeted to cities with more educational or welfare responsibilities (Pelissero, 1985). However, the direct link to revenue sharing is less likely to be significant. In fact, we may assume at this point that cities with more functional responsibilities for education or welfare will not receive larger amounts of revenue sharing, since the state may have already compensated them for these services through categorical aid programs. One might even argue that such cities will receive less revenue sharing money, since they receive more than average aid in the education and welfare areas, making their total state aid larger than cities without these functional responsibilities.

This chapter attempts to extend the state aid responsiveness literature by focusing on state revenue sharing programs. Given that need is a stated criterion in at least 23 state revenue sharing programs, it seems appropriate to analyze how well targeted are revenue sharing funds for large cities. The importance of state resources, revenue sharing distribution systems, and municipal government service obligations will also be examined to see if local need or state system factors are the more important determinants of state-city revenue sharing policy.

DATA AND METHODS

This chapter attempts to answer the general research question—is state-city revenue sharing targeted to the neediest cities? More specific questions include: Have states become better targeters of revenue sharing funds over time? Have particular dimensions of city need been more influential in state revenue sharing allocations than others? Or are state-level factors more important determinants of state revenue sharing with cities? To answer these questions, data have been collected on the 47 largest cities in the states. This sample includes all cities that had 1970 populations of 300,000 or more (but not cities that achieved a 300,000 population later than 1970.)[2] These large cities were chosen for the sample because the most serious problems that came to be associated with the urban crisis were and still are found among this group. For this reason, one would expect state governments to be somewhat better acquainted with the problems and distress in these cities. Such an

awareness could provide the opportunity for targeting state-city revenue sharing to these city governments.

The analysis of state-city revenue sharing covers three time periods.
The first year studied is 1962, a period before the awakening to an urban
crisis in this country, and one which also witnessed little in terms of an
active role for states in urban affairs. Consequently, one would not
expect significant targeting of state-city revenue sharing to have occurred during this time. The second time point is 1976, or 15 years later.
Following the peak of the urban crisis and the predominant federal role
in urban problem-solving, this period was chosen to reflect the evolving
state capacity and willingness to aid urban areas. Here one expects to
see somewhat better targeting of state revenue sharing to needier cities
because state legislatures have been reapportioned; adding more urban
legislators, many states have established state-level departments of urban affairs, and both the federal-local grant developments and the crisis
in cities during the previous decade forced states to take a more active
role in city problem-solving. The final time period is 1982 and was
chosen to assess targeting practices at the start of a more state-centered
federalism era. The expectation is that state responsiveness to city needs
will be most pronounced 20 years after the first period analyzed. Also, of
interest here is the degree of targeting taking place two years after President Reagan began signaling his intent to increase state responsibility
for local problems.

The dependent variable is state revenue sharing receipts of sample
cities in each of the three years, derived from Census Bureau reports.[3]
These include data by city on intergovernmental revenue received from
state governments for "general support." Among the sample cities, revenue sharing is a sizable component of total state aid for local governments. The average revenue sharing fund in the states in which the 47
sample cities are located and the proportion of total state intergovernmental expenditures for three times points are indicated below:

1962	$ 26 million	(7.7% of total state aid)
1976	$181 million	(10.1% of total state aid)
1982	$305 million	(10% of total state aid)

Not only is size of state revenue sharing important, but so is its growth
in state budgets. While state intergovernmental spending increased 800
percent from 1962 to 1982, revenue sharing grew by over 1,072 percent—
a faster growth rate than any functional category of state aid.

Because part of state revenue sharing is often allocated on the basis of
city population, a pattern typical of much intergovernmental aid (see
Copeland and Meier, 1984; Pelissero, 1984), total revenue sharing received by each city was regressed on population to produce a non-

population-determined measure of revenue sharing. Removing population from the dependent variable should not be interpreted as removing
the primary or sole basis for distributing the funds, however. Fifteen
states among those in which the sample cities are located use population
as a factor in allocating state revenue sharing to cities. But population is
the dominant factor in the allocation process of only seven cases. The
rest of the cities receive revenue sharing with population as only one
among as many as six factors weighed in the distribution process. The
new nonpopulation based residual revenue sharing measures for 1962,
1976, and 1982 allow for analysis of this form of state aid in light of the
differential needs of the sample cities. In other words, with population-
based factors removed from the measure, one can begin to examine how
much state revenue sharing was allocated on a needs basis and how
much according to state-level influences.

Since the focus of this study is upon city need, the independent variables used here represent one of three dimensions of need or distress in
communities. There is difficulty in defining exactly what constitutes city
need—a problem noted by the ACIR (1980) in its own work on state
revenue sharing with local governments. Need will be treated in this
study similar to its use in previous analyses of intergovernmental aid
responsiveness (Cuciti, 1978; Dye and Hurley, 1978; Stein, 1981). That
is, three dimensions of city need are included among the independent
variables: social need, economic need, and fiscal need. The three indicators of social need, taken from the 1960, 1970, and 1980 censuses, include: (1) elderly (total population 65 years or older), (2) poverty (total
families below the poverty threshold), and (3) crime rate (total serious
crimes reported). Since each measure is also highly correlated ($r > .90$)
with population, each was regressed on population to produce a residual measure of social need. Two economic need variables were also
derived from the above three censuses. City population growth rate is a
measure of population change in the cities for 1950–60, 1960–70, and
1970–80. Home ownership, the other economic need indicator, is measured by total owner-occupied housing during each period.[4] Finally,
two measures of the financial health of city governments have been
included. The first of these is city budget deficit or the difference between city revenues and spending in 1962, 1976, and 1982. The second
measure is fiscal effort in the same three years, measured as a ratio
between general revenue and total personal income in the city.[5]

If state revenue sharing money is targeted to needy cities, then residual revenue sharing will be positively related to the social need and
fiscal need measures and inversely related to the economic need measures. The expectation is that targeting did not occur in 1962, and therefore the relationships should be weak or opposite of the expected direction. On the other hand, residual revenue sharing in 1976 and 1982 is

expected to show stronger evidence of targeting, which would be consistent with research on aggregate state aid to cities (Dye and Hurley, 1978; Morgan and England, 1984; Pelissero, 1984).

Because we are confronted with 50 separate and distinct state aid systems (Stein, 1981), a series of indicators will be employed in the analysis that measure state differences. First, a dummy variable has been created for each of the three years that indicates whether or not the predominant criterion in a state's allocation system is municipal need. Since states use as many as six criteria in the revenue sharing distribution system, states that use local need as the major factor have been coded 1, all others are coded 0.[6] This variable will serve as a state-level predictor that is most directly related to each state's revenue sharing distribution system. The assumption here is that state use of a needs-based allocation system will be positively linked with more residual revenue sharing. To assess state resources, measures of both state tax capacity and tax effort will be included in the analysis.[7] We can assume that states making greater tax efforts and states with greater tax capacity will also provide more residual revenue sharing funds to cities. Finally, the assignment of major state service responsibilities at the local level will be examined. Cities have been coded according to whether they provide education or welfare services through municipal financing, both of these services, or neither service. This measure is labeled "functional comprehensiveness" (Liebert, 1974). Because functional comprehensiveness has been linked in the literature to both total state aid (Morgan and England, 1984) and categorical aid for education and welfare (Pelissero, 1985) in cities, we expect this variable to be negatively related to revenue sharing in cities.

ANALYSIS OF RESIDUAL REVENUE SHARING, 1962–1982

Multiple regression models were developed for residual revenue sharing and city need for each time-point. The initial models included all seven independent variables measuring need and are displayed in table 12.1. The regression for 1962 showed no significant effects for any of the seven need variables. The multiple correlation (R) of .44 suggests that only 19 percent of the variability in 1962 residual revenue sharing can be accounted for with these need predictors. And although the model is not statistically significant, the analysis is consistent with the expectation that residual revenue sharing would not be well targeted in this first time-point.

The results of the 1976 regression in table 12.1 suggest that some important changes may have occurred since 1962. Three of the seven predictors display stronger and significant standardized regression coefficients (Beta) in 1976 than in 1962. This suggests that state revenue

Table 12.1   Multiple Regression Models for Residual State-City Revenue Sharing and City Need, 1962–1982

Predictors	Coefficient	1962	1976	1982
Elderly Residual	b	.179	.221	.354
	Beta	.179	.235	.354
	t-ratio	.946	3.021*	1.792
Poverty Residual	b	.175	.016	-.043
	Beta	.175	.017	-.043
	t-ratio	.991	.195	-.286
Crime Residual	b	-.022	-.085	.178
	Beta	-.022	-.085	.178
	t-ratio	-.135	-1.040	1.388
Growth Rate	b	-.022	.004	.001
	Beta	-.118	.036	.056
	t-ratio	-.513	.485	.335
Home Ownership	b	-.000	-.000	-.000
	Beta	-.693	-.992	-.374
	t-ratio	-.276	-10.094*	-1.960*
Budget Deficit	b	-.000	.000	-.000
	Beta	-.284	1.109	-.290
	t-ratio	-1.642	10.330*	-1.555
Fiscal Effort	b	4.656	-.733	3083.715
	Beta	.252	-.060	.211
	t-ratio	1.153	-.778	1.205
(Intercept)	a	-.273	.930	-.309
	R	.44	.93	.70
	R^2	.19	.87	.49
	F	1.13	35.88*	5.30*
	(N)	(42)	(47)	(47)

*$p \leq .05$.

sharing was more targeted to need in this year than it had been in 1962, with more revenue sharing going to cities with more elderly, fewer homeowners, and larger deficits. What is surprising in this year is that among the need variables that were not significant predictors, the relationship between revenue sharing and fiscal effort, crime, and poverty moved further away from a pattern of targeting. Overall, the seven-variable model produced an $R = .93$ and accounted for 87 percent of the variability in 1976 residual revenue sharing.

The final model in table 12.1 is the seven-variable regression for 1982. In general, the 1982 analysis shows this to be a poorer model of residual revenue sharing than that for 1976. Although five predictors were stronger determinants in 1982, several displayed sign changes also. All three social need measures had higher Betas in 1982 than in either 1962 or 1976, but none was significant. And while the pattern of targeting to cities with more elderly and higher crime rates improved, there was a slight drop in the already weak targeting on poverty. Homeownership was the only significant predictor in this year, and its standardized regression coefficient was smaller ($-.37$) than in 1976 also. The most divergent changes occurred among the fiscal need predictors where revenue sharing seemed to improve its targeting to cities making stronger fiscal efforts while also being less responsive to deficits. Although neither variable is significant, this pattern is very similar to the finding for 1962. Overall, this seven-variable model accounts for 49 percent of the variability in residual revenue sharing—a significant drop from 1976. At the same time, the significant predictors in both 1976 and 1982 were those showing better targeting to need.

The next step in the analysis was to assess the importance of the four state-level measures. A first examination of the intercorrelations among these state-level variables demonstrated that all four could not be included in a multivariate model. Specifically, this was due to the high correlation between state tax effort and revenue sharing distribution system variables. In each year there was a strong positive relationship between the two measures, showing that states making strong tax efforts also tend to be states that distribute revenue sharing funds on a local government needs-basis.[8] Such a relationship is significant in itself and suggests that states with better tax efforts are also more likely to consider local government needs. The tax effort variable will be dropped in the succeeding analysis, though, to permit us to employ the revenue sharing distribution measure in the multivariate model.

Similar to the analysis performed with the predictors of city need, the remaining three state system variables were employed in a multivariate analysis. Table 12.2 displays one multiple regression analysis for each of the three time points. It is clear that in 1962 none of these predictors was a significant determinant of residual revenue sharing in the sample cities. The 1976 model is significant and warrants some discussion. The one statistically significant predictor was the revenue sharing distribution system measure (Beta$=.29$). This positive relationship indicates that by 1976 residual revenue sharing was somewhat determined by use of a needs-based allocation system in the states. The coefficient demonstrates an improvement over the 1962 model and reflects the wider use of needs-based allocation systems by the mid-1970s. Although not significant predictors, both state tax capacity and functional comprehensiveness displayed somewhat surprising relationships to revenue sharing. Contrary to the expectations, residual revenue sharing was larger among cities that carried a heavier municipal burden for local education and welfare services and whose states had smaller tax capacity.

Table 12.2   Multiple Regression Models for Residual State-City Revenue
Sharing and State System Measures, 1962–1982

Predictors	Coefficient	1962	1976	1982
Distribution System	b	.133	.681	1.240
	Beta	.040	.288	.517
	t-ratio	.215	2.09*	4.41*
State Tax Capacity	b	-.001	-.024	-.001
	Beta	-.165	-.212	-.210
	t-ratio	-1.02	-1.54	-1.79
Functional Comp	b	.124	.277	-.260
	Beta	.118	.250	-.365
	t-ratio	.627	1.84	-3.12*
(Intercept)	a	.910	2.16	.900
	R^2	.24	.49	.66
	R	.06	.24	.43
	F	.72	4.35*	10.57*
	(N)	(42)	(47)	(47)

*$p < .05$.

The 1982 analysis suggests the best model for residual revenue sharing. By that year, two of the predictors—the distribution system and
functional comprehensiveness—were significant. As hypothesized,
larger revenue sharing receipts in the sample cities were found where
cities had fewer functional responsibilities and the state used a needs-
based distribution system. Again, state tax capacity was negatively related to revenue sharing. This three-variable model explains 43 percent of
the variation in the cities' residual revenue sharing receipts, better than
either 1962 or 1976. The final time-point analysis also suggests a turnabout in this form of aid. No longer was more revenue sharing found in
cities that had more education and welfare services supported by the
municipal treasury. As expected, this may indicate that states gave less
revenue sharing to cities already receiving more total state aid (because
of the categorical assistance for these functions.) Finally, the trend over
the 21-year period is a positive one, with states making important
changes in the revenue sharing distribution system that resulted in a
stronger relationship with city need.

The final stage in the analysis is to examine the effects of both the city
need and state system variables on residual revenue sharing. A more
parsimonious set of predictors, including just two city need measures,
were chosen for this stage in the analysis. One is a measure of socioeconomic need in cities—elderly. This variable was positively corre-

lated with revenue sharing in each of the three years and is a good measure of dependency in the population due to its strong relationship to income and poverty. The second city need variable to be used is budget deficit. It appears to be a good measure of fiscal need in cities, and it was highly correlated with home ownership. For this reason home ownership was not included in the final analysis, but its effects will largely be represented by deficit and elderly (since most states permit property tax exemptions for elderly).

Table 12.3 shows the final multiple regression models using the combination of city need and state system variables. The weakest model is again that for 1962. The only significant predictor, budget deficit, is negatively related to residual revenue sharing—indicating that the revenue was not well targeted in that year. So as expected, state residual revenue sharing was not very responsive to need during this preurban crisis period. The changes observed in 1976 generally suggest better targeting on the part of the states. For example, there is the expected positive relationship between budget deficit and revenue sharing and,

Table 12.3   Final Multiple Regression Models for Residual State-City Revenue Sharing, 1962–1982

Predictors	Coefficient	1962	1976	1982
Budget Deficit	b	-.000	.000	-.000
	Beta	-.325	.256	-.054
	t-ratio	-2.09*	1.83	-.475
Elderly Residual	b	.122	.401	.384
	Beta	.122	.427	.383
	t-ratio	.751	3.25*	3.03*
Distribution System	b	.373	.000	.995
	Beta	.112	.256	.415
	t-ratio	.608	1.83	3.74*
State Tax Capacity	b	-.001	-.001	-.000
	Beta	-.152	-.080	-.072
	t-ratio	-.952	-.624	-.633
Functional Comp	b	.056	.080	-.200
	Beta	.053	.072	-.283
	t-ratio	.284	.544	-2.57*
(Intercept)	a	.816	.802	.260
	R	.41	.68	.75
	R^2	.17	.47	.56
	F	1.42	7.00*	10.06*
	(N)	(42)	(47)	(47)

*$p \leq .05$.

also, elderly and revenue sharing. Along with the positive effects of the distribution formula, there is clear evidence that states were doing a much better job of responding to city need by that year. The predictors representing city need are obviously more important determinants than the state system variables in this year; together the five predictors account for 47 percent of the variability in 1976 residual revenue sharing.

The importance of the state system variables is much more apparent in the final model, that for 1982. Although elderly was still a strong predictor, the strongest determinant in that year was the distribution formula. Again in this year we can note that higher residual revenue sharing monies were found among sample cities with greater socioeconomic need, fewer education and welfare burdens on the municipal budget, and where states emphasized city need in the allocation system for revenue sharing. Together, these variables account for 56 percent of the variability in residual revenue sharing in 1982—the strongest of the three models.

CONCLUSION

Local governments are turning to the states, expecting their parent government to pick up some of the slack left by the federal government's reduced role in local problem solving. A clear commitment to this need will be evident in the allocation of state aid monies to local governments throughout the remainder of this decade. One of the easier options for state aid, and one that will be most welcome in communities, is more extensive use of state-local revenue sharing. A strong argument can be made that these funds will be more effective if they are targeted to needier communities. The pattern of targeting that has occurred in residual revenue sharing for cities from 1962 to 1982 suggests that states have demonstrated that they can respond to urban needs.

For instance, the data for 1962 indicate that state-city revenue sharing was not targeted to needy cities. But the change occurring by 1976 generally supports the hypothesis that state revenue sharing would be better targeted following the peak of the urban crisis and restructuring/reapportionment in state governments. State revenue sharing was shown to be responsive to all three dimensions—social, economic, and fiscal—of city need in this period. One could reasonably attribute this change to such factors as the increased state capacity and willingness to play a more prominent role in urban affairs, the example set by the federal government through direct federal-local aid programs, as well as the initial movement toward a more state-centered federalism that began during the Nixon administration. More recently, the analysis for 1982 reveals that although residual revenue sharing does not appear to be as responsive to need as it was in 1976, there is still evidence of targeting in the 1980s. Yet it seems plausible that states did not actually alter their method of targeting between 1976 and 1982. Rather, by 1982 changing social conditions in cities, such as the growing number of elderly and poor elderly and the increase in reported crime, may have given these social need variables more importance than other need factors. At the same time, the revenue sharing aid mechanism may have become more popular for those large cities that wanted to avoid the additional "grantsmanship" often needed to secure categorical funds. And more states had included local need as a factor in the revenue sharing distribution system. The ease of receiving state revenue sharing funds may have allowed cities to rely upon these funds in lieu of seeking new forms of categorical aid.

In sum, city need is an apparent and important factor in state-city revenue sharing—particularly in the mid-1970s. State system explanations increase in importance over time such that the revenue sharing distribution system is the most important determinant of residual revenue sharing by the early 1980s. We should note that 1982 was only the first year that any New Federalism initiatives were in place. The pattern of targeting observed among sample cities in 1982 may be continuing and perhaps even improving as we move into the middle of the decade and states become more settled with the latest version of state-centered federalism. At a minimum, the evidence indicating that the state role in revenue sharing has been a positive one since the mid-1970s should provide local government officials with a positive outlook on state responsiveness for the foreseeable future. And, if states continue the trend toward wider employment of local government need as a criterion in the revenue sharing allocation process, this type of state aid may become the most responsive form of assistance for cities in need.

NOTES

1. Information was calculated from U.S. Bureau of the Census, *State Government Finances in (year)* for 1962, 1976, and 1982, (Washington, D.C.: Government Printing Office, 1963, 1977, 1983).

2. More exactly, the list is the 47 largest U.S. cities in 1970 exclusive of Washington, D.C., which, of course, receives no state aid.

3. Data for the state revenue sharing variables are taken from Table 7 in U.S. Bureau of the Census, *City Government Finances in (year)*, for 1962, 1975–76, and 1981–82, (Washington, D.C.: Government Printing Office, 1963, 1977, 1983).

4. Data for the social and economic need variables were taken from the 1960, 1970, and 1980 Censuses of Population and Housing.

5. Data for the fiscal need variables were taken from the 1960, 1970, and 1980 Censuses of Population, and *City Government Finances in (year)* for 1962, 1975–76, and 1981–82, Table 7.

6. The basis for distributing revenue sharing is found in U.S. Bureau of the

Census, *Census of Governments, 1962 (and 1977, 1982), State Payments to Local Governments* (Washington, D.C.: Government Printing Office, 1963, 1979, 1984).

7. Data were taken from ACIR, *Measures of State and Local Fiscal Capacity and Tax Effort* (1962); and *1981 Tax Capacity of the Fifty States*, (1983).

8. The correlations are as follows: r = .61 (1962), .56 (1976), .61 (1982).

REFERENCES

Advisory Commission on Intergovernmental Relations. 1980. *The State of State-Local Revenue Sharing* (Washington, D.C.: Government Printing Office).

Cohen, Neal M. 1982. "Community Assistance: The States' Challenge," *Intergovernmental Perspective* 8: 14–21.

Copeland, Gary W., and Kenneth J. Meier. 1984. "Pass the Biscuits, Pappy: Congressional Decision-Making and Federal Grants," *American Politics Quarterly*, 12: 3–21.

Cuciti, Peggy. 1978. *City Need and the Responsiveness of Federal Grant Programs.* Report to the U.S. House of Representatives, Committee on Banking, Finance, and Urban Affairs, Subcommittee on the City, 95th Congress, 2d Session (Washington, D.C.: Government Printing Office).

Dye, Thomas R. 1976. *Policy Analysis* (University, Ala.: University of Alabama Press).

Dye, Thomas R., and Thomas L. Hurley. 1978. "The Responsiveness of Federal and State Governments to Urban Problems," *Journal of Politics* 40: 196–207.

LeMay, Michael. 1973. "Expenditure and Nonexpenditure Measures of State Urban Policy Output: A Research Note," *American Politics Quarterly* 1: 511–28.

Liebert, Roland J. 1974. "Municipal Functions, Structure, and Expenditures: Reanalysis of Recent Research," *Social Science Quarterly* 54: 765–83.

Morgan, David R., and Robert E. England. 1984. "State Aid to Cities: A Causal Inquiry," *Publius* 14: 67–82.

Pelissero, John P. 1984. "State Aid and City Needs: An Examination of Residual State Aid to Large Cities," *Journal of Politics* 46: 916–935.

———. 1985. "Welfare and Education Aid to Cities: An Analysis of State Responsiveness to Needs," *Social Science Quarterly* 66: 444–52.

Stein, Robert M. 1981. "The Targeting of State Aid: A Comparison of Grant Delivery Systems," *The Urban Interest* 3: 47–59.

Stephens, G. Ross, and Gerald W. Olson. 1979. *Pass-Through Federal Aid and Interlevel Finance in the American Federal System, 1957–1977*, report to the National Science Foundation (August 1).

Stonecash, Jeffrey M. 1981. "State Policies Regarding Local Resource Acquisition: Disorder, Compensatory Adjustment, or Coherent Restraint?" *American Politics Quarterly* 9: 401–25.

Teitelbaum, Fred, and Alice E. Simon. 1979. *Bypassing the States: Wrong Turn for Urban Aid* (Washington, D.C.: National Governors' Association).

Ward, Peter D. 1981. "The Measurement of Federal and State Responsiveness to Urban Problems," *Journal of Politics* 43: 83–101.

13
Incremental and Abrupt Change in Fiscal Centralization in the American States, 1957– 1983

Jeffrey M. Stonecash

Change has been a fundamental part of state-local fiscal relations in the United States. Over the last 30 years states have assumed an increasing role in fiscal matters. States now raise a larger proportion of all revenue raised by states and their localities. States also provide a larger proportion of direct services, and local governments are more reliant than ever on state aid as a source of their revenue (Stonecash, 1983, 1985).

While change has occurred, how it occurs is not clear. Is it incremental with politicians making marginal adjustments that nonetheless produce significant cumulative change? Lindblom (1959) suggested that most policymaking is characterized by incrementalism. Beer (1973) argued that in the specific area of centralization the primary driving force is gradual change in the structure of the economy. This fits well with the argument of Dye (1966) that economic forces are primary in affecting state policies. If broad and gradual changes in society and the economy are important, then our explanatory focus might be on how political systems absorb and respond to gradual change.

Others, however, argue that change is just as likely to be abrupt. Jennings' reanalysis of Key's (1949) hypothesis about the "organization" of political groups supports this view. He found that changes in state taxation were abrupt and products of different coalitions gaining control of government (1977, 1979). Wirt (1983:307) and Due (1963:4) argue, respectively, that the Civil War and the Great Depression were sources of significant changes in fiscal responsibilities of state governments. Hansen (1983:149) finds a clear burst of state tax adoptions during the 1930s. From this perspective our theories and methods must be developed with a concern for detecting abrupt changes (Albritton, 1979; Bowler, 1974; Schulman, 1975).

The concern of this analysis is what kinds of changes have occurred in one area of fiscal centralization in the states, the proportion of all state-local revenue raised by the state government. Change in this particular area is important because it is crucial for the role that state governments can play within the state "system." If the state raises little revenue, its ability to play a dominant role is constrained. Change in this regard creates the likelihood that states will play a much more dominant role, either through direct provision of services or through greater aid to local governments (Stonecash, 1981; Gold, 1983:5–16).

AGGREGATE CHANGE

From 1957 to 1983 the states, on average, experienced a significant increase in their capacity to raise revenue vis-à-vis their local governments. The average proportion of state raised revenue increased from 55.9 percent to 63.9 percent. Not all states changed the same. Those that were the most centralized in 1957 changed very little over the 26 years (Stonecash, 1983:133). The major changes occurred among those states least centralized in 1957. States in the latter group increased state raised revenue as much as 28 percent (New Jersey), with five states increasing over 20 percent and another 14 states increasing from 10 to 20 percent.

While there have been major changes, it is the annual changes that are important. Table 13.1 shows the distribution of annual changes for all states grouped into six categories.[1] Two significant matters are evident.

Table 13.1   Distribution of Annual Change Scores, 1957–1983

Ranges	Proportions	Frequency
-3.0 and less	3.92	51
-2.9 to -1.5	7.31	95
-1.4 to less than 0	32.92	428
0 to 1.4	37.69	490
1.5 to 2.9	11.08	144
3.0 and greater	7.08	92
Totals	100.0	1,300

First, there is an enormous amount of positive *and* negative change within the states from year to year. Of all the changes, 44.2 percent are negative. While centralization has increased over time, it has not come about through a series of uninterrupted positive changes. Negative changes have been very common. Second, most changes are not large. If changes within plus or minus 1.5 of 0 are regarded as minor, then 70.6 percent of all annual changes have been of limited scale.

Proportionally, there are not many large changes. Eleven percent of all changes are greater than plus or minus 3.0. If only large positive change is examined, the proportion of changes greater than 3.0 is 7.08. This predominance of minor change is important and worthy of some exploration before focusing on the larger question of how the pattern of these annual changes are related to net changes from 1957 to 1983.

FISCAL CENTRALIZATION AND THE ECONOMY

The extent to which the state raises revenue is in large part a political decision. Revenue raising is also affected from year to year by the performance of the economy. Increases in economic activity enhance revenue flows to the state, while recessions reduce revenue. If state revenue systems are more responsive to these variations than local systems are, then the role of the state will fluctuate accordingly. This creates changes in the dominance of the state that are generally not major and are not the result of a specific decision to change the role of the state. They emerge largely from the state being passive. States are not always passive in the face of recessions (major tax increases were enacted in many states during the 1982–83 recession), but they are likely to be so when changes in the economy produce relatively minor fluctuations in their revenue.

The effect of these fluctuations can be seen in several ways. The staff of the Advisory Commission on Intergovernmental Relations (ACIR) has monitored changes in state tax collections for the last 20 years. They divide changes in taxes into those resulting from political actions and those from economic factors. From 1964 to 1984 the bulk of changes stem from economic changes (ACIR, 1985:72). This dominance and fluctuation of economic factors leads to minor variations in fiscal centralization. From 1957 to 1983 there were seven years in which the average change for all states for fiscal centralization was negative. A rough sense of the impact of economic fluctuations can be seen from regressing average state revenue changes on national unemployment levels. The bivariate association between the two is .33 and the relationship is negative.[2]

This sensitivity to the economy is likely to increase in the future. Over the last 30 years states have increased their role in raising revenue, and state and local tax systems have gradually increased in income elasticity (Rafuse, 1982:112–13). From 1951 to 1981 the change was from .93 to

1.03. This means that economic fluctuations produce corresponding changes in state and local revenues of greater than 1.0. That situation will produce continued minor fluctuations in state fiscal centralization in response to economic changes.

The significance of this is that a great deal of the minor negative and positive changes shown in table 13.1 are not the result of incremental "decision making" at the state level. A large proportion of small changes are likely the result of the passivity of the states as the economy changes. How many of them are of that nature cannot be assessed here without a detailed economic analysis of each state. That is beyond the scope of this analysis, but it is still important to note the importance of economic fluctuations in affecting fiscal centralization changes.

PROFILES OF SYSTEMS

While these aggregate figures are interesting, the important matter is how individual systems behave. To assess that requires examining change patterns that exist within states. Two types of change are particularly important. If change proceeds incrementally, then most changes should be positive and moderate. "Setbacks" may occur because of fluctuations in the economy, but significant net change should be associated with moderate changes. If abrupt changes are the primary source of significant change, a few large changes should predominate. These two types of changes can occur together, of course, which suggests several combinations of change.

With that in mind, each state was characterized according to the predominance of small-change scores and according to the extent of large-change scores in the state.[3] The former was done by first characterizing each state in terms of the *proportion* of change scores within plus or minus 1.5 of 0. These proportions were then grouped in terms of whether they were 80 or above, from 80 to 65, or less than 65. This characterizes states in regard to the dominance of small changes over the years. The characterization of states in terms of the extent of large changes was achieved by adding together the two largest changes experienced during the 26-year time span.[4]

Once these groupings were constructed, the groupings were cross-tabulated to examine the relationship between the two characteristics. The results are shown in figure 13.1. The figure shows which states fall into the various categories along with the mean change in centralization in that category. Below the mean value is the range of change scores for states within that category. Finally, the states in each category are listed.

Several interesting points emerge from the figure. First, something of a general pattern appears among the states. There is no necessity that it be the case, but those states that are highly stable (80 percent or more of

Figure 13.1 Distribution of States by Change Characteristics of Stability and Largest Changes

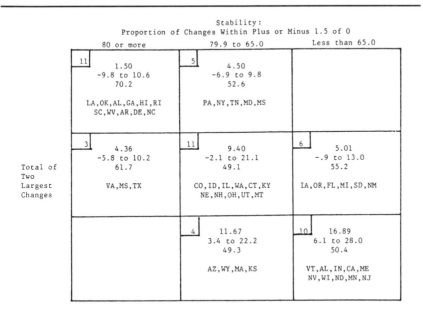

NOTE: The number in each cell is shown in the upper left. The mean centralization changes of each group is below that. The range of change scores is shown below that. Below that is the mean centralization level for that group in 1957. The states involved are at the bottom of each cell.

their changes are within plus or minus 1.5 of 0) are also those in which their largest changes are relatively small. Those states that have low stability are those for which the largest changes are relatively large. It is hypothetically possible that states might be largely stable with occasional abrupt changes of varying magnitudes. That is not the case. Instability over time tends to be associated with significant single positive changes. Finally, a large proportion of states with moderate stability also had moderate changes in their largest two changes. Not all states fall into the pattern, but it appears that a large proportion of the states follow a pattern of increasing instability associated with ever larger single changes.[5] This suggests that instability is not associated with many moderate changes.

This pattern suggests some clearly distinct change profiles among the states. No clear demarcation between types identifies states as one "type" or another, but there are pronounced differences. The states in the upper left corner are ones that were originally highly centralized and have changed very little since then. Most of their year-to-year changes have been contained within a narrow range. Their largest changes have not been large, and they have experienced very little net change. They are essentially "stable" systems.

This provides a first insight into what kinds of questions we might puruse regarding change. When it does not occur, why doesn't it? Almost all the states in this stable grouping are southern states, and they were highly centralized in 1957. Did they remain stable because their high level of centralization forms some sort of "natural" limit that is difficult to go beyond? Or is it that the level of centralization reached by 1957 has been supported by a strong consensus so that annual changes are very limited? Or is it that in most of these states major political differences are not "organized" into any clear coalitions so that elections bring change? Key (1949:308–10) argued that unorganized politics prevents issue emergence and that elections lose their relevance as a means of bringing about change. Jennings (1977) examined that hypothesis and found it to be true. Perhaps these states are ones where for some reason issue differences over fiscal centralization and the role of the state were not significant from 1957 to 1983.

There are other states that represent a quite different situation. They had a relatively low proportion of changes within plus or minus 1.5 of 0, and when change did occur, it was significant in magnitude. The low proportion of small changes also indicates that the other changes (aside from the largest two) were also rather significant. These are systems in which the state's revenue raising role is much less stable. That "instability" does not just refer to annual changes but to net changes. These are states that were relatively decentralized in 1957 and changed a great deal by 1983. Unlike the previous grouping, these states do not represent a particular region.

These states pose another set of questions in trying to understand change. Why have they changed so much? Why have they experienced so many large changes? Is there something about these particular political systems that prompts such changes? Or have actions of the federal government prompted these changes?

There are, of course, states that do not fall into these two opposite "types." The states in the other groupings manifest various combinations of stability and large changes. The variety of combinations reflects considerable diversity in the kinds of change patterns that exist in the states.

This diversity is also important to the first concern of this analysis: What kinds of change patterns exist? Clearly there is some variation of change patterns. All states have experienced minor increases and decreases in the role of the state due to economic fluctuations. Beyond that common experience there is considerable diversity. North and South Carolina have all but one of their changes within plus or minus 1.5 of 0.

Changes for Florida are distributed across the full range of variation. Indiana and Maine have many minor changes but a high number of changes of large magnitude. The diversity is difficult to characterize (and specific labels should probably be avoided), but the pattern shown in figure 13.1 does suggest that incremental increases in centralization do not characterize the majority of the states.

NET CHANGE AND PATTERNS OF CHANGE

The evidence shown in figure 13.1 also appears to answer the question about what *kinds* of change patterns produced significant net change over the 26 years. It is clear that the greatest net changes are among those states with lesser stability and larger nonincremental changes. That, however, is not an entirely valid conclusion. The data in figure 13.1 are organized around types of change patterns. The averages of net change contained in the various cells conceal a considerable range of net changes among the states in each cell. Many of the states that reflect patterns of low stability and moderate to large abrupt changes did not change as much as the average implies. To assess the characteristics of those changing varying net amounts it is necessary to organize the data in terms of those net changes.

Table 13.2 presents the states in terms of categories of net change and leads eventually to a slightly different conclusion about what brings about change and what kinds of change patterns exist in the states. The states are grouped into three change characteristics categories of less than 8, 8 to 14.9, and 15.0 or greater. Several other groupings were used, but this one seemed to differentiate them the most in terms of extent of change and types of change patterns.

From 1957 to 1983 most states (26) did not change much. Those states that did not change much have some strong similarities. They were relatively centralized in 1957. They are also states in which the bulk (75 percent) of annual changes were contained within the plus or minus 1.5 range. They also are states in which the largest two and three changes are small compared to the other groups. In contrast, those states that changed the most were low on centralization in 1957. They also were low on the proportion of changes contained within the range of plus or minus 1.5 (60.8%). Their largest two and three changes are also much larger than the other two groups. The conclusion that emerges from figure 13.1 and table 13.2 is that significant change in centralization emerges not from the cumulative effect of incremental changes, but from abrupt change. Those states that have patterns of low stability and significant large changes have changed (on average) the most from 1957 to 1983. Those that changed the most over the 26 years are also ones that had change patterns dominated by several large changes.

Table 13.2   Change Characteristics by Net Change

Change Characteristics	Net Change		
	0-7.9	8.0-14.9	15.0 or more
1957 position	62.9	48.3	48.1
Largest 2 positive changes	6.2	9.6	12.8
Largest 3 positive changes	8.4	12.2	16.5
Proportion within 1.5 of 0	75.3	69.8	61.4
N =	26	14	10

The evidence suggests that attempts to understand changes in fiscal centralization (in terms of the state's role in raising revenue) should focus on what brings about abrupt change. That is not to say that there are not cases of incrementalism, but when change comes about, it appears to emerge primarily from relatively dramatic change.

REFINING THE PROFILES OF CHANGE

This pattern is clear, but it is not uniform. There are still some exceptions contained in figure 13.1 and table 13.2 that are worth exploring. Not all the states with change patterns of low stability and large changes changed a great deal (Vermont is in this group but its net change is 6.1 percent.) Some states that did not have large changes did end up changing a great deal (Rhode Island and Kentucky). These exceptions are interesting not just to explore every unique variation but because they further illuminate how change proceeds.

The first interesting case involves states that have profiles of relative instability and large changes but no significant net change. These states can be identified by the fact that the ratio of their largest two or three changes to their net change is very high (over 2). These are states in which some significant positive changes occurred but the state ended up changing much less than these positive changes. The distinguishing characteristic of these states is that they have also experienced major negative changes. Indeed, all states have some negative changes and some have large negative changes. The important matter for net change is the relative magnitudes of positive and negative changes. Is it the case that some states have large positive changes offset by large negative changes? The data relevant for this issue are presented in figure 13.2. The change in the largest two positive changes was grouped as in figure 13.1. The net changes from 1957 to 1983 were then grouped into less than 8, 8 to less than 15, and equal to or greater than 15. The two groupings were then cross-tabulated. The concern was to assess the characteristics of those states that had large single positive changes but experienced different net changes. The figure contains the mean of the largest two and three negative changes experienced by states in each cell.

The variation within the figure shows a generally clear pattern. Those states that have large positive changes but do not have large net changes are the ones which also have large negative changes. These are states in which significant single positive changes are ultimately offset to some degree by large negative scores. These major negative fluctuations in the role of the state may be due to economic factors, such as when Wyoming experiences changes in oil revenues, or Michigan finds its revenue flows dramatically affected by the fortunes of the auto industry. It is also possible, of course, that the explanation of such negative changes lies with the political process within the state.

Multiple regression can also be used to assess the "independent" role of these characteristics. A regression was run in which the variables were the position of the state in 1957, the sum of the largest two positive

Figure 13.2   Negative Changes by Net Change and Positive Change
Characteristics

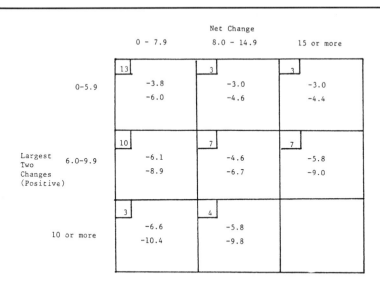

NOTE: The number in each cell is shown in the upper
         left corner. The two numbers in the cell are the
         mean of the largest of the two and three nega-
         tive changes experienced by each state.

Table 13.3 State Characteristics and Net Change

Characteristic	Unstandardized Coefficient	Standard Error
1957 Position	- .16	.06
Largest 2 positive changes	1.34	.17
Largest 2 negative changes	-1.45	.25

$$R^2 = .72$$

NOTE: All are significant at .01 or beyond.

changes, and the sum of the largest two negative changes. Together they explained 72 percent of the variation. The results indicate that: (1) the more centralized a state was in 1957, the less change since then; (2) the larger the two positive changes, the greater the extent of centralization since 1957; and, (3) the greater the two negative changes, the less the net change over time. The results of that regression are shown in table 13.3.

Those cases in which large negative changes play a role are significant for two reasons. They alert us to another pattern of change in state roles, and they dispel another notion that is often implicit in the incremental approach to change. Increases in the role of the state do not always become a "given," or a part of a new minimum. In some states there is a willingness to tolerate reductions in the role of the state or even to decide to reduce this role. This analysis does not provide any indication of whether the role of the state is reduced in these situations because the state specifically decreased its role or it allowed local governments to assume a larger role. Through whatever means, though, positive change does not necessarily imply a new minimum role for the state. Even states with large positive changes and net changes have some fairly substantial negative changes. It is just that the negatives are more than offset by instances of positive change. Some states simply have a more volatile role in the revenue raising process. Why that volatility exists is another matter worth exploring.

CONCLUSIONS

The predominant pattern of change among the states does not appear to be incremental in nature, at least as magnitudes of change are defined here. A careful review of individual state change patterns suggests that a few might fall into that category, but such cases are the exception. The evidence indicates that our concern should be to understand what brings about abrupt change.

While that point is clear, it should not be carried too far. This analysis indicates that change occurs primarily through abrupt transitions (which may be more or less permanent). It does not tell us anything about what causes change to occur this way. It still may be that it is the cumulation of gradual change in society that finally prompts abrupt change. It may well be that tensions build and are finally dealt with through some political action. Or it may be that it is the impact of differing political coalitions with long-standing differences largely unaffected by socioeconomic change that cause these change patterns. This analysis cannot answer those questions. It can only alert us to what we should be seeking to explain.

NOTES

1. Any grouping is somewhat arbitrary. To minimize any distortion of the image of change, several different groupings were tried. None altered the essential picture.

2. The relationship is that increases in unemployment lead to negative centralization changes. This relationship is somewhat stronger if allowance is made for the fundamental upward shift in unemployment levels that occurred around 1975. That shift raised the level of the relationship in the 1975–83 era. To allow for that, a dummy variable was created for the years 1975–83. When this dummy variable was included, the proportion of variance explained increased to .40. The dummy variable had a positive coefficient, indicating that the relationship between unemployment and centralization was still negative, but at a higher level from 1975–83.

3. It must be emphasized here that the designation of the magnitude of changes throughout this analysis is subjective. A major problem of the incremental-abrupt argument has been the issue of what constitutes an incremental versus a major change. Albritton (1979) focuses on this issue and provides some interesting and useful methodology for trying to resolve it. His method would be very involved for 50 states, however, so it is not used here. The intent of this analysis is to explore the nature of change patterns and not to definitively classify systems or specific changes.

4. The same was done for the largest three changes, and the results were virtually the same. The analysis was done using two changes to emphasize changes that might be the most unusual.

5. The same analysis was conducted using the largest three positive changes, and it was equally pronounced.

REFERENCES

Advisory Commission on Intergovernmental Relations. 1985. *Significant Features of Fiscal Federalism, 1984 Edition* (Washington, D.C.: Government Printing Office).

Albritton, Robert B. 1979. "Measuring Public Policy: Impacts of the Supplemental Social Security Income Program," *American Journal of Political Science* 23: 559–78.

Beer, Samuel H. 1973. "The Modernization of American Federalism," *Publius* 3: 49–96.

Bowler, M. Kenneth. 1974. *The Nixon Guaranteed Income Proposal: Substance and Process in Policy Change* (Cambridge: Ballinger).

Due, John. 1963. *State Sales Tax Administration* (Chicago: Public Administration Service).

Dye, Thomas. 1966. *Politics, Economics, and the Public: Policy Outcomes in the American States* (Chicago: Rand McNally).

Gold, Steven D. 1983. *State and Local Fiscal Relations in the Early 1980s* (Washington, D.C.: Urban Institute Press).

Hansen, Susan B. 1983. *The Politics of Taxation* (New York: Praeger).

Jennings, Edward T. 1977. "Some Policy Consequences of the Long Revolution and Bifactional Rivalry in Louisiana," *American Journal of Political Science* 21: 225–46.

———. 1979. "Competition, Constituencies, and Welfare Policies in the American States," *American Political Science Review* 73: 414–29.

Key, V. O. 1949. *Southern Politics* (New York: Knopf).

Lindblom, Charles E. 1959. "The Science of Muddling Through," *Public Administration Review* 19: 79–88.

Rafuse, Robert W., Jr. 1982. "The Outlook for State-Local Finance Under the New Federalism," pp. 99–149 in *Summary of Proceedings*, New York State Legislative Commission on State-Local Relations, Conference on New York's Fiscal System, April.

Schulman, Paul. 1975. "Nonincremental Policy Making: Notes Toward an Alternative Paradigm," *American Journal of Political Science* 69: 1354–70.

Stonecash, Jeffrey M. 1981. "Centralization in State-Local Fiscal Relationships," *Western Political Quarterly* 36: 301–309.

———. 1983. "Fiscal Centralization in the American States: Increasing Similarity and Persisting Diversity," *Publius* 13: 123–37.

———. 1985. "Paths of Fiscal Centralization in the American States," *Policy Studies Journal* 13: 653–61.

Wirt, Frederick M. 1983. "Institutionalization: Prison and School Policies," in Virginia Gray, Herbert Jacob, and Kenneth N. Vines (eds.), *Politics in the American States: A Comparative Analysis*, 4th ed. Boston: Little, Brown, and Company.

Part 6
The Future of
Intergovernmental Policy

14

Intergovernmental Relations and Public Policy: Down the Road

David R. Beam and J. Edwin Benton

As noted at the outset of this volume, it is indeed an exciting time to study intergovernmental relations (IGR). The American IGR system, though designed by the Founding Fathers to operate mainly with "minimal intergovernmental interaction and little 'sharing' of functional responsibilities" (Walker, 1981:xiii), has changed markedly in the last half century, particularly since 1960. The increasing frequency of interlevel contact and the constantly evolving level of complexity boggle the mind. Commenting on the nature of this change, Shapek (1981:vii) observes: "We have entered a new era of intergovernmental complexity, both vertically (between levels of government) and horizontally (between competing jurisdictions). Both internal forces (programmatic growth) and external forces (world and domestic events) have led to actions by the national, state, and local governments which are impossible to predict or control." Analagous change has also characterized IGR systems in other countries as well. Moreover, such dramatic change has necessitated a reinterpretation of the partnership between various actors comprising IGR systems. Amid all of the flux and change in IGR systems, both scholars and practitioners have been increasingly intrigued by and concerned with the public policies that are formulated and implemented in an IGR context. In fact, this subject has been at the center of each of the studies reported in this book.

These studies, of course, represent only a small fraction of the work that has been done recently in the field of IGR policy. Yet, we believe that they are representative enough of the larger body of literature from which they come to assist us in identifying recent developments in IGR and to suggest several trends to expect down the road. This kind of information should provide us with considerable insight as to those factors that are likely to set the tone for IGR policy formulation, implementation, and impact throughout the remainder of the 1980s. However, before speculating about future trends that recent IGR changes would seem to imply, a note of caution is in order as to the practice of identifying sources of such change.

CHANGE IN IGR

Usual practice is to attribute changes in intergovernmental relations to the influence of particular presidents. Thus, one speaks of the "Creative Federalism" of Lyndon Johnson and contrasts it with the "New Federalism" of his successor, Richard Nixon. By this standard of assessment, the nation was declared to have entered a new era in 1981. With the inauguration of Ronald Reagan, the historic trend toward governmental centralization was thought to be challenged and reversed. The president was said to be dismantling the social programs of the Great Society, or even those of the New Deal, depending upon the observer. In fact, there are those who predicted that future patterns of IGR would hinge on whether Ronald Reagan or Walter Mondale were elected in November 1984.

However commonplace, portrayals of these kinds hide as much as they reveal. First, they put far too much emphasis on a single official as the architect of the intergovernmental system. In fact, presidential influence in this area has usually been quite constrained. It is worth recalling, for example, that every president since 1968 has endeavored to reduce the size of the federal government's role in the intergovernmental system, but federal growth continued at a rapid pace throughout much of the 1970s. If real responsibility for shaping intergovernmental relations rests anywhere, it seems to be with Congress (ACIR, 1981).

Second, this overly presidential and partisan perspective ignores important continuities that often exist from one administration to the next. For example, the origins of each of the major intergovernmental initiatives associated with the Nixon years—including general revenue sharing, block grants, improved grants management procedures, and welfare reform—can be traced to the Johnson administration and usually to actors within the Johnson White House itself. In the same way, most of the proposals that are associated with the Reagan administration's New Federalism—federal aid cuts, grant consolidation, a tradeoff among domestic aid programs, regulatory relief, and the desire to balance the federal budget—had earlier, external origins. For example, federal aid as a proportion of state-local expenditures and as a share of federal outlays peaked in 1978. Certainly the tide of opinion had turned against the apparent inefficiencies of "big government" with the election of Jimmy Carter in 1976 and with California's Proposition 13 in 1978. Ronald Reagan was moving with this tide rather than swimming against it.

As in the past, some current trends in American IGR seem likely to persist, regardless of who occupies the White House. These trends, of which three are singled out here, will be the crucial influences shaping IGR for the balance of the decade. Students of IGR are quick to point out that similar trends are discernible in other federal systems, and they are likely to temper IGR in these countries.

A RESURGENCE OF STATES AND COMMUNITIES

From a long-term perspective, perhaps the most notable change has been a rehabilitation of the reputation of state governments. They are no longer widely regarded as "horse and buggy" governments, as they were in the 1960s, and are coming once again to be viewed as laboratories of innovation and democracy—as was true in the Progressive era. For example, Senator Kennedy (1982) has quite correctly observed that states took the lead in such policy areas as utility rate reform, freedom of information, public election financing, health care cost containment, and controls on nuclear energy. Similarly, although the environmentalists of a decade ago generally sought federal solutions to pollution problems, they now frequently look to the states, recognizing that Washington has no monopoly on environmental virtue (Conservation Foundation, 1984). Indeed, in such areas as acid rain, the states are filling the gap created by federal inaction. "It's developing into a national trend," according to the Environmental Defense Fund (Stevens, 1984:3A).

In other fields, too, state and local governments are moving ahead on problems that leave the national government deadlocked. The declining quality of education was the major national domestic concern of 1983. A half-dozen critical reports were issued, many calling for federal action. Senator Lawton Chiles joked that "having a math and science bill has become a requirement for membership in the U.S. Senate" (*Education Times*, 1983:6). Moreover, educational quality became a key issue during the 1984 presidential campaign.

In practice, however, nearly all of the remedial effort has been at the state level. "It was almost like magic," one observer commented. "Within weeks of the publication of a series of commission reports on alarming declines in American education, states began to adopt major improvement programs for their public schools. . . . The states' determination to improve education appears to be at unprecedented heights" (Stanfield, 1983a:1650). Educational improvement remained a state priority in 1984.

Some 275 state-level task forces on education have been at work during the past year. Many states have imposed tougher graduation requirements and upgraded curricula textbooks; some have begun master teacher programs or boosted state aid.

In the area of industrial policy, too, most of the real action is by state and local governments. The concept may be simply an undefinable "buzzword" in Washington (Auerbach, 1983), but most states and large cities have had one for years, as the *National Journal* has noted (Stanfield, 1983b). Many states have established gubernatorial task forces on technological development, bringing members of the business, academic, professional, and financial communities together to recommend new initiatives. Some provide venture capital for high-risk undertakings; others offer research grants, industrial training programs, or tax credits. Moreover, while Congress has been thinking about enterprise zones for the past four years, 21 states have followed the lead of Florida, Connecticut, and Maryland in adopting legislation, and more than 330 zones are now operating under state laws (Wiesenthal, 1984). Thus, as Merrill (1984:451) comments, "state governors have in a few years managed to accomplish much more in pursuit of economic development than succeeding national administrations. . . . Innovation policy initiative has shifted from the federal to the state level, perhaps for some considerable time."

Only in very small part is this state resurgence a consequence of the administration's New Federalism. Despite dramatic proposals and even more dramatic rhetoric, what President Reagan actually accomplished fell far short of his objectives. There has been no large-scale withdrawal of national power. To be sure, federal aid spending dropped for the first time in modern history in FY 1982 by some $6.6 billion, but it has since resumed an upward climb, though at a modest pace. Nine block grants were established under the same legislation, the Omnibus Reconciliation Act of 1981, but nearly all later proposals for consolidation have been rejected. Indeed, some of the administration's intergovernmental goals may now be more difficult to accomplish because of its rhetorical excesses and tactical blunders (Conlan, 1984; Eads and Fix, 1984). The administration itself seems to have lost interest in intergovernmental reform, while it seems unlikely that any new bill with the word "federalism" in its title will be adopted by Congress for years to come.

Instead, the reinvigoration of state and local government has been largely self-generated. Two decades of administrative, political, and fiscal reforms have made the states structurally much stronger and more "modern" than they were in the 1950s and 1960s (ACIR, 1985). Moreover, in the late 1970s, a new breed of state and local leaders arose that emphasized public-private cooperation and improved management to spur economic revitalization for their jurisdictions (see Stanfield, 1979; Peirce and Hagstrom, 1983). As the growth in federal aid was slackening, then, role models shifted from one of "grantsman" to "entrepreneur." Since these trends have deep roots, they are unlikely to prove transitory.

BROADENED INTERGOVERNMENTAL TENSION

Although state and local governments now enjoy a more prominent status in the intergovernmental system than previously, tensions between national and subnational governments have by no means subsided. On the contrary, they are now broader and thus more extensive than they were a decade ago.

Since the end of the New Deal, the key issues of intergovernmental relations have involved grants-in-aid: the need for new programs, the appropriate allocation of funds, and the desirability of consolidation or managerial improvements. This traditional area of concern has not disappeared, despite some premature declarations that the grant era was over. Although 137 separate grants were terminated or consolidated by the Reconciliation Act, over 400 still remain, with outlays totaling about $100 billion.

Disputes over grant expenditures and program performance will continue in the future, just as they commanded attention in the past. This conflict is apt to be heightened as grants are given close scrutiny as a result of deficit pressures (Posner, 1984). Indeed, mounting deficits—rather than any of the officially announced policies—are the most important legacy of the Reagan administration for the structure of federalism.

Still, conflict over grants is very old news. What has changed is that grants-in-aid are no longer the sole, nor perhaps even the chief, focus of intergovernmental attention. They have been supplemented by two newer areas of concern: regulation and revenues.

Beginning in the mid-1960s, but especially in the early and mid-1970s, state and local governments became the administrators or targets of a host of federal regulations (ACIR, 1984). The majority of these programs addressed environmental protection or nondiscrimination problems, but others involved such diverse functions as occupational health and safety, health care cost containment, and traffic speed laws. Concern about the fiscal burdens, administrative problems, and intrusiveness of these programs arose slowly, but by the late 1970s even liberal state and local officials were protesting Washington's "mandate millstone" (Koch, 1980). Leading concerns over recent years have included inconsistencies in federal nondiscrimination and environmental impact policies; bilingual and handicapped education requirements; the cost of providing wheelchair access to mass transportation; unnecessary rigidity in federal environmental policies; exposure of municipal governments to antitrust liability; and the assertion of federal control over cable television.

Although regulatory excesses and inefficiencies have been a target of every president since Nixon, and a move to deregulation in such industries as airlines and trucking captured bipartisan support under Presidents Ford and Carter, the Reagan administration was the first to stress the intergovernmental aspects of the problem. Mayors, governors, and other officials were invited to suggest rules in need of review, while Executive Order 12291—which established the administration's policies for regulatory review—called for the analysis of rules imposing large cost increases on state and local government agencies. However, despite the administration's claims of cost reductions totaling as much as $6 billion, overall results have fallen well short of expectations. Few major statutes have been modified, although such key laws as the Clean Air and Clean Water acts were up for renewal, and many attempted administrative changes ran afoul of legislative or judicial resistance. One review (Lovell, 1983) found the greatest successes were changes in the way agencies enforce regulations rather than a reduction in the rules themselves.

Now the regulatory relief effort seems to have been largely abandoned, while something of a backlash has arisen on Capitol Hill. Little further reduction of national controls appears likely; indeed, some 26 bills that would preempt state and local activities in one area or another are presently before Congress. The Reagan administration itself has sometimes abetted an expansion of federal authority, as witnessed by new rules on truck sizes, the care of handicapped newborns, and (most recently) the drinking age. In June 1984, President Reagan suddenly embraced a bill to penalize states with drinking ages below 21 by taking away a portion of their highway construction funds—an idea he had previously declared to be a violation of a state's rights. The decision was "government by Gallup poll," according to Representative James Howard, who sponsored the measure (see Tolchin, 1984:E5). "His political advisers told him it was a 'sleeping giant' of an issue, and he'd better get on the right side of it." At any rate, conflict on federal regulatory issues affecting state and local government may be expected to fuel debate in the political arena—as well as the courts—for many years ahead.

Even more important may be anticipated disputes over tax policies and other fiscal resource issues. The dramatic expansion of intergovernmental aid during the post-World War II era was always premised on the greater fiscal strength and equity of the national income tax. Now, given projections of $200-billion-plus deficits, federal officials are looking harder at many state and local revenue sources. State and local officials, for their part, have learned from experiences under the Economic Recovery Tax Act (see Cook, 1982) that they must keep a close eye on federal tax policy changes.

For several years now, many of the most important intergovernmental conflicts have revolved around revenue resources: mortgage revenue bonds (MRBs), industrial revenue bonds (IRBs), industrial development bonds (IDBs), the deductibility of interest on municipal bonds, and the unitary tax system. The 1982 five-cent hike in the federal gasoline tax— one of the tax sources that President Reagan had previously suggested turning back to the states—also brought protests from several governors.

Now, federal tax turnbacks are clearly *out;* revenue enhancements are *in* (see ACIR, 1984b). Walter Mondale pledged to raise taxes if he were elected to office, and Ronald Reagan's publicly stated opposition notwithstanding, even former Reagan administration officials, such as David Stockman, insist that tax increases are essential as part of a larger effort to reduce federal deficits. However, many of the alternatives being considered—including a "flax tax" or federal consumption (sales or value-added) tax—might threaten the strength of the state and local government tax base (see Kleine, 1984). As North Dakota's Senate majority leader David E. Nething (1984:2) has observed, "the challenge of the remainder of this decade may well be reconciling the many conflicting interests that can arise when federal state, and local governments vie for the same tax dollars."

THE LOCALIZATION OF NATIONAL PROBLEMS

A third quite recent trend that should be expected to persist involves rising state and local involvement in issues that once were almost the exclusive province of the national government. This reverses the traditional historical pattern of American intergovernmental relations, which may be summarized as growing federal participation in fields that once were regarded as chiefly local concerns—including education, law enforcement, waste disposal, and mass transit.

But, if local problems can be nationalized, the converse also holds, as was demonstrated by the hundreds of New England towns that debated resolutions favoring a nuclear freeze in the spring of 1982. Indeed, some 57 North American cities and towns have declared themselves "nuclear free zones," banning nuclear weapons within their borders. More significantly, the National Governors' Association in 1983 adopted, for the first time, a comprehensive statement on federal budget policy. Current fiscal realities mean that state leaders have reason to be concerned about such big-ticket items as military procurement and federal retirement benefits. Among other things, the governors' resolution set targets for defense spending and urged that any domestic budget cuts be concentrated on such non-means-tested programs as Medicare and pensions, rather than federal welfare aid. The plan was to reduce the federal budget deficit to about $90 billion by 1988 (see Matheson and Thompson, 1983).

State and local governments also find themselves much concerned with questions of international trade, which since 1960 has grown from $35 billion to $507 billion—or about one-fifth of the GNP. As Kline (1984) observes, "Global economic interdependence has overlapped the division of governmental responsibilities in the U.S. federal system. A variety of state government officials now face an expanding agenda of international concerns and possess a rather surprising potential for influencing results." States are now heavily involved in promoting job-producing exports and increasing foreign investment. Many quadrupled their budgets for trade promotion in the latter half of the 1970s. Indicative of the trend is the fact that some 19 states presently have established offices in Tokyo to try to encourage Japanese investments (*New York Times*, 1984). Cities, too, are developing their own "foreign economic policies" (Steinbach and Peirce, 1984). The mayor of New Orleans, for example, has headed trade missions to Senegal, Brazil, Japan, and Nigeria. One challenging consequence of this trend is that state and local officials are finding themselves under new pressures, as when a Japanese delegation led by the chairman of the Sony Corporation visited 23 states, threatening to withhold investment from those that did not end use of the unitary tax system (Behr, 1984).

The continuing and, in some ways, growing interlevel involvement belies the effort by the Reagan administration to restore some semblance of the traditional system of dual federalism, which was marked by separated rather than intricately shared functions. The key proposal, advanced in 1982, would have "traded off" federal aid to welfare and a number of other domestic functions to states in exchange for full federal financing of the costly Medicaid program. After months of debate, negotiations between federal, state, and local officials broke down, and the proposal never was drafted into legislation. Although rationalization of federal expenditure and service priorities might be a useful response to growing fiscal pressure, it seems unlikely that any new initiative will be advanced soon (see Benton, 1986).

CONCLUSION

In sum, the dynamics of American IGR have surely changed as mid-decade approaches. The growth of the national government has slowed, while state and local governments are recognized to be playing more innovative, activist roles. These are important trends, which may be expected to continue.

At the same time, the basic contours of the federal system are not markedly different. No real devolution of power has been accomplished, and intergovernmental relations, as of mid-1986, are no less complex and intertwined than they were when Ronald Reagan first took office. Growing concern about the impact of federal regulatory and tax policies on state and local governments means that there are now more areas of tension than there were a decade ago. Furthermore, state and local governments have found reason to become involved with federal budget, international trade, and even defense policies—areas once left to Washington. All of these characteristics suggest that American intergovernmental relations (as well as the making and implementing of public policies in such a context), through the balance of the 1980s, will remain as complex and conflict-prone as ever.

REFERENCES

Advisory Commission on Intergovernmental Relations. 1981. *An Agenda for American Federalism: Restoring Confidence and Competence* (Washington, D.C.: Government Printing Office).

———. 1984a. *Regulatory Federalism: Policy, Process, Impact and Reform* (Washington, D.C.: Government Printing Office).

———. 1984b. *Strengthening the Federal Reserve System: Implications for State and Local Taxing and Borrowing* (Washington, D.C.: Government Printing Office).

———. 1985. *The Question of State Government Capability* (Washington, D.C.: Government Printing Office).

Auerbach, Stuart. 1983. " 'Industrial Policy' Newest Buzzword," *The Washington Post* (June 10, 1983): D1, D11.

Behr, Peter. 1984. "Japanese Group Attacks Unitary Taxation Method," *The Washington Post* (June 14): E10.

Benton, J. Edwin. 1986. "Economic Considerations and the Reagan New Federalism Swap Proposals," *Publius: The Journal of Federalism* 15: (forthcoming).

Conlan, Timothy J. 1984. "The Politics of Federal Block Grants: From Nixon to Reagan," *Political Science Quarterly* 99: 247–70.

Conservation Foundation. 1984. *State of the Environment: An Assessment at Mid-Decade* (Washington, D.C.: The Conservation Foundation).

Cook, Robert F. 1982. "The Economic Recovery Tax Act and Its Effects on State and Local Revenues" in John William Ellwood (ed.), *Reductions in U.S. Domestic Spending* (New Brunswick, N.J.: Transaction Books).

Eads, George C., and Michael Fix. 1984. *Relief or Reform?: Reagan's Regulatory Dilemma* (Washington, D.C.: The Urban Institute).

Education Times. 1983. "Federal Legislation: 'It Looks Like Having a Math and Science Bill Has Become a Requirement for Membership in the U.S. Senate' " (April 11, 1983): 6.

Kennedy, Senator Edward. 1982. "Kennedy Addresses Conference on Federalism," *Congressional Record* 128 (July 1): S 7923–S 7925.

Kleine, Robert J. 1984. "Juggling Intergovernmental Revenue Concerns," *Intergovernmental Perspective* 10: 8–17.

Kline, John M. 1984. "The Expanding International Agenda for State Governments," *State Government* 57: 2–6.

Koch, Edward I. 1980. "The Mandate Millstone." *The Public Interest* 61: 42–57.

Lovell, Catherine. 1983. "Effects of Regulatory Changes on States and Localities" in Richard P. Nathan, Fred C. Doolittle, and Associates, *The Consequences of Cuts: The Effects of the Reagan Domestic Program on State and Local Governments* (Princeton, N.J.: Princeton Urban and Regional Research Center, Princeton University).

Matheson, Scott M., and James R. Thompson. 1983. "The States Need a Resolution Now." *The Washington Post* (May 15, 1983): B8.

Merrill, Stephen A. 1984. "Knowledge and Politics in Innovation Policy Design," *Policy Studies Review* 3: 445–452.

Nething, David E. 1984. "View From the Commission," *Intergovernmental Perspective*, 10: 2.

New York Times. 1984. "States Seek Business in Japan" (May 21): D14.

Peirce, Neal R., and Jerry Hagstrom. 1983. *The Book of America: The Changing Face of Politics Across America* (New York: W. W. Norton).

Posner, Paul L. 1984. "On the Brink of a Torrent?" *SIAM Intergovernmental News* 7: 1, 2.

Shapek, Raymond A. 1981. *Managing Federalism: Evolution and Development of the Grant-in-Aid System* (Charlottesville, Va.: Community Collaborators).

Stanfield, Rochelle L. 1979. "A New Breed of Mayors With a New View of Washington," *National Journal* (May 26): 866–70.

———. 1983a. "Learning From the States," *National Journal* (August 6): 1650.

———. 1983b. "An Industrial Policy for Cities and States," *National Journal* (February 26): 434–35.

Steinbach, Carol, and Neal R. Peirce. 1984. "Cities Are Setting Their Sights on International Trade and Investment," *National Journal* (April 28): 818–21.

Stevens, Carol. 1984. "Acid Rain Cleanup Is Led by NY," *USA Today* (July 12): 3A.

Tolchin, Martin. 1984. "States Face a Carrot or a Stick on the Drinking Age," *New York Times* (July 1): E5.

Walker, David B. 1981. *Toward a Functioning Federalism* (Cambridge, Mass.: Winthrop).

Wiesenthal, Eric. 1984. "States Take Initiative in Enterprise Zone Laws," *Public Administration Times* (June 1): 1, 8.

Selected Bibliography

Anderson, William. 1960. *Intergovernmental Relations in Review.* Minneapolis: University of Minnesota Press.

Bailey, Stephen K., and Edith K. Mosher. 1968. *ESEA: The Office of Education Administers a Law.* Syracuse, N.Y.: Syracuse University Press.

Bardach, Eugene. 1977. *The Implementation Game.* Cambridge, Mass.: The MIT Press.

Bardach, Eugene, and Robert A. Kagan. 1982. *Going by the Book: The Problem of Regulatory Unreasonableness.* Philadelphia: Temple University Press.

Barfield, Claude E. 1981. *Rethinking Federalism: Block Grants and Federal, State, and Local Responsibilities.* Washington, D.C.: American Enterprise Institute.

Bendiner, Robert. 1965. *Obstacle Course on Capitol Hill.* New York: McGraw-Hill.

Berke, Joel S., and Michael W. Kirst. 1972. *Federal Aid to Education: Who Benefits? Who Governs?* Lexington, Mass.: D. C. Heath.

Bush, George. 1981. *Year-End Summary of Actions Taken by the Presidential Task Force on Regulatory Relief.* Washington, D.C.: Office of the Vice President.

Caputo, David A., and Richard L. Cole. 1974. *Urban Politics and Decentralization.* Lexington, Mass.: D.C. Heath.

Comfort, Louise K. 1982. *Education Policy and Evaluation: A Context for Change.* New York: Pergamon Press.

Committee for Economic Development. 1970. *Reshaping Government in Metropolitan Areas.* New York: Committee for Economic Development.

Dillon, John F. 1911. *Commentaries on the Laws of Municipal Corporations.* 5th ed. Boston: Little, Brown and Co.

Dommel, Paul R., Victor E. Bach, Sarah F. Liebschultz, Leonard S. Rubinowitz, and Associates. 1980. *Targeting Community Development.* Washington, D.C.: Department of Housing and Urban Development.

Due, John. 1963. *State Sales Tax Administration*. Chicago: Public Administration Service.

Dye, Thomas R. 1966. *Politics, Economics, and the Public: Policy Outcomes in the · American States*. Chicago: Rand McNally.

———. 1976. *Policy Analysis: What Governments Do, Why They Do It, and What Difference It Makes*. University, Ala.: University of Alabama Press.

Eads, George C., and Michael Fix. 1984. *Relief or Reform? Reagan's Regulatory Dilemma*. Washington, D.C.: The Urban Institute.

———, eds. 1984. *The Reagan Regulatory Strategy: An Assessment*. Washington, D.C.: The Urban Institute.

Edwards, George C., III. 1980. *Implementing Public Policy*. Washington, D.C.: Congressional Quarterly Press.

Eidenberg, Eugene, and Robert D. Morey. 1969. *An Act of Congress*. New York: W. W. Norton.

Elazar, Daniel J. 1962. *The American Partnership*. Chicago: University of Chicago Press.

———. 1982. *American Federalism: A View From the States*. 3d ed. New York: Harper and Row.

Elsner, Hermann. 1979. *Das Gameindefinanzsystem*. Cologne: Verlag W. Kohl-hammer.

Glendening, Parris N., and Mavis Mann Reeves. 1984. *Pragmatic Federalism: An Intergovernmental View of American Government*. 2d ed. Pacific Palisades, Calif.: Palisades Publishers.

Gold, Steven D. 1983. *State and Local Fiscal Relations in the Early 1980s*. Washington, D.C.: The Urban Institute Press.

Goldwin, Robert, ed. 1974. *A Nation of States*. Chicago: Rand McNally.

Graves, W. Brooke, 1964. *American Intergovernmental Relations*. New York: Charles Scribner's Sons.

Grodzins, Morton. 1966. *The American System: A New View of Government in the United States*. Chicago: Rand McNally.

Gunlicks, Arthur B. 1986. *Local Government in the German Federal System*. Durham, N.C.: Duke University Press.

Hale, George E., and Marian Lief Palley. 1981. *The Politics of Federal Grants*. Washington, D.C.: Congressional Quarterly Press.

Hansen, Susan B. 1983. *The Politics of Taxation*. New York: Praeger.

Hanus, Jerome L., ed. 1981. *The Nationalization of State Government*. Lexington, Mass.: D. C. Heath and Co.

Hawkins, Robert B. ed. 1981. *American Federalism: A New Partnership for the Republic*. San Francisco: Institute for Contemporary Studies.

Hawley, Amos H., and Basil G. Zimmer. 1970. *The Metropolitan Community: Its People and Government*. Beverly Hills, Calif.: Sage.

Howitt, Arnold M. 1984. *Managing Federalism: Studies in Intergovernmental Relations*. Washington, D.C.: Congressional Quarterly Press.

Kaufman, Herbert. 1967. *The Forest Ranger*. Baltimore: Johns Hopkins Press.

Kettl, Donald F. 1980. *Managing Community Development in the New Federalism*. New York: Praeger Publishers.

Lave, Charles A., and James G. March. 1975. *An Introduction to Models in the Social Sciences*. New York: Harper and Row.

Lawson, Michael W., and Karen M. Benker. 1985. *Significant Features of Fiscal Federalism: 1984 Edition.* Washington, D.C.: Government Printing Office.

Leach, Richard H. 1976. *American Federalism.* New York: W. W. Norton & Co.

Lieber, Harvey. 1975. *Federalism and Clean Waters: The 1972 Water Pollution Control Act.* Lexington, Mass.: Lexington Books.

Lipsky, Michael. 1980. *Street-Level Bureaucracy.* New York: Russell Sage Foundation.

Lowe, Jeanne R. 1972. *The Near Side of Federalism: Improving State and Local Government.* New York: Ford Foundation.

Lowi, Theodore. 1979. *The End of Liberalism: The Second Republic of the United States.* 2d ed. New York: W. W. Norton.

MacMahon, Arthur W., ed. 1955. *Federalism: Mature and Emergent.* New York: Macmillan.

Martin, Roscoe C. 1965. *The Cities and the Federal System.* New York: Atherton Press.

Mazmanian, Daniel A., and Paul A. Sabatier. 1983. *Implementation and Public Policy.* Glenview, Ill.: Scott, Foresman and Co.

Mercanto, Philip. 1967. *The Politics of Federal Aid to Education in 1965: A Study in Policy Innovation.* Syracuse, N.Y.: Syracuse University Press.

Mitnick, Barry M. 1980. *The Political Economy of Regulation.* New York: Columbia University Press.

Mogulof, Melvin B. 1971. *Governing Metropolitan Areas: A Critical Review of Councils of Governments and the Federal Role.* Washington, D.C.: The Urban Institute.

Munger, Frank J., and Richard F. Fenno, Jr. 1962. *National Politics and Federal Aid to Education.* Syracuse, N.Y.: Syracuse University Press.

Nathan, Richard P., ed. 1979. *America's Changing Federalism.* Washington, D.C.: Brookings Institution.

Nathan, Richard P., Paul R. Dommel, Sarah F. Liebschultz, Milton D. Morris, and Associates. 1977. *Block Grants for Community Development.* Washington, D.C.: Department of Housing and Urban Development.

Peterson, Paul E. 1981. *City Limits.* Chicago: University of Chicago Press.

Reagan, Michael D., and John G. Sansone. 1981. *The New Federalism.* New York: Oxford University Press.

Riker, William H. 1964. *Federalism, Origin, Operation, Significance.* Boston: Little, Brown and Co.

Ripley, Randall, and Grace Franklin. 1982. *Bureaucracy and Policy Implementation.* Homewood, Ill.: The Dorsey Press.

Rosenschon, Jürgen E. 1980. *Gemeindefinanzsystem und Selbstverwaltungsgarantie.* Cologne: Gemeindeverlag.

Rubin, Irene. 1985. *Shrinking the Federal Government.* New York: Longman.

Savas, E. S. 1982. *Privatizing the Public Sector: How to Shrink Government.* Chatham, N.J.: Chatham House Publishers.

Schattschneider, E. E. 1960. *The Semi-Sovereign People.* New York: Holt, Rinehart, and Winston.

Shapek, Raymond A. 1981. *Managing Federalism: Evolution and Development of the Grant-in-Aid System.* Charlottesville, Va.: Community Collaborators.

Sharpe, L. T., ed. 1981. *The Local Fiscal Crisis in Western Europe*. Beverly Hills, Calif.: Sage.

Sundquist, James L., and David W. Adams. 1969. *Making Federalism Work*. Washington, D.C.: Brookings Institution.

Teitelbaum, Fred, and Alice E. Simon. 1979. *Bypassing the States: Wrong Turn for Urban Aid*. Washington, D.C.: National Governors' Association.

Tribe, Laurence H. 1978. *American Constitutional Law*. Mineola, N.Y.: The Foundation Press.

Walker, David B. 1981. *Toward a Functioning Federalism*. Cambridge, Mass.: Winthrop.

Wikstrom, Nelson. 1977. *Councils of Government: a Study of Political Incrementalism*. Chicago: Nelson-Hall.

Wood, Robert C. 1958. *Suburbia: Its People and Their Politics*. Boston: Houghton Mifflin.

Wright, Deil S. 1982. *Understanding Intergovernmental Relations*. 2d ed. Monterey, Calif.: Brooks/Cole Publishing Co.

Wright, Deil S., and Harvey L. White, eds. 1984. *Federalism and Intergovernmental Relations*. Washington, D.C.: American Society for Public Administration.

Zimmermann, H. 1981. *Studies in Comparative Federalism: West Germany*. Washington, D.C.: Government Printing Office.

Index

About the Contributors

DAVID R. BEAM is Issue Management Coordinator with United Airlines. A former Director of Research for the Naisbitt Group and former staff member of the Advisory Commission on Intergovernmental Relations, he has contributed to several studies of federal grant and regulatory policies. Recent projects include an assessment of the Reagan Administration's New Federalism initiatives and an analysis of the impact of news media on federal-state-local relations.

J. EDWIN BENTON is Associate Professor and Chair of the Department of Political Science at the University of South Florida. His research has centered around state and local fiscal policy, governmental reorganization, Reagan New Federalism policies, and contextual voting behavior. He has published articles in the *Social Science Quarterly, Urban Affairs Quarterly, Policy Studies Journal, Policy Studies Review, State Government,* and *Midwest Review of Public Administration.*

MICHAEL CLARKE is Professor of Public Administration at California State University, San Bernardino. He is the editor, along with Sheldon Kamieniecki and Robert O'Brien of *Controversies in Environmental Policies,* SUNY Press 1985. His research has been published in *Public Administration Review, International Journal of Public Administration, American Review of Public Administration* and the *Journal of Health & Human Resources Administration.* His current research focuses on the effects of plant closings on the public sector.

OSBIN L. ERVIN is Associate Professor of Political Science and Director of the MPA Program at Southern Illinois, Carbondale. His research has focused primarily on municipal finance and administration. Recent articles have appeared in the *American Review of Public Administration, Water Resources Research,* and *Public Productivity Review.* He is currently completing a second manuscript on the Community Development Block Grant program.

ARTHUR B. GUNLICKS is a professor of political science at the University of Richmond. He has contributed to a number of edited works, and he is the author of numerous journal articles on German government and politics. He is the contributing editor of *Local Government Reform and Reorganization: An International Perspective,* published by Associated Faculty Press-Kennikat.

DAVID M. HEDGE is Associate Professor of Political Science at West Virginia University. His research has focused on intergovernmental fiscal relations, deregulation, and implementation. Recent articles appear in *Journal of Politics, American Politics Quarterly,* and *Women and Politics.*

SHELDON KAMIENIECKI teaches political science at the University of Southern California. In addition to publishing articles on environmental politics in numerous journals, he has written *Public Representation in Environmental Policy Making: The Case of Water Quality Management* and coedited *Controversies in Environmental Policy.* He is currently working on a book concerning the implementation of the Hazardous and Solid Waste Amendments of 1984.

CATHERINE H. LOVELL is professor of management in the Graduate School of Management, University of California, Riverside. Her research and writings have centered on issues in intergovernmental relations particularly on the costs and benefits of mandating by federal and state governments on local governments.

DONALD C. MENZEL is the Director of the Public Administration program at the University of South Florida. He is presently completing a book on policy implementation and is conducting research on the implementation of merit programs in Florida's public schools.

LOUISE BYER MILLER is currently an Adjunct Professor of Political Science at the Nelson A. Rockefeller College of Public Affairs and Policy of the State University of New York at Albany. She recently received her doctorate from that institution's Graduate School of Public Affairs. She also is a faculty member at Russell Sage's J.C. of Albany. Her interests include constitutional and administrative law, American federalism, state and local government, and American legislatures.

DAVID R. MORGAN is Director, Bureau of Government Research, and professor of political science at the University of Oklahoma. His work on state and urban politics has appeared in a number of professional journals. The second edition of his book *Managing Urban America* appeared in 1984.

ROBERT M. O'BRIEN is Professor and Head of the Department of Sociology at the University of Oregon. He has published in the areas of measurement, criminology, stratification, and decision-making processes in toxic waste management. He is a coauthor of *Urban Structure and Criminal Victimization* (with David Decker and David Schichor), author of *Crime and Victimization Data* and coeditor of *Controversies in Environmental Policy* (with Sheldon Kamieniecki and Michael Clarke; forthcoming). O'Brien received his Ph.D. in sociology from the University of Wisconsin (Madison) in 1973.

JOHN P. PELISSERO, formerly of Texas A&M University, is an Assistant Professor of Political Science at Loyola University of Chicago. His research has focused primarily on urban policy and state and local finance. His recent articles have appeared in the *American Political Science Review, Journal of Politics*, and *Social Science Quarterly*.

MICHAEL J. SCICCHITANO is Assistant Professor of Political Science at West Virginia University. His research interests include regulatory policy, implementation, legislative politics, and decision making.

CHARLES P. SHANNON serves as a legislative analyst for the Joint Budget Committee of the Colorado General Assembly. He was employed by the Denver Regional Council of Governments for 12 years, including five as director of the Division of Local Services. His work on local government has appeared in several scholarly journals.

JEFFREY M. STONECASH is Associate Professor of Political Science at Syracuse University. His research interests are intergovernmental relations and state politics, and he has published articles on these matters in *Publius, American Politics Quarterly, Western Political Quarterly*, and *Political Methodology*.

FRANK J. THOMPSON is Professor of Political Science and Department Head at the University of Georgia. His published work includes books, articles, and book chapters focused on policy implementation, health policy, bureaucratic politics, and personnel administration. His book, *Health Policy and the Bureaucracy: Politics and Implementation*, with MIT Press was recently reissued in paperback.

PINKY S. WASSENBERG is an Assistant Professor of Political Science at Central Michigan University. Her research focuses on the implementation of environmental and natural resources policies.

MARY H. WATSON is a Project Specialist in the Office of Project Development, Management, and Evaluation in Southern Illinois University's School of Technical Careers. Her work and research interests are oriented around issues in acquisition of federal funds for state and local projects. She holds the M.P.A. degree from Southern Illinois University at Carbondale.

**Policy Studies Organization publications
issued with Greenwood Press/Quorum Books**

Intergovernmental Relations and Public Policy
J. Edwin Benton and David R. Morgan, editors

Policy Controversies in Higher Education
Samuel K. Gove and Thomas M. Stauffer, editors

Citizen Participation in Public Decision Making
Jack DeSario and Stuart Langton, editors

Energy Resources Development: Politics and Policies
Richard L. Ender and John Choon Kim, editors